Fags, Hags and Queer Sisters

Fags, Hags and Queer Sisters

Gender Dissent and Heterosocial Bonds in Gay Culture

Stephen Maddison

First published 2000 by
MACMILLAN PRESS LTD
Houndmills, Basingstoke, Hampshire RG21 6XS
and London
Companies and representatives
throughout the world

ISBN 0–333–77661–5 hardcover
ISBN 0–333–77662–3 paperback

A catalogue record for this book is available
from the British Library.

This book is printed on paper suitable for recycling and
made from fully managed and sustained forest sources.

10   9   8   7   6   5   4   3   2   1
09 08 07 06 05 04 03 02 01 00

Printed and bound in Great Britain by
Antony Rowe Ltd, Chippenham, Wiltshire

*With love and thanks
to the women who brought
me up to be a Nice Boy:
Mary Gibbs, Lil Worrall, Lottie Charlton,
Doreen Maddison, Betty Chilcott,
and Patricia Maddison.*

And to AH, who's a very Nice Boy.

Contents

Acknowledgements

I came into academia because I understood it to be a place where I could explore what it meant to be gay, and the investments I have made in this piece of writing have been so important because they have been about trying to understand how my identity works. Of course, academia is not a free place for thinking about the world in deep and meaningful ways, it is a highly regulated institution where you have to learn to be resilient if you want to write about anything that has any emotional value whatsoever: in academia intellectual endeavour is surplus labour. Indulging in the luxury of intellectual exploration has entailed the negotiation of a number of governing institutional frameworks, from funding applications and the professional induction process of PhD examination, succumbing to the competitive frenzy of job interviews where a monograph accrues added status, to the mechanical league tabling of my department's RAE profile.

In the process of all these negotiations (oh, and in the intellectual pursuit too) I have notched up a considerable number of favours in the last seven years, and there are many people who I want to thank. I am grateful for the financial support I have received from the British Academy, who awarded me a three year studentship, without which I could never have taken this seriously. I am also grateful for the financial support I have been given by my dad, Phil Maddison, and my mum, Pat Maddison, and by Andrew Hutton.

The following people helped me on my way. They read drafts, bits of drafts, scribbles on envelopes, they gave me places to stay, they gave me references, they inspired me, or gave me confidence, or got me going. Love and thanks to: Helen Barlow, Jonathan Dollimore, Alex Doty, Richard Dyer, Nicky Harper, Val Hill, Kate Lacey, Vincent Quinn, Linda Rozmovits, Corinne Shirman-Sarti, Jane Valentine, Sue Wiseman and Alicia Wood.

Thanks go to staff and students I have worked with in the department of Cultural Studies at the University of East London and at Sussex University who have taught me much more than seven years of reading could have. Special thanks to the Information Services Department at Sussex University Library who provided a service far in excess of what budgetary realities might lead us to expect. Thanks to Bette Bourne who graciously read bits of *Belle Reprieve* to me over the phone before it was published and whom I was too shy to thank properly at the time (*there is a seriously bona Queen for you*).

Spectacular, sequin-encrusted thanks to Alan Sinfield who has offered tremendous support, institutional back up and vigorous intellectual stimulation. Thanks to Andy Medhurst who reminded me that being a Queen is the highest form of life we can aspire to. Thanks to my fierce sister, Nick Dearden. Thanks to Ben Gove, with whom I shared every hand-wringing detail of this. Thanks to Paula Graham, whose emotional and intellectual judgement I always trust implicitly. Thanks to my mum, Patricia Maddison, a queer icon if ever there was one, and my dad, Phil Maddison, who have both supported me throughout. Lastly, big hugs and kisses to Andrew Hutton, who makes me feel like I've come home.

Introduction

Fags, female icons and Stonewall

> Friday, June 28, 1969. 1:45am. There was a full moon. Judy Garland had been buried that afternoon. And the queers on Christopher Street had had enough.[1]

The riots that took place outside the Stonewall Inn in New York's Greenwich Village in June and July 1969 have become understood as the key moment in the emergence of contemporary gay politics. The obstinacy and militancy of the Stonewall's mainly black, Hispanic and drag clientele on those nights has become appreciated by disparate constituencies of queers as an homogenizing moment in which a liberationary attitude was birthed. Throughout the intervening thirty plus years the Stonewall riots have become a queer myth to be drawn upon and recirculated at times when we are in need of empowerment. The twenty-fifth anniversary of the uprising, which came at a time of emergency, during an epidemic when our numbers are continuing to be decimated, and during a period when Western democratic and economic systems seemed to be sliding ever further to the right, was appropriately marked then, with considerable levels of gay and lesbian Pride, expressed not only in commemorative marches and demonstrations, but with scholarly and experiential commentary, and, in keeping with the character of modern gay urban life, a volume of merchandising, produced, distributed and bought by gay people. The level of investment made in celebrations of Stonewall might be variously understood as the expression of an ever more diverse, sophisticated and confident subculture in touch with its history, or as the commodified, sanitized and nostalgic reminiscences of a modern political movement which has

1

failed to maintain the militancy so briefly expressed in a couple of civic disturbances twenty-five years earlier. Whatever the meaning ascribed to Stonewall, its importance as an identifiable moment of authentic queer activism remains indisputable.

A particularly marvellous elaboration of the Stonewall narrative comes in an eponymously titled film, directed by Nigel Finch and adapted as fiction by Rikki Beadle-Blair from Martin Duberman's historical-experiential account, was released in 1996.[2] *Stonewall* opens with a close up shot of an Hispanic drag queen applying her lipstick. It cuts to a documentary montage that displays original footage of Greenwich Village queer[3] life in the late 1960s, interspersed with sound bites from people present on the scene at this time. One of these participants, with the status of an 'eye-witness', says 'I think [the riot] had to do with Judy Garland's death'. This documentary sequence serves to set an historical context for the narrative, but it is very short: we quickly return to the now fully lip-sticked drag queen, who we later learn is called La Miranda. Her head fills the screen, as she tells us:

> See, there's as many Stonewall stories as there's gay queens in New York: and that's a shit load of stories, baby. Everywhere you go in Manhattan or America, or the entire damn world, you're gonna hear some new legend. Well, this is my legend, honey. Okay? My Stonewall legend.

The film cuts to the fictionalized interior of the Stonewall Inn where three drag queens are lip-synching to the camera, and we understand that the narrative is now structured as a function of La Miranda's perspective on Stonewall. La Miranda's legend follows the experiences of three participants in the riots: La Miranda herself, Matty Dean, the new boy in town with whom the drag queen is in love, but for whose affections she must compete with the assimilationist and respectable Ethan; and Bostonia, a matriarchal black drag queen who is kept by Vinnie, a closeted gangster who runs the Stonewall Inn. We follow our protagonists through their brutalization by the New York police, who raid the Inn, and by the Government, who call La Miranda to the draft, and by the Ordinances on Fire Island which circumscribe what Ethan promises Matty Dean will be 'heaven on Earth'. We also follow the diverse attempts of these characters to make sense of this brutalization – physical, cultural and emotional – and their differing attempts to survive and to formulate political resistance. Matty Dean is the outsider through whose eyes these political expressions are tested. The Homophile movement, of which Ethan is a part, stages a ludicrously understated, silent and respectable protest in Philadelphia, while the drag queens offer a magical, reverent and celebratory initiation of a new young sister.

It is clear that this complex, fabulous film favours the flagrancy of the drag queens, whose lip-synched, highly choreographed performances of songs by 1960s girl groups, such as the Shangri-Las, work as a kind of camp chorus that frames the events of the narrative. These segments underpin queer ownership of the narrative which *Stonewall* unfolds: the outlandish precision of the miming and the choreography, and the perfectly balanced tension in these performances between dead-pan camp and sequinned excess, which disrupt and segment the narrative progression, ensure that the film never slips into a ventriloquism of documentary authoritarianism. As a consequence, the rendering of these lives that are ruthlessly mediated by powerful and hostile agencies is always more than a mere elaboration of oppression. The appalling difficulties of queer life are represented without effacing the bravura and distinctiveness of queer culture and resistance.

The script reinforces this celebration of the way in which the drag queens relish their queer expression in the face of authoritarian intervention. When the police first raid the Stonewall, its patrons accept a posture of grudging acquiescence, removing jewellery and keeping their heads down. La Miranda refuses an order to go to the washroom to remove her makeup and has her face pushed into the filthy water in a tub on the bar used for cleaning glasses. But she takes control of this humiliation: after the cops have released her, she shoves her own head back into the water, holding it there while her tormentors look on in disbelief. Finally, La Miranda flings her head back out of the water, tossing back the locks of her coiffure. Then she returns to her seat and takes out her lipstick for a touch up, as the cops move in for further brutality. The queen behind the bar addresses her sister:

> *Princess Ernestine*: 'La Miranda girl, why do you always put yourself through this?'
> *La Miranda*: 'Why, Princess Ernestine? Just for the sheer, irresistible god-damn glamour of it all.'

Much later, La Miranda has confessed to Matty Dean, who is now her lover, that she fears the doctors she has been sent to for assessment by the draft officers, as she once underwent aversion therapy. Matty Dean steps in and impersonates his lover for the interview, wearing her Afro wig and loud makeup:

> *Matty Dean* (As *La Miranda*): 'Oh doctor, how fifties you be! Me, I'm living in the *other* state, between maleness and femaleness.'
> *Doctor*: 'Which is?'
> *Matty Dean*: 'Fabulousness!'

The need for such fabulousness is great. After a fascinating exchange between Bostonia and her lover Vinnie, who wants the drag queen to have a sex-change operation so that they may acquire respectability, Vinnie seems to accept his non-normative desires and identity. He rushes to Bostonia's apartment the night of Judy Garland's death to comfort his lover, who is bereft. Vinnie insists they go out for ice cream, and the couple end up in an up-market restaurant. When they are asked to leave, Vinnie throws over the table and Bostonia flings money for the bill on the floor. Later, after some tender, revealing moments between the lovers in bed, seemingly still unable to tell Bostonia that he loves him, Vinnie shoots himself, having scrawled the words in lipstick on a mirror. Meanwhile, Matty Dean has returned to La Miranda, having temporarily deserted her for Ethan's respectability, seeming to understand the limitation of assimilation.

The night of the riot leads our protagonists to the Stonewall, emotionally bruised by personal traumas caused by having to negotiate illegality and cultural and social oppression. Before we join them, dancing through their sorrows, the film interrupts their narrative with some documentary footage of Judy's funeral. As we re-join the Stonewall's queers, our perception of their trauma is heightened by this reference, the knowledge of which is sustained as 'Zing! Went the Strings of My Heart' is playing on the jukebox as the police make their fateful raid. The queens move into a more discretionary mode as the cops barge in, but Bostonia restrains one sister from removing Judy's song from the juke box. Later it is Bostonia who first strikes out against an officer, igniting the repressed fury which leads to the mass uprising.

None of the major accounts of the Stonewall riots and the emergence of Gay Liberation in their aftermath directly attribute the uprising to queer grief at the death of Judy Garland, but it is striking that most, like Michael Bronski's, make an association between them:

> Judy Garland is at the pinnacle of the gay male pantheon of idolized women. ... By the time of her death she had become so much of a gay institution that many New York City gay bars draped themselves with black crepe in mourning. More than 22,000 people paid their

respects at the funeral home. Some attribute the Stonewall Riots to
the distress gay people felt at Judy's death.[4]

Bronski makes no explicit judgement about an implied causal relationship between Garland's death and Stonewall, but it is clear that for him
the telling of the riots requires an account of Judy's funeral and her
importance for gay men.

It does not make much sense politically or historically to reduce the
complex circumstances which fuelled the uprising to an event which,
of itself, is not related to years of brutal oppression; although we may
convincingly argue that Judy's life, work and death are clearly granted a
symbolic relationship to that oppression. Her death was hardly necessary as the justification of civil disobedience. Finch's film works the idea
of Garland's death into a tapestry of other pains and humiliations so as
to give our political struggles dignity, but also to insist on our cultural
specificity. The emotional context *Stonewall* offers for the riots, refracted
through the idea of Judy, remains quintessentially queer: it is a device
which substantiates queer culture and eludes any crude reductionism to
mandarin discursiveness. Of course La Miranda was standing up for her
rights when she re-applied her lipstick, of course the rioting drag
queens, performing their high-kicks in the face of police batons and riot
shields, were defending their rights, but much more than that, these
acts of dissent are queer acts: they are never *just* political. Moreover, one
of the most satisfying elements of *Stonewall* is the way in which it gen-
ders male homosexuality so fabulously. These aren't just men sexually
into other men, or men in frocks: they are great, gorgeous pouting
Queens.

Here then, we can see that this epochal event in the history of homosexual people is associated in a functional, if not causal way, with the
death of a woman, and the grief her passing elicited in men who adored
her. Yet what about the meaning of this symbolic relationship between the
reality of being a homosexual man and the veneration of Judy Garland?
Why should a culture apparently founded on same-sex desire be so interested in forming an adoring relationship across sex difference?[5] Dennis
Altman notes the symmetry in the synchronism of Garland's funeral
and the riots, which the *Stonewall* film so perfectly capitalises upon:

> It was amidst the exuberance that followed the riots – they began,
> almost too perfectly symbolic a coincidence, the day Judy Garland,
> favorite of so many 'queens', was buried – that the New York Gay
> Liberation Front was founded.[6]

In the impressive documentary series *Over the Rainbow/The Question of Equality*, produced in America by the Testing the Limits Collective, and screened in the UK by Channel 4 in 1995, veteran activist Karla Jay notes that:

> I do remember that Judy Garland died, and Judy Garland of course was a great icon, particularly of gay men, so a lot of people thought that there was a lot of added tension because people were upset because Judy Garland had died. Personally I think it was a coincidence.

Altman and Jay are understandably circumspect about emphasizing the Garland connection: they wish to stress the historical decisiveness of the uprisings, and the repellent conditions endured by homosexual people which caused them. The effect of this circumspection, however, is to dismiss the importance of Judy as a taste preference, at the same time as it is clearly necessary that both bring Garland's funeral into the discussion. Bronski goes much further than these understandings of Judy and similar iconic women stars as mere *taste* for queens:

> Gay men responded emotionally to films and to the men in films through identification with women stars. In film semiotics, women are the vehicle of emotion and sexual passion. . . . There are hosts of female actors, singers and personalities with whom gay men have strongly identified. Some have been practically deified: Judy Garland and Barbra Streisand.[7]

Here there are two possible explanations for this association gay men have with women film stars: that they are the vehicle through which gay audiences could understand and organise their desire of male film stars, and that women stars embodied emotion and sexual passion. Both sound fairly plausible: straight women and gay men do share a common sexual interest in men, and women's desire is ascribed cultural legitimation and widespread representation, so desiring men through an identification with similar desires in women would not only give gay men a much wider range of places to locate culturally, but would also provide a potentially greater diversity of narratives with which to make sense of that desire. Yet what about women being the 'vehicle of emotion and sexual passion' for gay men? Is this level of emotional identification a necessary requirement for desiring men? If this is the case, might we not deduce that gay men's interest in women as the 'vehicle of emotion and sexual passion' is merely a function of our interest in *men* and not in women at all? Or is the expression of passion and emotion an end in itself for gay men and therefore an imperative of our interest in women and what they stand for in and of themselves? If so, why should homosexually oriented men have any more of an investment in emotions and passion than heterosexual men, who after all, do produce passion in their desire for women? Is all that we share with women our common sexual desire for men? If female stardom is a personal taste, why is it one shared by so many queens, and why is this taste represented as being so emblematic, constitutive even, of queer identities and history?

In 1980, in a volume written by members of London's Gay Left Collective, Richard Dyer and Derek Cohen offered terms that widened this understanding of gay men's interest in women. Their chapter is divided into two sections, with the former being mainly the work of Dyer, which questions the association between high cultural taste and homosexual expression, and presents a much more discursive and analytical treatment of gay men's apparent interest in women.

> But the rightness of being cultured and hence queer, or vice-versa, went further into an area I still have not disentangled. Somehow to me cultural sensitivity was 'feminine'; and being queer was not being a man – that was why the two went together.[8]

Here there is a suggestion that the association gay men make with women, at a level of investment we may see in the ubiquity of Judy Garland's presence in narratives of Stonewall, arises out of something much more fundamental than a subculturally derived, shared *taste* among gay men. While for Bronski an identification with women by queers is the opportunity for experiencing sexual and romantic desire of men, for Dyer there is here a much more profound proposal of queerness and its association with women as a gender refusal, 'not being a man'. Dyer goes on to say:

> It is clear that, as I experienced it then, the equation of artistic queerness with femininity downgraded both femininity and men. I negate myself by identifying with women (hence refusing my biological sex), and then put myself down by internalising the definition of female qualities as inferior ...[9]

There are complex historical factors at work here: Dyer is referring to attitudes to which he was subject at a point before he became active in gay and women's politics; yet his self-directed criticism also bears the marks of Gay Liberation anti-sexist politics of the late 1970s, whose stance on camp is noted by Corey K. Creekmur and Alexander Doty:

> In its 'closeted', less overtly political forms, camp has frequently been denigrated and maligned as self-oppressive and misogynistic ever since the Stonewall rebellion of 1969 made gay culture more publicly visible on the evening of Judy Garland's funeral.[10]

Yet it is too easy to reproduce presumptive cultural narratives:

> ... Yet, with the women's and gay movements, it became possible to turn these values on their heads while preserving that art–gayness–femininity link.[11]

For Dyer, it is the *proximity* of Gay Liberation politics and feminist politics that enables a questioning ownership of gay tastes and practices in which we can see the formulation of gender dissent. This questioning is also characteristic of Dyer's assessment of camp, in an article first published in *Playguy*, where he talks about the gay practice of calling men 'she':

> Calling gay men 'she' means I don't think of them, or myself, as straight men (with all that that implies). But given the actual situation of women in society, and given that however hard I try, there's still plenty of male chauvinism about me, there is something rather suspect about this habit.... I'd rather gay men identified with straight women than with straight men.[12]

Later, in *Heavenly Bodies* published in 1986, Dyer used a variety of first-hand accounts of gay admiration for Judy Garland to set up a complex analysis of how she signified as star, and how queer reading set up a series of empathies through which she was accessible as ordinary, and yet sufficiently stellar and beleaguered to symbolize both the frustration of queerness, and its resilience.[13] Dyer makes a persuasive and influential insistence upon the social and cultural contingence of gay adoration of Judy.

Despite the prevarications in Stonewall narratives, which minimize the constitutive effects of Garland's funeral upon the birth of Gay Liberation, Judy's very ubiquity within these accounts, if only to be dismissed in favour of more weighty considerations, offers us a very substantial marker of the importance of relationships between gay men and women. But what kind of relationship is this? Why has the adoration of strident, emotionally resilient, privileged, tenacious and plucky women become so powerfully understood as a cultural expression of men who sexually desire other men? What does this tell us about gay men? What *is* homosexuality when it is the practice of an identification with women? Dyer's work, and that of Michael Bronski, enables us to situate such questions in a context cleared of pathological debris, where we may draw upon a whole range of negotiations which validate gay practice.

Elsewhere however, we might not find that much lucid discussion of gay men's identification with women that advances on this pioneering work and begins to answer the kinds of question I offer here. This is not to say that much of the work which has been done on this kind of queer iconography is not valuable: for example, during the early 1990s there was considerable, often highly politicised, discussion by gay men on both sides of the Atlantic about the suitability of that Ambitious Blonde, Madonna, as a representative of our identificatory practices in relation to women.[14] Rather than address the issue of gay men's relationships with women, both iconic and fictional, and with real people, many critics and academics have engaged with the complex question of camp, which we might understand as a performance mode for handling hostile cultural conditions and which often involves some level of female identification.[15] Others have approached the notion of gay male effeminacy or drag performances as a strategic homosexual expression.[16] Both of these approaches are discussed further in later chapters: they clearly inform a territory that seems to be constituted by gay men's expressions of gender refusal, gender indeterminacy and gender de-naturalisation. Yet we still lack analysis which systematically maps the conditions through which relationships between gay men and women are meaningful, and relates the formation of such relationships to questions about the nature of gender, and the nature of homosexuality itself. As Alex Doty has noted, 'clearly, we need more popular and academic mass culture work that carefully considers feminine gay and other gendered queer reception practices.'[17] This book attempts to address this need.

Fags, hags and queer sistership

The title of this book is provocative on several counts. The reference to sistership appropriates a designation of familial relationships between women, and applies it to relationships conducted by gay men, and in the process exhibits an exercise of power, which is a function of my maleness and intellectual privilege. Similarly, the use of the word fag may upset those gay men who feel that we should always refer to ourselves in respectable or dignified terms. Bollocks to that: as I make clear in this book, our desire for respectability is an assimilationist trap, and I reject it. I am not a decent homosexual, I'm a flaming fag.

The use of the word hag is more problematic, particularly in the context of fag, and it is not my intention to be insulting towards those women who associate themselves with gay men, far from it. However, in aligning themselves with gay culture, or with feminism, women reject particularly dominant, respectable notions of femininity and femaleness; effectively they are undertaking acts of gender dissent. This is the context in which Mary Daly refers to women as Hags in her *Gyn/Ecology: The Metaethics of Radical Feminism*, as women contesting patriarchal ideas of womanhood, who create Hag-ography or Hag-ology, and this seems to me to be an appropriate use of the word in this context; I will go on to argue that women who bond with gay men do so as a form of political resistance.[18] I am not unaware that my use of the term hag here will solicit (Radical) feminist dismay. Marginal and oppositional positions across a spectrum of identities and experiences are compelled to jostle for cultural space: different kinds of identities, invoking gender, class and ethnic categories all inhabit similar and overlapping spaces. All of our articulations necessarily invoke the identities and positions of others. We have a responsibility to allow such jostling to challenge our own complicity with the oppressions of others: that is one of the key projects of this book, to examine the ways in which the oppression of women and the oppression of gay men are structurally linked. However, I am never going to be able to articulate myself in a way which will ventriloquise any form of feminism, and I don't want to try. I want to use feminism not to gain the approval of feminist critics, but to assess the ways in which my own practices (and those of other gay men) can be contextualized and understood through the knowledge they produce. My intention in this book is to engage as incisively as possible with the gender politics of both women and men.

Yet this book is about (largely male) gay culture, and terms such as hag and fag have had meaning in this context, and I want to associate my discussions here with those kinds of subcultural discourse, not to necessarily condone them, but to address them. The call to sistership has been an important affirmation in many feminist strategies, as I will go on to discuss in Chapter 2; again, this use of the idea of sistership and queerness is not without precedent or relevance in gay subculture.

As we have seen, Richard Dyer has suggested that the process by which gay men designate each other as 'she' is about expressing an identification against straight men and *with* straight women. Among the collegial and formal acknowledgements in Alex Doty's *Making Things Perfectly Queer* lies one which calls upon the honorary sistership of those two little girls from Littlerock and thanks a friend (queer sister?) who's 'the Lorelei to my Dorothy.'[19]

In his passionate and politically fierce eulogy to Vito Russo, 'Right On, Girlfriend!', Douglas Crimp picks up many of the issues raised by speakers such as Larry Kramer, Arnie Kantrowitz and David Dinkins at Russo's memorial service in 1990 and uses them as the opportunity to assess strategies of activism used by gay people during the AIDS emergency.[20] Crimp reports that Kramer used the memorial as an opportunity to affirm Vito Russo's commitment to AIDS activism by lambasting the decision by AmFAR to hold a benefit screening of the then recently released film *Silence of the Lambs*, on the grounds of its representation of the mass-murderer, Jame Gumb as a 'gay man'. Crimp's essay covers a number of issues germane to Kramer's criticism and related to the contemporary context of AIDS activism, but he concludes with an incisive consideration of the differing, and contesting, responses lesbians and gay men have had to *Silence of the Lambs* and its star, the lesbian icon Jodie Foster. Crimp's deliberations return to the cultural context of the memorial service, and several times he marks Vito Russo's 'unashamed worship of Judy Garland'. Crimp does not specify the identity of the girlfriend he salutes in the title of his piece: by their name, gender or sexual orientation. We may deduce that Crimp's 'girlfriend' is Russo, the adored film critic who 'pointed his finger at queers only to tell us how much he loved us and to praise our courage.'[21] The girlfriend certainly isn't Jodie Foster, nor even Larry Kramer or Mayor Dinkins, but 'she' might be Judy Garland:

> . . . Vito's was a feistier kind of dignity, not Jodie's idea of dignity but Judy's, a survivor's dignity. If we really want to honor Vito's memory – as a film scholar and movie buff, as a queer, an activist, and a friend – we shouldn't forget that he loved Judy, and that his identification with her made *him* queer, not her.[22]

In the kinds of relationships constituted in the use of 'she' by gay men referring to each other, and in Doty's fantasy of he and his friend as the Marilyn Monroe and Jane Russell characters from *Gentlemen Prefer Blondes*, as well as in Crimp's designation of Vito Russo as his girlfriend (and/or of Judy Garland as Vito Russo's girlfriend), femininity or womanliness is used as a marker of affiliations which resist hetero-sexualized manhood. It is my project here to investigate the kinds of representation made by gay men who would reject identification with straight men. These kinds of representations would seem to call upon a kind of bonding which I initially refer to as queer sistership, in the spirit of gay men's long-standing affirmations of solidarity with one another expressed through feminine designations; in Chapter 2 I theorize such acts of sistership as heterosocial bonding, a term I introduce to signify how queer sistership resists male homosocial subjectivity. In as far as this designation of sistership is controversial, this is intentional: these investigations will attempt to be as candid and as self-reflexive as possible about the effects of gay male bonding with women. This enquiry is not conducted through an analysis of sociological relationships between groups of gay audiences and specific star images, but it attempts to uncover some of the structural conditions that shape these relationships by assessing the kinds of knowledge reproduced through specific texts, and the kinds of contests enacted over the meanings of those texts.

The methodological tool used in this investigation is cultural materi-alism, whereby texts, in the form of literature, television and film, but also reviews, interviews and other cultural artefacts, are themselves seen as instances of cultural reproduction. Textual material offers relatively tangible opportunities for making an assessment of the conditions through which knowledge is being reproduced. Cultural materialism assumes that no text can adequately account for the culture which it represents: that is, its representation of that culture will not be coher-ent, and will not be able to contain all the possibilities it necessarily brings into play. As the social order reproduces itself it cannot but throw up contradiction and conflict. It is the job of culture to produce knowledge with which to handle that level of complication: more reac-tionary artefacts may strive to explain away contradiction and abrasive conditions, smoothing away incoherence to attain plausibility; while more radical and oppositional interests may attempt to maximize the effect of incoherence and contradiction. It is very important to assess the conditions for interpretation by analyzing not only texts them-selves, but the debates they attract and the criticism with which their meaning is managed. Systems of knowledge in which we make sense of our lives abound with what have been called faultlines, that are a prod-uct of abrasion between often competing locations of authority.[23]

This is not a book about star icons, nor is it a history of divas, dames, bitches, martyrs, sirens, victims, bombshells, nymphettes, goddesses, tramps, vamps and tarts beatified by gay men. Rather, what I want to do is to try and understand the nature of gay men's interest in women and demonstrate the importance of gender in understanding gay identities. I am not after a big, totalizing history, but a more detailed, intimate account of relations and structures. These concerns are pursued through four chapters, each of which works to historically and politically situate its arguments. Chapter 1 uses the contests enacted by disparate constituencies over the meanings of Tennessee Williams's play *A Streetcar Named Desire* to look at the models available for understanding gay men's representation of women. 'From Pathology to Gender Dissent' tracks a number of different reading strategies that have been deployed by hostile dominant critics, feminist critics, queer avant-garde performers, gay academics and gay subcultural audiences in their investments in *Streetcar*. The chapter concludes with a new reading which attempts to exploit gay understandings of the relationship between Williams and his character of Blanche DuBois, by associating them with a de-naturalization of male power, that facilitates an incisive critique of heterosexuality and an alignment with the interests of women.

Chapter 2 takes up the questions about male power and the structure of heterosexuality from the first and maps out some of the conceptual and political struggles which have organized our understanding of feminist politics and gay politics. It attempts to understand in detail the structural relationship between straight men, women and gay men by undertaking a detailed consideration of male homosocial narratives and the functionality within them of women and queerness. This chapter uncovers heterosocial tendencies which may offer a model for understanding relationships between women and gay men.

The latter half of the book then attempts to apply this model to representations which seem deliberately to make this affiliation as described in 'Heterosocial Tendencies'. Chapter 3 notes the extent to which straight women attempt to form alliances with gay men, and looks in detail at the representations made of lesbians and gays in the American situation comedy *Roseanne*, which has a considerable queer address. The analysis of *Roseanne* processes the extent to which heterosocial dissent is a function of faultlines within narratives of male homosociality. Chapter 4 looks at the work of gay director and writer Pedro Almodóvar in order to judge the extent to which gay male representations of women are able to overcome homosocial narratives (and the inducements these make to gay men to assimilate themselves within patriarchal interests) and make promising and useful heterosocial affiliations.

1
From Pathology to Gender Dissent: Tennessee Williams's *A Streetcar Named Desire*

In December 1996 a new production of *A Streetcar Named Desire* opened at the Haymarket Theatre in London. It was directed by Sir Peter Hall, a pillar of the English theatre, and it starred the noted, Oscar-winning American film actress Jessica Lange in the role of Blanche DuBois. Big guns for a play first performed in 1947. Yet as critics of the Haymarket production indicated with varying degrees of hyperbole, *Streetcar* 'is one of the great American plays of the century',[1] even 'one of the great plays of the century',[2] 'a masterpiece'[3] and of Blanche 'possibly the greatest part created for a woman in the modern American theatre',[4] 'one of the supreme roles of drama'.[5] *Streetcar* is a work for which critics, directors, actors, theorists and filmmakers maintain a tenacious interest that seems to be continuing beyond the fag-end of the millennium. Indeed Tennessee Williams himself seems to remain a figure through whom considerable cultural capital can be exchanged. In 1992 the prestigious University of Minnesota Press published David Savran's study of masculinity in the plays of Williams and Arthur Miller, while in 1993 a new collection of essays *Confronting Tennessee Williams's 'A Streetcar Named Desire'* was published, as well as a new coffee table biography of Williams, by Ronald Hayman.[6] Another biography concentrating on the writer's early life, *Tom: The Unknown Tennessee Williams* appeared in 1995.[7] In the summer 1994 London's National Theatre staged a highly prestigious and sumptuous revival of *Sweet Bird of Youth* and he remains a consistently produced playwright. The cinematic adaptations of Williams's plays continue to be shown on television from time to time, and in early 1997 the BBC broadcast a season of them to mark the West End production of *Streetcar*.

Yet if Williams remains a figure that elicits notions of artistic greatness, worthy of revivals and national acclaim fourteen years after his death, he also remains implicitly understood as a homosexual, with an emblematic fixation on his women characters. The National's opulent production of *Sweet Bird of Youth* was the occasion for the resuscitation in the British broadsheet press of a discourse about the particular significance of Williams's female characterizations, a discourse which reappeared in critical appraisals of the Haymarket's *Streetcar*. In 1994 the *Independent*, which ran a full page feature headlined, 'Tennessee Williams and His Women', suggested that:

> Williams's women, more than those of any other 20th-century dramatist, only truly exist in performance. That they are merely feminised men has been disproved time and again.[8]

That such disproving needs to be stated, again, might indicate that the *Independent* was uncertain how conclusive the denial has been. There is also considerable slight of hand here: the allusion to 'feminised men' feigns an indeterminacy about the ideological narrative in question, which actually suggests that Blanche, Maggie, the Princess and company specifically represent the playwright himself. In her *From Reverence to Rape* Molly Haskell offers a more incisive and ingenuous account of the *Independent*'s apparently disproved notion:

> In the case of Tennessee Williams' women, there is little confusion. His hothouse, hot-blooded 'earth mothers' and drag queens – Blanche DuBois, Serafina, Maggie, and Alexandra Del Lago – are as unmistakably a product of the fifties as they are of his own baroquely transvestised homosexual fantasies.[9]

This suggestion that Williams's notable female characters were dragged-up versions of himself seems tenacious, even when it is being denied or supplanted. For Alistair Macaulay, 'Blanche's displays of femininity are so self-dramatizing, and her confusions about masculinity are so emphatic, that her role – as it is written – is very nearly that of a drag-queen, albeit highly poignant. Just how much self-projection was there for Williams in creating her?'[10] Writing about *Streetcar* at the Haymarket in 1997 it seems clear that John Gross wants to acknowledge the denial, even as he finds it difficult not to recirculate and invest in the 'disproved' notion:

> Even if [Williams] hadn't acknowledged as much, there would be no prizes for guessing how closely he identified with [Blanche]. It would

be too cut and dried to speak of a homosexual subtext – she is emphatically a woman, not a man in disguise – but the story of her ill-fated early marriage to a young 'degenerate' (her sister's word for him) strongly signals the presence of transposed homosexual feelings.[11]

The Observer's Michael Coveney refuses even to acknowledge the sell-by date of the proposition in which he invests, that *Sweet Bird*'s Princess 'can be viewed as a metaphoric version of Williams himself on a bad day'.[12]

These critical responses offer particularly clear examples of what David Savran has called the 'virtual ubiquity' of Stanley Edgar Hyman's notion of the 'Albertine strategy', which refers to Proust's Albert-made-Albertine transposition, and describes the transvestism of the authorial position.[13] This transaction exemplifies a preponderant strain of knowledge through which homosexuality is socially understood, but which has not just sustained for mainstream critics: it has also become an enduring part of gay men's pleasures in plays like *Streetcar*. Blanche DuBois, Alexandra del Lago, Maggie the Cat and Amanda Wingfield have inspired and thrilled generations of homosexual men, like Mike Silverstein, who wrote his 'An Open Letter to Tennessee Williams' in 1971: 'You were among the first to teach me that women are my sisters, fellow-victims. Blanche DuBois, Hannah Jelkes, above all the Gnadiges Fraulein . . . these were the first sisters I had encountered'.[14] But it's not just sistership that gay men have found in works like *Streetcar*. The iconography of brutish, irresistible machismo that is crystallized in the character of Stanley Kowalski and refracted through those of Chance Wayne, Brick and the rest, has provided a defining imagery for contemporary homosexual culture, as Derek Jarman has noted: 'The modern Queer was invented by Tennessee Williams. Brando in blue jeans, sneakers, white T-shirt and leather jacket. When you saw that, you knew they were available.'[15] If *A Streetcar Named Desire* can be understood as presenting women as the opportunity for gay sistership and identification, then it may also be understood as presenting men as the opportunity for gay desire.

It would seem then, that Tennessee Williams's *A Streetcar Named Desire* is an ideal vehicle with which to look at how dominant, that is heterosexual, groups and marginal, homosexual groups, have handled competing notions about the nature of gay identity and its relationship to identifications with women. Not only has the play elicited critical responses of an extraordinary tenacity and passion, but was written before the emergence of Gay Liberation: the considerable attention it has generated spans key historical shifts in the nature of gay identity.

This gives us the opportunity to draw out the kinds of knowledge implicated in the contests enacted over the meanings of the play.

1.1 *Streetcar*: Perversion or great American (queer) art?

The ways in which mainstream American theatre criticism, and indeed the US cultural establishment generally, has handled Tennessee Williams show us that he has been a source of considerable anxiety. On the one hand his works were showered with acclaim and awards: when *A Streetcar Named Desire* opened on Broadway in 1947 it won the New York Drama Critics' Circle Award and the Pulitzer Prize, and in 1952 Elia Kazan's film version won the New York Film Critics' Circle Award; *Cat on a Hot Tin Roof* was first performed in 1955 and eventually ran for 694 performances, winning the Pulitzer Prize, the Drama Critics' Circle and Donaldson Awards. In the West the emergence of cold-war ideology in the early 1950s insisted on the moral, spiritual and cultural superiority of the American way of life over communism. Williams's success, both at home and abroad, which we may in part attribute to a degree of controversy about the sauciness of his depiction of heterosexual relations, made it necessary for him to be embraced as emblematic of that American superiority. Yet by the 1960s, critics such as Howard Taubman and Stanley Kauffman began to question the way in which understandings of American culture were being handled by Williams; they also challenged the work of Edward Albee and William Inge, homosexual dramatists who were also hugely popular and successful. In 1963, shortly after the Broadway debut of Albee's *Who's Afraid of Virginia Woolf?*, Taubman wrote a piece for the *New York Times* in which he claimed to want to help the people of America recover their 'lost innocence'. He entreated them to:

> Look out for the baneful female who is a libel on womanhood.
> Look out for the hideous wife who makes a horror of the marriage relationship.
> Be suspicious of the compulsive slut ... who represents a total disenchantment with the possibility of a fulfilled relationship between man and woman.[16]

By the 1970s, Stanley Kauffman was more explicit:

> we have all had much more than enough of the materials so often presented by the three writers in question [Williams, Albee, Inge]:

the viciousness towards women, the lurid violence that seems a sublimation of social hatreds, the transvestite sexual exhibitionism that
has the same sneering exploitation of its audience that every club
stripper has behind her smile.[17]

I think Kauffman's comments about female sex workers make it fairly
clear that the 'three writers in question' are not perhaps the only ones
harbouring a sublimated viciousness towards women. In a deft move of
patriarchal recuperation (his presumptive 'we'), homosexuals are positioned as pathologically bitter in the same moment at which women
are reinstated into the protective and parochial fold – as long as they
don't compromise the duplicity upon which male authority reproduces
itself (hence the alleged 'sneering exploitation' of the sex worker). But
Kauffman is rattled by these writers: his recuperation of patriarchal
effects into gay male misogyny is but a thin veil for his discomfort – the
fluidity and integrity of his authority is straining at this point, and
requires a violent reinstatement ('viciousness', 'lurid violence', 'hatreds',
'sneering') which betrays his anxiety.

Molly Haskell's work in *From Reverence to Rape* showed how homosexual representations of women might facilitate patriarchal purposes
in their negotiation of repression and in their desire to express erotic
excess. Very quickly her feminist analysis of Williams's female characterizations was re-appropriated however, by criticism with a dominant
project. An example of such an appropriation is offered by Stephen
S. Stanton in his collection of critical essays published in 1977.[18]
Haskell's thesis proposed a feminist analysis of filmic representation: it
was precisely this kind of work that gave strength and encouragement
to similarly critical discourses enacted by lesbians and gay men, and yet
only three years after *From Reverence*, Haskell's repudiation of Williams's
women as lustful cyphers of homosexual histrionics and her reticence
about acknowledging them as representations of a de-naturalized heterosexuality makes a recuperative assimilation of her work for homophobic purposes disconcertingly smooth. Whereas the tone of Haskell's
analysis is invigoratingly pejorative, Stanton's introduction strikes an
oily balance between outright bigotry and hegemonic liberalism. In a
volume hysterically concerned with rescuing Williams's canonical stature from the twin nemeses of diminishing 'artistic' quality and homosexual vice, it is clear from the opening paragraph which poses the gravest
challenge for Stanton's project.

The increasing openness with which Williams represented himself in
interviews through the early 1970s, culminating in the highly explicit

Memoirs of 1975, is attributed by Stanton not to the political and social shifts engendered by several years of Gay Liberation agitation but to the playwright's personal 'confession', prompted not by political conscious-ness or an alignment with liberationary activity, but by 'courage' that was permitted by a 'new tolerance' in the media.[19] Such terms deftly disempower Williams's agency as a flourishing 'gay' man whilst they veil Stanton's recuperative intentions in liberal condescension, secured by the smug insistence upon his distance from earlier critics, who with considerably more ingenuousness dismissed Williams's work as what has been described as a 'Fetid swamp'.[20] Stanton magnanimously acknowledges Williams's 'shortcomings' which, if they are to become great drama must 'be better distanced and universalized'. He considers Stanley Edgar Hyman's notion of the Albertine strategy to be 'percept-ive' because it enables this universalization:

> [Tennessee Williams's] plays are frequently transvestite since they substitute women for men in the sexual relationships; and the best of them succeed in transforming homosexual into heterosexual relationships . . . in drawing on his private experience, he has univer-salized it.[21]

This circuit of incorporative recuperation is secured with reference to an instance of Williams's own attempt to incorporate: 'A true faggot does not like my women. I do not have a faggot, a homosexual, a gay audience. I write for an audience.' Here, Williams's strategic retreat, itself a function of the homophobic terms under which the playwright had to negotiate the public reception of his work (if not his own homophobia), isolates the 'gay' audience from the universal fold to which Stanton welcomes Williams – as long as he is really writing about universal heterosexuals and vilifying faggots.

The difficulty which Taubman and Kauffman were attempting to bludgeon, and which Stanton was attempting unctuously to connive away resides in Williams's homosexuality being so proximate to under-standings of him as a great American playwright. Cold war ideology rested on policing the virility of the imperialist nation state, that is, on upholding the naturalized integrity of the heterosexual patriarchal sub-ject. The rise of psychoanalysis as popular discourse through the 1950s in America all too clearly manifested homosexuality as tangible and unsettling to the internal confidence of that subjectivity. As Alan Sinfield has shown, Freud's reference to the notion of bisexual latency 'meant that *anyone* might be subject to deep-set homosexual inclinations. This was convenient for witchhunters'.[22] The idea of latency provided ample opportunity for the exploitation of anxiety in potential subjects, for it implied that the unspeakable homosexual urge may possibly reside deep in the subconscious of even the most manly American: certainly the more anxious that subject the more he would attract an aura of paranoia and guilt. Yet, as Sinfield suggests, 'latency was too good; once you started looking, no one was exempt'[23] and this could explain the gradual turn from an opportunistic celebration of Williams as a great American artist to a systematic demonization of him that Taubman and Kauffman exemplify. It became necessary to turn the anxiety from the threat within to the threat without; hence Kauffman's instructive guidelines: 'look out for the baneful female' for she is a sign of homosexuality, of un-Americanism.

For US cold-war ideology this 'baneful female', the woman with sexuality, personality, presence is not only unacceptable as the bearer, enabler, of American manliness, she is in fact not even a woman, but a product of a warped homosexual imaginary. It is also clear that while the preoccupation of Kauffman and Taubman with the women characters in the plays of Williams and his colleagues is an index of their Freudian understanding of the homosexuality of these playwrights, it also represents an unease about the ideological relationship between naturalized heterosexual gender roles and homosexuality. Freudian notions of inversion, appropriated from the work of the earliest radical homosexual writers and assimilated within Freud's system of sexual aberrations, provided a way for hostile critics to make *Streetcar* about homosexuality – allowed them to render it perverse – which rescued them from the difficulty offered by Williams's problematizing representation of heterosexuality. The abhorrence that is present in *Streetcar* for Taubman and his chums is not actually a *product* of Williams's homosexuality, but is rather *revealed* by its de-naturalising effect upon systems of gender. The playwright's sexuality enables an uncomfortably incisive critique of heterosexuality. This idea will be developed throughout this chapter and consolidated in a reading of the play which closes it.

Inversion: *Maurice* and unrequited desire

Stanley Kauffman, Molly Haskell and Stephen Stanton would seem to want to situate Williams's own identifications as being uncomplicatedly through Blanche as a desirer of Stanley.[24] It is important to be highly sceptical of such accounts, not only because they pathologise homosexuality, or render it as an eternal state of victimisation, but because they uphold homosexuality as an abnormal reflection of heterosexuality whose function it is to normalize gender roles. Williams's *Memoirs* make it clear that he liked to dominate men, not the other way round, and while this does not provide conclusive evidence of the nature of his identificatory or fantasy practices, it certainly enables us to problematize accounts of homosexual desire that position gay men as necessarily locked into a masochistic erotic relationship with an ultra-masculine stud.[25] The undercurrents in such accounts suggest a cultural, rather than particularly homosexual, fascination with the authority and legitimacy of the butch male as the appropriate, proper male as sexual subject, in relation to which feminine subjects (be they homosexual male or heterosexual female) must simper in passive admiration. In the logic of their paranoia these critics subscribe to a prevailing psychoanalytic construction of homosexuality as an inversion of physical and psychic sex identity: Williams's female characters express his morbid (and un-American) homosexuality which is a pathological inversion of normal masculinity and femininity. However, the pathological and heterosexist notion of inversion made popular through psychoanalytic discourse in the 1950s was itself an appropriation of models of inversion or of a third sex which emerged in the nineteenth century and were separately proposed by the likes of Krafft-Ebing, Karl Heinrich Ulrichs and Havelock Ellis, who were attempting to make sense of their desires.[26]

Inversion was initially proposed by early homosexual writers as a way of naturalizing what had been perceived first as sinful, and then later, perverse behaviour. Ironically the later appropriation of inversion, or third sex, theories by Freud provided a whole new clinical, and later institutional, context for the legitimation of the idea of homosexuality as perversion. The concept of inversion is predicated on a 'natural', biological division of the species along gender lines, and the idea subsequently circulated culturally as an expression of the need to suggest the inevitability of camp stereotypes for gay men and butch stereotypes for lesbians, and then explain that stereotype as scientific (medical) fact.

Karl Heinrich Ulrichs, a German lawyer, began to write about what he called the third sex in an attempt to intervene in the juridical regulation of 'unnatural fornication' in the 1860s. Ulrichs' notion of the third sex, or Uranism, was based on a dichotomy of body and soul in which a mismatch has taken place in the first three months of foetal development; the same period in which the medical profession was asserting that physical hermaphrodism became manifest: indeed, inversion was called a 'hermaphrodisy of the mind'. The foetus is then left with the body of one sex and the soul of the other; however, Ulrichs had little conception of how this mismatch would constitute the characteristics of a third sex: the only area in which the concept really appeared to interest him was that of the reversal of normal sexual preference.[27]

A crucial aspect of Ulrichs' contention was that sexual relations between Uranians and what we would now call heterosexual youths ('Dionians') should be decriminalized because he believed that most Uranians desired sexual relations with heterosexuals:

> 'Is a Uranian sexually attracted to a Uranian? A little or not at all.' They were as little attracted to each other as they were to women, for whom they felt abhorrence in sexual matters. The Uranian's object of desire was a person who was male in body and soul, that is, a Dionian. Ulrichs recast the dichotomy of female and male desire into a theory of the Uranian lover and his Dionian beloved.[28]

Ulrichs' conceptualisation of homosexuality as a third sex became the prevailing structure of knowledge on the subject for much of the next century. As George Chauncey has noted, the end of the nineteenth century was a crucial period in the emergence of understandings of homosexuality as the characterisation of certain identifiable individuals rather than as a form of sinful behaviour in which anyone might engage.[29] Repudiated or moderated, Ulrichs' notion predominantly organised the discourse on homosexuality until the rise of social problem discourses in the 1950s and 1960s.[30] Indeed, one of my contentions is that Ulrichs' propositions, and the idea of inversion, continue to be deeply implicated in ideological work in relation to sexuality, and specifically so in the consideration of Tennessee Williams's relationship to women as a sex, and femininity as a sign of gender.

We can perhaps see the force of Ulrichs' work in E.M. Forster's post-humously published homosexual (Uranian?) novel *Maurice* which translates many of Ulrichs' preoccupations into an English class context; and which, although not published until 1971, remains an important indicator of the prevailing knowledges of the time it was written – a mere thirty years after Krafft-Ebing's initial scientific consideration of Ulrichs' work, and fourteen years after Ulrichs' own later writings.[31] We could perhaps suggest that *Maurice* was the first important novel in English literature to assemble a 'modern' male homosexual identity; *The Well of Loneliness* occupying a similar place in relation to lesbianism. It is, of course, lamentable that Forster's novel was not published earlier (especially after the prosecution of *Lady Chatterley's Lover* under the Obscene Publications Act in 1960), its latency is a depressing but compelling missed opportunity: the possibilities for mobilization and cultural shift might have been diverse and substantial. Nevertheless, even though the novel did not have the opportunity to circulate as *The Well* did, it remains an important indication of the thinking prevalent at the moment of its conception, and since 1970 it has circulated widely and visibly. It remains an important instance of an attempt to assemble a matrix of homosexual identities at a notably early point. I want to suggest the strength of the influence that Ulrichs's understanding of abnormal sexual object choice, as a confusion of sex and gender, had at the turn of the century, in order to then demonstrate how subsequent negotiations of this model were remorselessly caught up in its concerns.

Maurice was famously inspired by a visit to the socialist writer and self-proclaimed Uranian Edward Carpenter (who was heavily influenced by Ulrichs), and his comrade and lover, George Merrill, who touched Forster's bum, sending a sensation 'straight through the small of my back and into my ideas'.[32] Written at a time during which the very possibility of homosexual desire as a discursive notion was still in its infancy, *Maurice* necessarily exhibits the incoherences that are held within the models of homosexuality Forster was mobilizing, and which are displaced across other models disputed and incorporated into those which he favoured. John Fletcher offers a reading of the complex inter-sections the novel exhibits around divergent Platonic models of manly love which are themselves inconclusive.[33] Fletcher asserts that Forster's imperative happy ending is a vision of sexual sameness, a 'virile doub-ling', possible only because of two crucial textual absences:

> *Maurice* is notable for the absence of a theory of inversion, of inter-mediacy or of cross-gendering such as marks the writings of many of Forster's homosexual contemporaries, e.g. Proust, Radclyffe Hall and especially Edward Carpenter. Also noticeable is its sexual inexplicit-ness, the absence of the theme of sodomy so crucial to Forster's other suppressed homosexual fictions which turn on the act of sodomy as the symbolic act of male inversion through which a range of other differences – barbarian/christian, missionary/native, officer/half caste, milkman/baronet – are played out.[34]

I would suggest, however, that this is not strictly the case. Forster's text is haunted by inversionist structures, and consequently by an ideological imperative Ulrichs exemplified in his manifestos of Uranism, and which he reproduced so eloquently (albeit with the most transgressive of motives) which gestures towards a gendering of difference across desire.

Present among the counter-currents of Greek ideals in the romance between Maurice and Clive is the spectre of class difference, which carries with it a connotation of gender, paradoxically in a reverse formation to that which Uranism enacts. Homosexuality, most noticeably of the effete, dandy variety, was associated with the leisure classes: they had the material means to enact an aesthetic – an identity, and they had the money with which to procure working class men.[35] Consequently a cultural association of effeminacy, which we could suggest was locked into place by the Wilde trials, was enacted around upper-class identity.[36] In tracking the construction of the desires at play in Forster's plot and character system we find a substantial incoherence which pivots around the class, intellectual, and thus, gendered identity of the protagonists. Clive is upper class and a literary intellectual during his relationship with Maurice at Cambridge, although he is noticeably, necessarily, not a dandy. He is a figure in whom the text invests considerable anxiety: he mustn't be a dandy in order to suggest a mutual manliness in his relationship with Maurice, but he must be enough of a literary intellectual to be familiar with the Platonic dialogues. Further there is Risley, in whose literary intellectual circle Clive is implicated, and who is a powerful background figure in the Cambridge part of the novel. Risley represents a classically effete leisure class dandy; a figure situated perversely in relation to the heroic manliness of our protagonists. It is in the measure of Clive and Maurice's difference from Risley at Cambridge that we gain an orientation as to the sexual character of the principals: Risley is the known quantity, the foppish, sissy dandy ('They sat down, and Risley turned with a titter to Maurice and said, 'I simply can't think of a reply to that'; in each of his sentences he accented one word violently.')[37] in relation to whom Maurice appears as a rough, rugger playing man, and for whom we are led to believe Risley has a sexual desire: '[Maurice] had not spoken before, and his voice, which was low but very gruff, made Risley shiver' (p. 33), and furthermore an attraction which is conceived through a collapse back into Uranism – Risley of the aesthetic sensibility (feminine soul?) and male body desiring the gruff Maurice, who at this point is nominally Dionian, partially by virtue of the fact that he is the object of the leisure-class effete homosexual's desire and therefore he must be 'masculine'.

Leaving university, Clive also leaves the leisure class and becomes, quite literally, landed gentry, a responsible lord and estate owner. Maurice is distinctly middle class at Cambridge and beyond, thus during his affair with Clive the arrangements suggest a seduction of the Dionian Maurice by the effete, inverted Clive, whose strategy of seduction is itself literary ('I knew you read the Symposium in the vac' p. 56). As I have suggested, however, this inversionist structure must be unstable, given the diverse deployments of Platonic ideals Forster enacts, Clive's ultimate refusal of physical love ('"I? It's appalling you should attribute such thoughts to me", pursued Clive. Had he corrupted an inferior's intellect?'),[38] and our knowledge as readers of Maurice's troubled feelings. Nevertheless, among the diverse notions implicated in Forster's schema, inversion, and its attendant gender structure, are to be found, latently and crucially festering. Upon Maurice's consensual progress into the relationship with Clive his status as Dionian 'other' must dissipate – the mutuality of their desire produces sameness, and their love cannot be sustained. Although, with Greek heroism and unlikely forwardness, it is Scudder who initiates the sex with Maurice, their relationship, before the transcendent retreat to the Greenwood, is characterized by the fear and exploitation that is a function of their class identities.

Again, alongside the Greek ideals, the organization of the homosexual relationship is shot through with gendered notions of Uranism–Dionism. Forster doggedly attempts to neutralize this tendency, but his vision of manly sameness is destabilized by a rupture along the lines of class difference in which the desire is constituted. There is a suggestion in John Fletcher's analysis that Forster's imperative was the writing of a narrative in which his own paradoxical absence from the happy ending could be conceptually, or at least fantasmatically, reinstated. As Carpenter's ideal of Greek and manly comradeship is shot through with implicitly (although suppressed) gendered class difference, and posits a desire which is compromised by similarity, and enflamed by difference ('my ideal of love is a powerful, strongly built man ... preferably of the working class. ... Anything effeminate in a man ... repels me very decisively'),[39] so we could say the same of the desire that he inspired in Forster,

> I want to love a strong, young man of the lower classes and be loved by him and even hurt by him. That is my ticket ...[40]

and which is represented in Maurice:

> 'This too has gone wrong' began flitting through his brain. ... He was back in the smoking-room at home with Clive, who said, 'I don't love you any more; I'm sorry', and he felt that his life would revolve in cycles of a year, always to the same eclipse. [...] They must live outside class. (p. 208)

What the text does not, cannot, acknowledge, is the position which the writer holds in the structures of Uranian desire that are being consciously disavowed in all this manly Greek love, which can adequately be used to handle platonic friendship (the kind to which Clive is referring in his last meeting with Maurice when he says 'But surely – the sole excuse for any relationship between men is that it remain purely platonic.' p. 213) but cannot do the job when the text requires something a little more carnal. In order to participate successfully in the consummation of virile sameness, Forster (and arguably Carpenter as well)[41] must disavow his own upper middle class literary effete intellectualism, in the process suppressing the Uranian inversion that constantly informs and structures the desire he represents in *Maurice*, and mitigates against the happy ending. The retreat into the Greenwood cannot sustain the weight of the desire for transcendence that the conflicting currents of identity in which Forster is bound up in the novel require. Crucially for the plausibility of his manly and symmetrical lovers, Forster is unable successfully to supplant Ulrichs's Uranian model with a Greek one – partially because of the instability of the notion of manly Greek egalitarianism, and partially because of the anxiety Forster had about the identity he perceived himself to inhabit in the Uranian model, which for him, we may now suggest, necessitated its suppression.

We might suggest that Forster's anxiety is one precipitated by the acknowledgement of a disjunction, particularly troubling in homosexual arrangements, between identification and desire. Because he identifies himself as not being what he values and exalts as a sexual being, the desired, the 'strong young man of the lower classes', the implicitly masculine Dionian figure, he exhibits a need to re-locate his identification away from the Uranian model in which his desire is constituted, and closer to that which is the desired, desirable: the masculine Dionian. The urgency with which *Maurice* seeks to secure its symmetrical 'virile doubling', is an index of the degree to which Forster found himself enmeshed in a structure which gendered his desire, and which his class and value system rendered him unable to be empowered by. Classified by his own desires and tastes as a feminine man, a Uranian, Forster was locked into a continually unrequited search for a plausible Dionian identification. It is for its exemplification of this quite particular difficulty in the negotiation of homosexual desires to be and to have that *Maurice* is useful.

Over half-a-century later, this inversionist model is still being used to enmesh homosexual writers, with, it seems, little more opportunity allowed for the possibilities of subverting or contesting a system still entrenched in Uranian principles. While Williams states in the *Memoirs* that he wasn't attracted to camp men,[42] there is no reason to believe that he had a masochistic orientation towards Stanley (or Brando for that matter) as a 'real' (heterosexual) man. Such latently inversionist accounts elide the power relations within and across homosexual desires and identities, merely positing gay desire as a unitary position, reflexive of a self-loathing desire for the unattainable 'real' man (Dionian): unattainable as both an ego ideal or sexual partner. Inversionism cannot conceptualize a man's 'active' masculine desire for a 'passive' feminine male partner; nor, for that matter, a sissy's desire for another sissy. Homosexual men must be locked into a struggle simultaneously to find both acceptable points of identification in the available systems which offer only the abjection of effeminacy, and to find the possibility of imagining a requitable object of desire when the cultural imperative offers only the endless unrequitability of 'real' heterosexual (Dionian) men. We can see the mirror of this formulation in Radclyffe Hall's melodramatic *The Well of Loneliness*, which was first published in 1928. Among its many strategies, it offers the immutability of inversion as God-given and inverts are represented as inevitably suffering – but with the worthiness, even holiness, of martyrs: Hall's protagonist is named after the first Christian martyr, is born on the eve of the Redeemer who saved by suffering and the novel is suffused with religious motifs and language.[43] The novel posits lesbianism as inversion, and has little trouble conceptualizing the desires of its butch protagonist, Stephen Gordon, but collapses under the strain of attempting to position the desire of her femme partners, Angela or Mary, who behave all wrong: Stephen desires them because they are women with the consciousness of men, and thus they have to be femme-acting; yet if they behave in a 'feminine' way, how can their desire for Stephen be explained by the inversion of a male consciousness in women's bodies? They can either be femme-acting or desire women, but within an inversionist account, they cannot be both.

This is of course one of the contradictions through which the heterosexual hegemony proceeds, which allows for multiple accounts of the identities which is its project to contain – inversion theories portray gay men as all limp-wristed Uranian femmes in pursuit of a Dionian real man (lesbians as masculine butches inevitably unrequited in their desire of feminine women), while disease models portray gay men and lesbians as infectious, predatory figures, sin models absolve the desire but damn the sexual practice and so on. These models are activated by culturally-situated needs to police the boundaries of gender. While each specific discourse may prove to be disabling within its own frame, the diversity of accounts that must proliferate, in order to attempt to contain all threatening possibilities, produces faultlines in the cultural landscape.[44] It is at the point of rupture, when these discourses or stories collide, that ideological work is most anxiously and viciously undertaken to secure the hegemony and (re)contain the contradictions: these moments are opportunities for mobilization and dissidence. Dominant authority does not necessarily collapse under the weight of these contradictions, but they are potential breaking points, at which new formations are possible, as the terms of cultural reproduction are contested and negotiated. Thus it is not sufficient merely to comment upon the difficulties that ensue when we attempt to make sense of our practices and validate our identifications or desires; we need to be sensitive to the complexity of the power structures in which we are positioned and in which we are jostling. If the rise of psychoanalysis as popular discourse in America gave the narrative of inversion an authoritative invigoration in the 1950s and 1960s, then the growing cultural confidence and political activism of homosexual subcultures enabled a dissident assault upon such hetero-patriarchal knowledge.

Coming out: Stonewall and gay politics

As we have seen, Gay politics emerged in the liberationary aftermath of the Stonewall riots of June 1969 in Greenwich Village in New York. The riots acted as a catalyst for the burgeoning political awareness and anger among homosexuals which was engendered by a climate of heightened social unrest that characterized 1960s radical politics in America. The political character of the Gay Liberation Front, which emerged within a month of the Stonewall riots, could be said to be largely influenced by the strategies and rhetoric of the black power, feminist, student and anti-Vietnam war movements that shaped the face of a dissident politics in the US during the 1960s. A similar movement emerged in Britain, influenced by the ardour of American post-Stonewall militism, but distinct in its negotiation of the crucial 1967 Sexual Offences Act, which instated containing and liberally tolerant notions of public and private, and opened but a small window of legal acceptability for certain male homosexual practices in private.

One of the characterizing principles of Gay Liberation was the development of a politics of coming out, which sought to contest the reorganization of dominant regulation that had occurred in Britain with the premise of liberal toleration of homosexual behaviour in private.

Similarly, in America, an uneasy combination of post-1950s hysteria about manliness, homosexuality and Communism, alongside the veneration of citizenship in the ideology of the Constitution brought about a state in which homosexuality could be tolerated, but only in private. Coming out of the closet was a crucial Gay Liberation strategy and involved reversing the terms of the public silence on sexual orientation and of coming together in unity. The effect of mounting a politics around 'coming out', as Eve Sedgwick has pointed out, however, is to reverse the process through which the containment is effected, rendering 'closetedness' itself as a 'performance initiated as such by the speech act of a silence'.[45]

The boundaries of the normal, of heterosexuality, are policed by the continuing connotation of homosexuality as an abjection; but this connotation is an open secret, which naturalizes the 'normal' by continually conjuring, but not speaking, homosexuality. Instating the notion of the closet as a site of contestation, out of which one can emerge, and through the invocation of which normality is secured, was one of the ways in which the particular politics of Gay Liberation came into intelligibility. Crucial to the movement was the assertion of an identity politics, similar to that of the women's movement, whereby what had been perceived as personal, possibly pathologised behaviour, became a political, positively affirmed identity; slogans used by the movement included 'Gay is good' and 'Gay is proud'. This mobilization also entailed the celebration of cultural forms that were considered to be intrinsically gay and rejecting of 'straight' norms and values. These forms eventually included drag, cruising, promiscuity, anonymous and public sex, camp, aestheticism and theatricality, sadomasochism, pornography, body building and body worship and a whole range of other practices problematically melded into an identifiable 'gay sensibility'.[46]

However, there was a tendency for the new liberationists to dismiss earlier political interventions, such as the Homophile Movement when, as John D'Emilio has pointed out, it seems apparent their work was a precursor to that of Gay Liberation and in part enabled its existence.[47] Thus, although we could say that there were distinct and fundamental discontinuities between the pre- and post-Stonewall eras, we need to emphasize the particular character and tenor of the Gay Liberation rhetoric and activity, rather than ascribe the earlier Homophile period to conservatism and the later Liberationism to radicalism. It is also important not to subtend a neat model of history which attributes the degree of political progression in direct proportion to the passing of time and the emergence of new and distinct movements. Although post-Stonewall activity within the Gay Liberation movement did represent a break with the terms of the earlier Homophile movement, Gay Liberation did not become the only rhetoric in circulation, even after Stonewall homosexual women and men continued to mobilise around political material that enabled them to manoeuvre and gain some leverage or respite in the precise conditions in which they were embedded. We could now suggest that these could be intelligible as an intersection of geographical and spatial concerns (urban, rural, metropolitan, national) with issues of class, age, ethnicity, education, affluence, marital and parental status, all of which, among others, function as the determining conditions for access to dissident, intellectual and sub-cultural materials. An analogue of this trajectory of negotiating political and cultural models can be found in an analysis of the contests over the emergence of Queer politics in the 1990s which sought to critique what was represented as liberal and comfortable Gay politics; yet Queer activism precisely mobilized the same kinds of political rhetoric and direct action used by Liberationists twenty years earlier. The key to Queer was that it attempted to sell radicalism and dissent to a newer generation who had to own their own involvements.[48]

An important part of the negotiations that entail cultural change and progress is the claiming of texts as indicative of particular moments or movements. This claiming involves a negotiation between existing reading positions and the newer position elaborated by the text that necessarily produces absences or loose ends: those parts of the text that are suppressed or glossed over, the characteristics which strain against the older position from the newer. Gay liberation partly came into intelligibility through the claiming of writers and other cultural producers as gay. Not only did this legitimize the liberation project, but the action of claiming itself was axiomatic, in that it brought the chosen subject out of the closet, and brought them into a process of positive affirmation and collectivity. This activity has been incalculably important in the development of gay identity as a positivity, as a way of conceptualizing a positive space in which to produce and imagine a life in which same-sex desire is possible.

In one of the collections of writings from the National Lesbian and Gay Survey, 'Andrew' writes of the moment at which he came out.[49] Taking part in a community play, a fellow cast member overhears him talking about the film *Torch Song Trilogy* and asks him if he is gay. It seems to be the collective acknowledgement of *Torch Song Trilogy* as a 'gay' film and as something valued within that collectivity that enables 'Andrew' to identify himself. The knowledges through which *Torch Song* is here secured as a gay text are context specific and rely on the apparently positive image the film suggests of a New York drag queen's homosexual lifestyle, and the relative rarity of such imagery. Yet this action is also historically specific: the particular importance of *Torch Song* is embedded in the cultural domain in which 'gay' circulates at the moment of which 'Andrew' is speaking and we may presume is secured by an elaboration of its positive elements (dramatization of a coming-out narrative in which the gay man is autonomous and dignified, depiction of harmonious and humorous domestic arrangements, the opportunity for shared anger and politicization in Alan's murder, and so on), and a suppression or glossing over of its less positive elements (the awkward and pejorative representation of anonymous or promiscuous sex, the primacy of normative, possibly heterosexualized domestic values, the fact that the women have to lose out for the gays to triumph, so that Arnold may be the best woman). Similarly when 'Simon' comes out to his father by extending his gayness back through history, he must suppress Oscar Wilde's marriage and children, Auden's resistance and Tchaikovsky's suicide to elaborate the notions of collectivity and positivity that define that gayness:

> I said, 'What do Proust and Auden, Oscar Wilde, Somerset Maugham, Alexander the Great and Tchaikovsky, Michelangelo, Cole Porter, Noel Coward, Housman, John Gielgud and Marc Almond have in common?' He stared at me. 'Add me to the list', I said.[50]

Identifying the moments of suppression or of glossing that enable the elaboration of a cultural position is an important way of being able to track cultural projects historically. But any cultural criticism must remain aware of not only the theoretical stakes involved, but the emotional ones as well. To vilify 'Andrew' in his alignment with *Torch Song* would be to perpetrate a vast and heinous injustice: *Torch Song Trilogy* is a titanic edifice of fabulousness. However, the circumstances that precipitate our identifications need to be identified in order that we can assess the scope our cultural negotiations have for dissidence or social change.

A Streetcar Named Desire: a gay play?

For those critics who have aligned themselves with the Gay Liberation project and who have engaged with Tennessee Williams, that engagement has been structured by the pathologizing accounts instated by Taubman and company in the 1960s. In keeping with the defining notions of gay politics, writers such as John Clum have attempted to displace the inversionist readings of *Streetcar, Sweet Bird of Youth* and others, with a reading that judges Williams's work by gay criteria; that is, as negotiations of the closet. Alas this project is grounded on a precarious terrain: whatever the enthusiasm with which gay critics may wish to claim Williams, or recognize his works as emblematic expressions of the knowledges and practices of gay culture, they remain products of a pre-liberation time.

Thus we can see that for gay theatrical critic John Clum, the principal concern in the work of Tennessee Williams is the extent of his closeted-ness: this is a marker of the degree to which he is useful to the agendas of Gay Liberation in speaking openly about homosexuality. Clum writes that the playwright 'was much more successful at dramatizing the closet than at presenting a coherent, affirming view of gayness.'[51] For Clum, the closet is an intrinsically problematic realm that it is the project of Gay Liberation to dissipate; yet his model of the closet itself perhaps bears an unfortunate resemblance to a psychoanalytically con-stituted concept of latency operative in American nationalistic para-noia: '*A Streetcar Named Desire*, though *without a living homosexual character or overt gay theme*, depicts in a codified fashion a paradigmatic homosexual experience.'[52] Even apparently radical critical manoeuvres do not necessarily escape the entrapment of dominant and heterosexist ideologies. So, *Streetcar* may not realise any homosexual representation or characterisation, but holds an inherent, and latent, form of homosexu-ality. For Clum, as for other gay critics, the homosexual-ness of char-acters like Blanche DuBois is an effect of the operations of the closet and not of a psychoanalytically ascribed pathology of inversion.[53] The knowing, fallaciously feminine disposition of Blanche then becomes a cloaking of the playwright's homosexual expression, hidden 'within the actions of a heterosexual female character' and this is a function of historical conditions (rather than psychic ones) which censored the open representation of coherent homosexuality (p. 150).

In both the earlier article published in 1989 and also in his book, *Acting Gay: Male Homosexuality in Modern Drama*, first published in 1992, Clum elucidates Williams's dramatisation of the closet in lengthy discussions of how the theatricality of Blanche constructs a series of gay codes that identify her as 'the quintessential gay character in American closet drama'.[54] This theatricality is played off against an eroticisation of the male characters, such as Stanley Kowalski, which makes them the objects of the gaze, and Clum notes that 'straight men could fantasize about the sexual attractiveness and power these male characters had.' This is true, although it is a feature of male sexuality that is not limited to homosexual representations. As Eve Sedgwick famously posits in *Between Men* and Craig Owens discusses in 'Outlaws: Gay Men in Feminism', the maleness of men, which is to be consumed by men through the male gaze, is a central component of the reproduction of masculinity.[55] The constant presence of the threat of homosexuality functions to police the precarious identificatory relationships that men are encouraged to form with idealised forms of masculinity. Thus the suggestion that the eroticisation of Stanley alone signals *Streetcar* as a gay, but closeted, text is a little premature. Clum's suggestion of *Streetcar*'s representation of a 'paradigmatic homosexual experience' seems an equivalent concept to that of 'gay sensibility', in that it calls on the recognition of certain subcultural practices as defining a homogenous gay identity.

Of the characteristics I noted earlier that in part seem to constitute this sensibility, Williams's work and *A Streetcar Named Desire* in particular, exemplify cruising and promiscuity (in Blanche's behaviour with wagon loads of soldiers in Laurel), camp, theatricality and aestheticism (Blanche again, as well as the theatrical and dramatic nature of *Streetcar* as a cultural form in itself), and eroticism of the male body and body building (Stanley, with his shirt off, torn, wet or in the process of being taken off). For Clum this archetypal gay construction is Williams's defence from the homophobia to which the playwright feared he would succumb:

> [Blanche] knows about paper moons and cardboard skies and paper lanterns, but she also knows that performance is both her allure and her protection. And William's [sic] protection of his homosexual subtext is achieved by hiding it within the actions of a heterosexual female character. (p. 150)

Clum is a little more indulgent of Williams in his later book than he is the article, but his criticism is a little barren in that he does not anticipate particular audiences for Williams's work. He says:

> The works of William Inge and Tennessee Williams are closet dramas in their evasions, silences, and invisibilites [sic] and in heterosexist language with which they surround their homosexual characters. They are also plays about the closet itself and about the terrors of being uncloseted. (p. 173)

Part of the problem here is an insufficiently cultural approach to both the terms and conditions that were organizing Williams' own ability to conceptualize his sexuality, and to the reading skills and subcultural strategies that typified gay liberation activity. Proceeding from the understanding that Williams was not writing explicit gay drama, Clum deduces that he must be writing closet gay drama because this is a notion consistent with Clum's own politics. In reading Williams this way, he has to be selective in his account of, for example *A Streetcar Named Desire*, in order to produce the coherence of his 'closet drama' approach. Clum does not discuss the role of Stella or Mitch in the closet economy of the play: if Blanche operates as a gay man, and Stanley is an object for the gay male gaze, how can this account handle the positions of Mitch, who is a heterosexual man and who desires Blanche, and Stella who is a heterosexual woman married to Stanley? As I shall be discussing shortly, Mitch's masculinity is not unmediated itself – through a certain passivity and connotations of Freudian homosexuality – and Stella is represented as a desiring, sexual woman. These factors at the very least trouble Clum's reading: within his own logic the audience for Blanche's theatricality needs to be masculine, in order not to rupture the ironic authority of her performance, and if it is the men in whom Williams is apparently constructing the drama's eroticism, then how come Stella, as a nontheatrical woman is shown to be actively sexual – what happens to the matrix of gender and sexual representation that Clum describes in this instance?

Further, in vilifying Williams for not making less closeted dramas, Clum is anticipating Williams as a mainstream playwright and a subcultural one simultaneously. Here the radical critique of Williams's heterosexism is collapsing back into liberal notions of sameness and equivalence. Clum's frustration with Williams is that he doesn't treat his gay characters, who admittedly do not fare well (they are dead, subtextual or self-oppressed) in the same way as his straight characters. Clum's assumption is that all Williams had to do was open the doors of his creative closet and liberation would flow through his pen and on to the American stage. This is the limitation of gay liberation perspectives, which insufficiently conceptualize the extent of the threat of homosexuality, and the degree to which it is already being conjured by dominant ideological discourses. Clum does acknowledge the brutal forces that make it difficult to be open, but he does not conceive that these forces are not just merely producing silence precipitated by the closet. In as far as the difficulty in openness is constituted by the active production of sexual categories, rather than the mere suppression of disclosure, Clum is unforthcoming. His model only adequately accounts for enforced silence as the mechanism through which homosexuality is circumscribed.

The particular terms in which Clum mobilizes the closet as an analytical tool have a tendency to be ahistorical and essentializing: given that the notion of the closet and the ideology of disclosure and secrecy that it discursively proposes came into being with gay liberation of the early 1970s, and has been brought into question by recent queer initiatives, it seems curious to extend that tool back into a consideration of texts written before 1970, in order to bring Williams to account in the late 1980s and early 1990s. Of *Cat on a Hot Tin Roof*, first performed in 1955, Clum says:

> *Cat* . . . contains Williams' most interesting attempt at measuring his characters' troubled relationships against the potential of an abiding love between two men, an attempt that is mitigated by Williams' inability, or disinclination, to forge a positive language for the homosexual love the play tries to affirm. (p. 156)

Here the Williams that Clum conjurs is a figure wilfully trenchant in his closetry (note the 'disinclination'). Clum does note the bind the playwright is caught in: on the one hand the troubled relationships are his 'most interesting attempt', yet they are 'mitigated' by his own personal whim or failing in not forging positive language. The rhetoric of positivity is one of gay liberationism. Clum's failure is in the way in which he situates the playwright outside the structures of knowledge that are manifested in the play – if the play is apparently negative about homosexual love, then this must be determined by Williams himself. A little earlier in his consideration of *Cat*, Clum notes that the motif of arrested development characterizes Brick's homosexual feelings. This is a Freudian notion in which same-sex desire is emblematic of an insufficiently matured development out of infantile polymorphous perversity. Yet despite having identified this as knowledge structuring the depiction of homosexual desire in the play, Clum situates Williams outside the cultural forces which made such knowledge the abiding terms for conceptualizing homosexuality in 1950s America, and blames him for not conjuring a more 'positive' representation.

A more imaginative attempt to locate Williams in relation to gay male culture comes in Neil Bartlett's production *Night After Night*. Vince, the barman addresses the audience:

> I fancied a change and I did go and see a more dramatic piece. I don't know if any of you saw it, it was that *Streetcar* with Miss Leigh. *Streetcar Named Desire*, what a fabulous title. Oh, and she was

fabulous in it, I thought, although I know some people thought otherwise...[56]

In the preface to his work Bartlett lists *A Streetcar Named Desire* among the sources used to form a popular image of the gay man at the time in which the production is set, 1958. Bartlett seems to be situating Vince through *Streetcar* in two ways: firstly as a tragedy queen preoccupied with the idea of suicide as the represented fate of homosexuals ('...the kindness of strangers is all very well, thankyou, but Miss Leigh's husband in *Streetcar Named Desire*, what happened to him?...Well, he killed himself didn't he?') whom Vince cannot even name as homosexual; and secondly as identifying Vivien Leigh's portrayal of Blanche DuBois as 'fabulous' and 'marvellous' (twice). It is telling that Leigh-as-Blanche is more memorable to Vince than Stanley, that apparently archetypal object of queer desire (note Jarman's lechery towards Stanley, noted below...). As a point of identification it is clear that Blanche is preferable to her dead husband ('I didn't find that very uplifting, actually'), but not quite so apparent why Blanche would be preferable to Stanley. In this characterization of Vince as an archetypally mincing bar queen it seems to be more important in securing the historical and cultural authenticity that he identifies with Leigh-as-Blanche, that he desires to be like her, than he sexually desires Stanley, and not just as a safer subject position from which to desire the husband (Vince does not articulate any sexual desire from the position of 'Miss Leigh'), but as a textual position that is 'marvellous' and 'fabulous'.

In other words, given the range of possible responses that a gay man might be expected to produce in relation to *Streetcar*, Bartlett elects to represent one in which his character chooses not to identify with the only 'homosexual' in the play, and does not represent a desire of Stanley, but who does find a meaningful and affirmative identification in Leigh-as-Blanche. Of the four subject positions available to Bartlett in order to signify Vince's homosexuality (Allan, Stanley, Mitch and Blanche), he chooses the identification with a woman. Blanche is not merely a position of identification because she desires men, but because she is a woman, a 'fabulous' and 'marvellous' subject position rather than an abject who is identifiable only as a function of the presence of somebody else in the room ('By coming suddenly into a room that I thought was empty...').[57] In so far as the identity of Blanche's husband is 'visible', that visibility is only conceivable as a connotation, as is Vince's own homosexuality. Vince does not come out as homosexual, cannot, and he is not named as such: 'people like me do meet at

parties . . . but they have come to terms with the, you know, situation.'
In Bartlett's judgement, what can be made explicit by this homosexual
man in 1958 is his identification with the starring actress, but more
than that, this is the identification that will make Vince meaningful to
a largely subcultural audience in the late 1990s.

From gender to libido (and back again?)

As we saw earlier, one significant problem homosexual writers like
Forster exhibit in their attempts to negotiate around inversionism is that
they enact a suppression of any connotation of effeminacy or female
identification. In Forster's case this necessitates his own absence from
the transcendent ascent into the Greenwood. This suppression represents a preponderant strain of post-liberation gay cultural activity. It
was partly in an attempt to shift the security of the effeminate construction consolidated by Freudianism that the macho clone image became a
predominant one in many urban contexts in which gay liberation flour-
ished. This strategy is less popular currently, but it was successful in
installing a different notion of homosexual men, one in which they
could be masculine. However, clone culture was less successful in shifting that part of the inversionist construction which imagines homosexual men locked into an endless desire of the Dionian ideal, the 'real'
man. Indeed, in some ways clone culture re-secured this structure, and
made it even more difficult to envisage the effeminate homosexual
as an object of desire – largely because it mobilized contest around dis-
puting the idea that homosexual men could not be masculine, rather
than around a challenge to the idea that masculinity should be the
central quality to aspire towards or desire. Gregg Blachford argues that the
masculinisation of American and British gay subcultures in the late 1970s
did not preclude the idolization of masculinity before this time, but
that 'for the first time homosexuals themselves moved away from the
previous stereotype of "swish and sweaters" towards a new masculine
style which has become the dominant mode of expression in the subculture'.[58] In other words, in the 1970s gay men learned how to identify
as masculine as well as to desire the masculine.

Yet while this clone culture may have become a predominant manifestation of urban gay life for a while, it would clearly be a mistake to
suggest that it was the only operative mode of homosexual expression,
even as it continues to maintain. But as Blachford suggests we may be
able to characterize this movement as instating a libidinous notion of gay
identity that no longer acknowledged the implicit relation between homosexuality and gender dissent or dysphoria. This relation was established

by the early exponents of the third sex model: homosexuality was not merely an existing sex with an alternative sexual object choice, but constituted a different gender all together. As we have seen, subsequently this conception of homosexuality as an alternative gender became understood as an inversion of sex and gender which produced the proposition of male homosexuality as a pathological manifestation of femininity. Gay politics and cultural activity has been strenuously engaged with this complicated and often repellent set of knowledges, and our subcultural negotiations are not consistent. While the rise of macho clone expressions has replaced the apparent fixation of the invert upon the unattainable heterosexual Dionian ideal with a more acceptable, requitable homosexual object of desire, gay culture continues to proliferate a remnancy of the gender structure inversionism implicated us within.

Gay culture no longer depends for its erotic satisfaction upon the willingness or corruptibility of 'trade', but has proliferated diverse expressions of the gendering of that relation: the cult of Jeff Stryker and other impenetrable porn icons, active and passive fantasies advertised on phonelines, the gendering of personal ads in the gay press around maturity/youth, active/passive, top/bottom, master/servant, occidental/oriental, black/white, trade/queen, hirsute/smooth, dominant/submissive, daddy/son, employer/houseboy. This reproduction of the primacy of masculinity, both as an image with which to identify (to be), and as a body to desire (to have), is a process we might describe as embodying the notion that hegemonies of oppression operate through rearticulation. In this instance, the oppressive and dominant structure of masculinity is rearticulated by a marginal group as something pleasurable, empowering, desirable. In the moments of rearticulation the structure becomes stronger as the power of its ideological centrality is reinforced, not by those who necessarily profit from it, but in this instance by those who inhabit an identity continually invoked in order to police the homosocial continuum. In *Bodies that Matter*, Judith Butler suggests that this rearticulation is a performative act, a participation in the process by which dominant ideology is secured hegemonically, by conjuring the possibility of dissent and contest.[59] This is a development beyond her performative thesis in *Gender Trouble*, which was widely interpreted as suggesting that gender is a performance and that performances which parody dominant gender constructions fragment their power.[60]

One of the reasons why *Gender Trouble* proved to be so popular, especially with gay male writers and activists, was that it was interpreted as promising an intrinsic subversiveness to subcultural practices that lesbian feminism had traditionally been critical of, such as gender-bending and drag, transsexualism, sadomasochism and sexual role play. Sheila Jeffreys comments on what she considers to be the dilemma facing the stars of 'lesbianandgay' theory:

> How, for instance, is the phenomenon of drag to be made not just acceptable but even seen as revolutionary in lesbianandgay theory when it has stuck in the craw of feminist theory ever since lesbians dissented from gay liberation? It is to be accomplished by a return to gender, and invention of a harmless version of gender as an idea which lesbians and gay men can endlessly play with and be revolutionary at the same time.[61]

Jeffreys decries what she sees in *Gender Trouble* and lesbianandgay theory generally as the elaboration of gender as merely a series of drag effects in which power becomes little more than a discursive metaphor. She argues that feminist lesbians have fostered these theories as a way of building authority and success in an academic environment where gay male sexuality has accrued a revolutionary chic that Jeffreys suggests amounts to a reinvestment in liberal and individualistic ideals.[62] The trajectory of lesbianandgay or queer politics in Britain would certainly bear out Jeffreys' arguments about the erosion of gender as a vital and urgent category of concern.[63]

However, Jeffreys' dismissal as politically compromizing practices such as lesbian butch and femme role-playing, sadomasochism and drag produces an analysis dangerously simplistic in its failure either to imagine the seductiveness and pleasure of such practices and their expedience in given cultural conditions, or the complex ideological contests through which such practices become the site of subcultural formation, resistance and dissidence. As Butler suggests in *Gender Trouble*:

> gender practices within gay and lesbian cultures often thematise 'the natural' in parodic contexts that bring into relief the performative construction of an original and true sex.[64]

There is clearly a problem with some of the ways in which ideas derived from *Gender Trouble* circulated culturally, which gave rise to an assumption that in our gender performances we might shrug off troublesome power relations as easily as one might strap on a dildo, apply a bit of lippy or slip on a frock.[65] Lesbian feminist writers have questioned Butler's investment in gay male cultural activity, suggesting that in making gay performances equivalent to queer ones, she erases the distinction between gay and lesbian and subsumes lesbian women into gay men.[66]

In *Belle Reprieve*, a queer adaptation of *A Streetcar Named Desire* by Split Britches and Bloolips, the roles of Blanche, played by the drag performer Bette Bourne, and Stanley, played by lesbian performance artist Peggy Shaw, exhibit both the kind of queer performativity that Butler suggests is a dissident intervention into the process of hegemonic rearticulation, and the terms under which this dissidence is both troubling to the natural effect of heterosexuality and necessarily caught up in the force of dominant rearticulation. When Stanley and Blanche emerge from boxes on stage at the beginning of the play and confront each other, Blanche must assure Stanley of 'her' credentials: before they can 'get on with the scenes of brutal humiliation and sexual passion' – Stanley must find her 'motive' in the trunk from which she emerged. As 'he' searches the trunk he asks, 'what are little girls made of?' while Blanche frames the terms under which we are to view identity in the play:

> *Blanche*: I assure you that is who I am. My namesake is a role played by that incandescent star, Vivien Leigh, and although the resemblance is not immediately striking I have been told we have the same shoulders.
> *Stanley*: (looking at passport photo) Then who's this here?
> *Blanche*: The information in that document is a convention which allows me to pass in the world without let or hindrance. If you'll just notice the message inside the front cover, the Queen of England herself not only requests this but requires it.[67]

Bette as Blanche here self-consciously asserts her right not only to reinterpret the iconic performance of the role by Vivien Leigh, but to perform Blanche's gender as any other performer would: this is the convention, the stage, that enables him to 'pass' as a woman character. *Belle Reprieve* exhibits the subcultural knowledge of which it is a product, reflecting as it does the significance *Streetcar* and Williams have in gay culture. A few lines later Stanley retorts,

> Look, have you any idea how many people we have come in here saying they're Blanche DuBois, clutching tiny handbags and fainting

in the foyer? I'm afraid I'll have to subject this case to the closest possible scrutiny before I allow any of you to pass any further. (p. 9)

Here in the licensed space of the alternative stage, Peggy as Stanley
performs with the authority of male power, identifying the gay practice
that inscribes the iconography of Blanche's dainty southern belle
femininity. Those gay male performers who come 'in here', into the
subcultural space, who clutch tiny handbags and faint, are deploying
femininity. Later, Stella, the woman-as-feminine performer in *Belle
Reprieve* (played by Lois Weaver), rearticulates the natural values of that
femininity and how she learned their characteristics from her (queer?)
sister, waiting for her to come home from Woolworth's, observing her
mannerisms and affectations, admiring her entrance down the staircase
to receive her 'gentlemen callers'. The irony in this performance space is
that (Lois as) Stella's admission comes but a few lines after we have
heard her role model in the bath:

> *Blanche*: One day I'll probably just dissolve in the bath. They'll come
> looking for me, but there'll be nothing left. 'Drag Queen Dissolves
> in Bathtub', that'll be the headline. (p. 13)

In an alternative, avant-garde political theatrical convention, to an
audience subculturally conversant with the Brechtian levels of irony
employed in these exchanges, and aware that they are being invited to
participate in disrupting the rearticulation of 'natural', conventional
gender structures, *Belle Reprieve* reinscribes Williams's play with a sense
of artifice which validates queer subcultural gender play, and troubles
the categories of normality in which all our knowledges are necessarily
located.

Yet it is interesting to note that the play coheres much more successfully around its presentation of Bette as Blanche and Peggy as Stanley
than it does around that of Lois Weaver as Stella and Paul Shaw as
Mitch. The underlying identities that validate these performances are
congruent with dominant models of homosexuality: Peggy playing a
butch dyke being Stanley, a man renowned as an icon of machismo,
and Bette playing a drag queen being Blanche, the archetype of the fey
southern belle, are both instances – performances – of the inversionist
conceptualization of homosexuality. Peggy performs Stanley so that she
can desire the feminine Stella, and Bette performs Blanche so that she
can be subjugated by Stanley. Lois' femme lesbian interpretation of
Stella desiring Peggy as Stanley, and Paul's fey straight interpretation of

Mitch desiring Blanche are much less satisfying: Lois can signify as lesbian or as feminine, but the potential to convincingly unite both terms, one conjuring the natural, one standing for perversity, is limited.

However, the constitution of the theatrical space is not consistent: the play shifts genres from avant-garde fairy-tale through political didacticism, realism and back again. One crucial point of shifting is when Blanche is about to be attacked and raped by Stanley. Bette has been flouncing around, rebelling against the group's avant-garde pretensions: 'she' aspires towards an authenticity that will validate her gender performance as Blanche, she wants to be in a 'real' play, one that her mother can come and see her in:

> *Stella*: You think you can play it?
> *Blanche*: I have the shoulders. (p. 34)

Yet as they progress into realism and return to Williams's *Streetcar* where Blanche's fate is sealed by the narrative and by her gender identity, Bette again steps out of the convention, rupturing the narrative, the rearticulation of patriarchal values, by reinvoking the specific performative context in which 'she' is embedded. 'She' foregrounds the avant-garde and the subcultural domain in which they are performing, and fragments the convention of the suspension of disbelief, inviting 'her' subcultural audience to see her as a gay man performing femininity, but not wanting to be treated like a woman, not wanting to be raped and humiliated:

> *Stanley*: Drop the stiletto!
> *Blanche*: You think I'm crazy or something?
> *Stanley*: If you want to be in this play you've got to drop the stiletto.
> *Blanche*: If you want to be in this play you've got to make me!
> *Stanley*: If you want to play a woman, the woman in this play gets raped and she goes crazy in the end.
> *Blanche*: I don't want to get raped and go crazy, I just wanted to wear a nice frock, and look at the shit they've given me! (p. 35)

In rendering his 'womanliness' as unnatural, the gay Bette enables us to catch a glimpse of the gender order being reinstated, but it is a glimpse that momentarily shatters the invisibility of the structure, catching its moment of rearticulation, a moment when the hegemony is being re-secured. In restoring his masculinity Bette takes control of his destiny once again, his performance of apparently authentic feminine representation, of subjugation, is over. Similarly, if Peggy as Stanley truly wishes to perform as a man, to be masculine, then she necessarily adopts a position of dominance in relation to identities positioned as feminine in the space. Here the performances constitute power rela- tions: to perform is to cloak oneself with the trappings of a culturally produced identity, it is to situate oneself in relation to other performers, other identities. To perform gender is to perform, to reproduce, power relations: as Hilary Harris notes: 'Sexuality may be about fucking, but getting fucked is still about gender, even if "only" metaphorically.'[68]

1.2   *Streetcar*: a play with gender?

A Streetcar Named Desire dramatizes the arrival of a middle-aged south- ern belle, Blanche DuBois, in licentious New Orleans, and her intrusion into the libidinous domesticity of her younger sister Stella, and her husband, Stanley Kowalski, a working-class second generation Polish immigrant. The DuBois plantation, Belle Reve, and the aristocratic status it represents, has been lost to the indulgent 'epic fornications' of Blanche and Stella's male relatives, and Blanche arrives unmarried and homeless. Despite her aristocratic bearing, which infuriates Stanley, it is apparent that Blanche is traumatized. However, she strikes up a roman- tic relationship with one of Kowalski's friends, Harold Mitchell, who lives with his mother, which promises to abate both her material pre- cariousness and her emotional vulnerability. Mitch appears enchanted by Blanche's bearing and grace, his affection growing in proportion to the frustration and violence of Stella's husband, who is being deprived of his raucous sex life and domestic nuclearity by Blanche's continuing presence: this becomes more evident when we learn that Stella is about to have a baby. Stanley discovers that Blanche was sacked from her position as a teacher of English for seducing a 17-year-old pupil, and that her reputation for sexual excess at the Hotel Flamingo got her hounded out of her home town of Laurel. At the dramatic climax of the play on the night of Blanche's birthday Stanley becomes violent and confronts Blanche with his knowledge of her history; he gives her a bus ticket back to Laurel. While they wait for Mitch's arrival, it transpires that Stanley has told his friend about Blanche's past and he no longer wants her. When Stella challenges Stanley about his behaviour he hits her again and she goes into labour. While her sister and brother-in-law are at the hospital, Blanche gets drunk and parades around in a swirl of satin and romantic fantasies. Stanley returns and the two fight; as Blanche continues to resist him, Stanley rapes her. The play ends after

Stella has returned home with her new baby, refusing to believe Blanche's accusation of her husband. Blanche retreats into delusions of former romantic gentility and is taken off to a mental institution.

Part of the task of an agile and dissident reader, one who wishes to formulate an interpretation which is culturally challenging, is to pose questions suggested by the ideological and narrative arrangements of a text that conventional wisdom and dominant productions and criticism have not posed or answered. One key incoherence around which the dominant formations at work in *A Streetcar Named Desire* destabilize, arises out of the question that if Stanley just wants Blanche out of the house so that he and Stella can keep those 'pretty lights going', which is how he justifies his actions to Stella, then why does he sabotage her chances of marrying Mitch (which would certainly get her out of the house), and why does he rape her? Why does he need to subject her to such behaviour? What destabilizing 'queerness' does she represent that must be dominated physically and medically removed (she is taken away at the end by a doctor) from the apparently threatening proximity to his identity and his homosocial matrix?

Within those accounts of *Streetcar* which position Stanley as the object of Williams's own masochistic homosexual desire it is axiomatic that the Kowalski conjured is indefatigably brutish and powerful, an unassailable potency. Ronald Hayman speaks of the way Williams apparently endowed his male characters 'with the same qualities that had excited him in men he had known', Mark Lilly feels that the playwright made it plain how far his male characters were his own homoerotic icons, while Christopher Bigsby is positively salivating as he suggests that Stanley 'dominates existence and as such in a way commands Williams's respect, even if he represents a brutalism which frightens'.[69] It is my intention here to develop a reading of *Streetcar* which attempts to address Stanley's need to annihilate Blanche, and which also invests in the constructive notion of gay men's identification with her. As part of this project it is important to look much more closely at the apparently robust masculinity with which Tennessee Williams imbued Stanley Kowalski.

Stanley Kowalski: Polack, stud, husband

In his biography of Williams, Donald Spoto recounts an erotic fascination the future playwright had for a man he worked with at International Shoe in 1934. He was dark and burly, and for that period became Tom's (Williams only became known as Tennessee after the publication of his first story in 1939) closest companion. He was called Stanley Kowalski:

It is perhaps hard to know how much of his character and personality are represented by the character with that name in *A Streetcar Named Desire*, but the attraction to him by Blanche DuBois is certainly something that the playwright himself first knew.[70]

Such precise biographical knowledge lends a greater credibility to suggestions about Williams' erotic fascination with the character of Stanley in the play, although this is a proposition about which we must remain suspicious; what it suggests however, is that Stanley seems to be invested with a particularly significant sexual character. Throughout the unfolding drama Stanley is constructed as being aggressively, animalistically sexual; this is not merely a reflection of the cross-currents of desire and gender that the play sets up: those cross-currents are themselves articulated through a construction of ethnic and racial difference. The notions of racial difference in *Streetcar* intersect with pre-existing and recirculating knowledges about the history of slavery and racism in the American south and the powerful myths that enable these oppressions to become plausible.

The heady, licentious and lyrical atmosphere that the play establishes in the opening stage direction calls upon an exoticism invested in New Orleans, which in this dramatic context, 'is a cosmopolitan city where there is a relatively warm and easy intermingling of races in the old part of town.'[71] The racial identity that is being particularly called upon here, it seems, is a 'soulful' Afro-American one; we may note the 'redolences of bananas and coffee' in the warm air, with their exotic connotations of the Caribbean, matched by the 'infatuated fluency of brown fingers' (p. 115) who add their own redolences of blues piano to the already heady atmosphere. The steamy, sensual *mise en scene* in which the play creates a space of passion and violence is to a large extent a function of ethnic exoticism, secured through an elaboration of the racial difference of New Orleans' apparent blackness. So, what the text identifies as a cultural image, an ethnic stereotype, is specified through the elaboration of racial difference – an apparent biological difference in physiology. As Sander Gilman points out, 'the association of the black with concupiscence reaches back into the Middle Ages.'[72] We might suggest, then, that the quality of licentiousness that *Streetcar* invests in New Orleans is secured through this evocation of a racial stereotype.

Lionel Kelly has pointed out that

[Stanley] is presented as an ethnic intruder in a site in which two prevalent other ethnicities, the southern white and the southern black, prevail. Both of these he seeks to subordinate, the one through an appeal to a legality that surmounts ethnic specificity, the other through a braggart appropriation of their modes of social being.[73]

There is clearly a danger in making Stanley's Polishness equivalent to the blackness with which the idea of New Orleans' licentiousness is secured and in the process rendering invisible the particular ethnic location he occupies. However, there is a slippage in *Streetcar* around Stanley, that is symptomatic of the contradictory racial and ethnic messages the play produces and the complex historical context of the play's setting. New Orleans is understood to have a particular ethnic identity as a place, secured through its mix of black and white, a place where normal boundaries are obscured, where the principal cultural conflict is not between black and white. As a southern city New Orleans was on the losing side in the Civil War, and so conjures an air of loss, and of the conflict between old aristocratic, colonialist values and those of the ascendant new America. It is in this milieu that Stanley makes his claim as a citizen of 'the greatest country on earth': claims his right to participate in the American dream, predicated on the promise of inclusion and immigrancy. However, *Streetcar* positions Stanley unevenly: it manifests a space coded as black and points towards Stanley's occupation of it, and yet simultaneously and contradictorily positions him as a Polish immigrant. Even before Kowalski appears on stage an effect of his difference from Anglo-Saxon whiteness is produced; Stella makes a point of telling her sister that Stanley is Polish and Blanche suggests that this is like being Irish, 'Only not so – highbrow?' and they laugh together (p. 124).

Here Stanley's ethnic difference and inferiority is secured at the same moment as Blanche's and Stella's superiority and sameness: they laugh 'in the same way'. This exchange helps to secure the sisters' social superiority: they represent the old (and lost) money of the aristocratic southern white family. Later we can see that this difference is secured through a conflation of primal sexual passion and bestiality. When it becomes apparent that Belle Reve is lost, Blanche's defensiveness leads her to suggest that Stella was in bed with her 'Polack' while Blanche struggled alone (p. 127). And later still Blanche's view of Stanley seems directly shaped by Victorian racial taxonomy:

> *Blanche*: There's something downright – bestial – about him! . . .
> There's even something – sub-human – something not quite to the
> stage of humanity yet! Yes, something – ape-like about him, like one

of those pictures I've seen in – anthropological studies! . . . Don't –
don't hang back with the brutes! (p. 163)

It is difficult not to conflate the racial work the play is undertaking
here with the kinds of knowledge about black sexuality produced in
Victorian racial taxonomies – Blanche even refers to anthropological
studies. Sander Gilman notes how such work 'commented on the lasci-
vious, ape-like sexual appetite of the black'.[74] This view of Blanche's,
that Stanley is an animalistic sexual beast, a primal figure, seems to be
endorsed by the text in the famous stage description which heralds his
entrance into the play:

> Animal joy in his being is implicit in all his movements and attitudes
> everything that is his . . . bears his emblem of the gaudy seed-bearer.
> (p. 128)

Not only is Stanley an animal sexual figure metaphorically, even
iconically, but by the end of the play he is also a rapist. In her now
classic book *Women, Race and Class*, Angela Davis explores the force of
the myth of the black male rapist, which imbues black men with a
predatory sexual drive, particularly in relation to white women. She
argues that the content of this myth is in direct opposition to the reality
endured under slavery where 'the right claimed by slave owners and
their agents over the bodies of female slaves was a direct expression of
their presumed property rights over Black people as a whole.'[75] Following the end of slavery, the myth of the black male rapist was used to
control and terrorize the black populations of the South. Lynchings,
justified with reference to the apparent insatiability and animality of
black sexuality, were used to parochially protect white women, and
strike fear into black ex-slaves. Given the particular kinds of imagery
Streetcar is calling up, and its setting in the south, it is difficult not to
read the play as buying into this kind of mythicization. *Sweet Bird of
Youth*, written twelve years after *Streetcar*, similarly points to a space
circumscribed by white myths of racial difference but situates the
young, beautiful and white Chance Wayne there instead of the anticipated black male sexual aggressor. Chance has returned to the small
southern town where years earlier he venereally infected his childhood
sweetheart, Heavenly, daughter of Boss Finley, the town's patriarch. At
the end of the play, Chance will be castrated for defiling her, in the
name of Boss Finley's appeal to keep the south segregated: his daughter
Heavenly is no longer convincing as a 'shining example [. . .] of white

Southern youth – in danger' from 'them that want to adulterate the pure white blood of the South.'[76]

Yet in *Streetcar*, this conflation of Stanley with blackness is not consistent throughout the play. While it continues to position him as an outsider, the speech in which Stanley makes a claim for his identity as an American citizen, reaffirms both his Polish ethnicity and his belief in the American dream:

> *Stanley*: I am not a Polack. People from Poland are Poles, not Polacks. But what I am is a one hundred per cent American, born and raised in the greatest country on earth and proud as hell of it, so don't ever call me a Polack. (p. 197)

This celebration of the aspirational potential America offers is related to Stanley's working-class identity: here his ethnicity is functioning in a way that signifies Eastern-European second generation immigrancy rather than associations of blackness and post-slavery racist rhetoric. However, this elaboration does reproduce both his primal sexuality, and his class difference from Stella and Blanche: he reminds his wife how common she thought he was when they first met, as she showed him pictures of Belle Reve, 'the place with the columns'. Stanley taunts Stella with her own desire for his common sensuality: he pulled her down off the columns, and she loved it, 'having them coloured lights going!' And he's explicit about what has ruptured this libidinous domestic harmony: it's the intrusion of Blanche, with her airs, likening Stanley to an 'ape' (p. 198).

So, at points the play relies on a construction of Stanley's sexuality through ethnicity somewhat distant from white supremacist notions of blackness and bestiality, in as far as that (Polish) ethnicity denotes working-class immigrancy and the ascendant industrialization of the new America. It is this distance from 'blackness' and the idea of him being working class that facilitates the possibility of an eroticization of Stanley by Stella (or Blanche), which would otherwise have been unthinkable, given the fears of miscegenation we would expect old family aristocratic southerners like Stella and Blanche to have: it is worth noting that they are a fallen, white trash version of the identity occupied by Boss Finley in *Sweet Bird of Youth*; he would no doubt see their poverty as what happens when you don't police your daughters rigorously enough. Yet part of the play's appeal is the way in which it represents Stella's active desire and the possibility of her pleasure in Stanley's sexuality, indeed this was one of the elements that was perceived to be most shocking when it first opened.

The racial and ethnic implications of Stanley's character in *Streetcar* are deeply embedded in the play's context and in its principal dramatic tensions. The iconic stature of Stanley's masculinity, and its contestant position in relation to Blanche's southern belle femininity, her status as white goddess, are to a large degree manifested through, and secured by a rhetoric of racial difference, reproduced through myths originated to secure the plausibility of white supremacy. However, this racial difference is not positioned in the text as a unified discourse, and there is a contradictory relationship between the notions of blackness and animalistic sexuality, and Stanley's (Polish) ethnicity, which jostle in the text. This ethnicity has a different cultural trajectory to that of the discourse of racial difference: it is positioned in such a way as to be aspirational to the values of the American nation ('born and raised in the greatest country on earth') and although it still occupies a subordinate position, this is a function of class, as well as ethnicity. The effect of this complexity of ideological imperatives is to render Stanley's masculinity as simultaneously dangerous and exotically sexual, but objectifiable: by Blanche as part of their contest over authority, by Stella as his social superior and wife, and by a potential audience (or Williams himself) as an object of sexual beauty. This last position of spectatorship, enabled by Stanley's ideological manifestation, is particularly important when put into the context of a performance of *Streetcar*. This play is notorious for its displays of male physicality: Stanley appears constantly to be undressing, dressing down and coming on stage in wet clothes. As Jarman notes, Marlon Brando as Kowalski secured a performative context for that character that is largely intelligible as a visual sign of sex;[77] indeed this was one of the features of Williams's work that was considered to be particularly shocking, and at least for Howard Taubman, such a scopophilic presentation of the male was an indication of the homosexuality of the playwright.[78] Both the power of the spectacle and the complex cultural knowledges he inscribes coalesce to offset Stanley's authority as an apparently unassailably masculine and authoritative figure. This modulates the possible meanings we may make from Blanche's presence in Stanley's life, and makes the notion of Blanche as a threat to his position and authority, one which requires substantial repression by him, more plausible. This is central to my interpretation of the play.

Miss DuBois: queer defiance?

If the prevailing account of Stanley we inherit from those of Williams's critics who buy into Freudianism highlights his unassailability, then their accounts of Blanche foreground her neurotic, vaporous powerlessness. One key problem identified by several critics of the Haymarket production of *Streetcar* was that Jessica Lange was too strong for the role. Charles Spencer wrote:

> Lange proudly proclaims in her programme note that she has 'built her distinguished career portraying strong and independent women', which sounds like the worst kind of preparation for Blanche, who is weak to the point of disintegration and famously dependent on 'the kindness of strangers'.[79]

Michael Billington agreed:

> But, although Lange works hard at the role, I still find it hard to believe in her as the delicate creature of Williams's imagination.[80]

Both critics exhibit considerable investment in the fragility of Blanche, an interpretation of her which they make Williams responsible for inscribing (rather than, say, their homosocial expectations of women), and which they resent Jessica Lange with her presumptious programme notes and strong independence, for disrupting. Hence, it is her performance that is inauthentic, rather than their reading.

Christopher Bigsby has offered an account of Stanley's attempted destruction of Blanche, which attempts to explain why he wouldn't rather just settle for her marriage and removal from his household. Bigsby has suggested that Stanley's sabotage of Blanche's relationship with Mitch repays her attempts to ruin his marriage, 'for she has indeed set herself to undermine a relationship whose honest and open physicality repels her.'[81] He could be referring to Stanley's violence towards his wife, which is both honestly and openly physical, but his intention is to naturalise the heterosexuality of the Kowalskis by reflecting it against Blanche's apparently duplicitous prudery. This neurotic Blanche, too genteel for sex, too delicate for reality, too hysterical to survive, is authenticated by the most famous and widely disseminated production of *Streetcar*. Vivien Leigh's portrayal in Elia Kazan's film of 1951 is all tremulous voice, downcast glances and widely frightened eyes: her affectations do not seem earthbound. Often it appears that those who have commented on Williams's play, are in fact referencing Leigh's performance in Kazan's film. Similarly, Jessica Lange's performance in the CBS television film of 1995 is so preciously, insistently neurotic that it seems perfectly sensible to violate her and cart her off to a lunatic asylum just to shut her up. Both readings of Blanche have her flee towards fanciful excesses of madness in order to be able to reconcile those elements of the play which doggedly oppose the plausible rendering of her as simply victimized.

For all its ubiquity and prestige, and potent iconography, Kazan's film remains, necessarily, a partial reading of *A Streetcar Named Desire*, which fails to make sense of Blanche's character or of the enmity between her and Stanley. Vivien Leigh's frail, almost translucently white Blanche hardly seems capable of drawing breath, let alone seducing wagon loads of soldiers, disposing of an aristocratic estate or of threatening Stanley to the point where the ferocity of their enmity can no longer be restrained. The English actress Sheila Gish, who played Blanche, has said that she always thought that they made Blanche 'tiresome' in Kazan's film, even though she is 'the greatest single part ever written for an actress' because 'they took all of [her spirit] away.' She goes on:

> So come the second half of the film, you really like Stanley a lot. You sit there thinking, 'Go on, get her out of there.'[82]

Both the 1951 and 1995 filmed versions retain Stanley's line from scene eight where he is justifying Blanche's exposure and expulsion to Stella. He says, 'Don't forget all that I took off her': yet as he is played by Brando and by Alec Baldwin, Stanley takes little more than a squirt of jasmine perfume and some carping off her. What is it that she has she done to him? Afterall, how bad can it be when she is supposed to be so delicate and weak? Lange's performance crystallizes those frustrating elements of Blanche's characterisation, as I have suggested, in such a way as to make the necessity of her expulsion from Stanley's domestic territory clear. But can such annoyance bear the dramatic and conceptual responsibility for the vicious and destructive response it garners, even accounting for an assumption about the ethical naturalization of man's authority in his own home?

At the end of Scene 5, Blanche is alone in the apartment, waiting for Mitch: it's Saturday night, Stella and Stanley have gone out with Eunice and Steve from upstairs. A young man appears: he is collecting for the *Evening Star*. Blanche greets him: 'Well, well! What can I do for *you*?' The young man is shy and self-conscious. Blanche doesn't give him any money, but gently and purposefully she flirts with him, turning up the heat as she holds him in her presence. As the boy is leaving, Blanche calls him back and asks him for a light, using the opportunity to close the gap between them. She asks him the time as she draws upon him:

> *Blanche*: So late? Don't you just love these long rainy afternoons in
> New Orleans when an hour isn't just an hour – but a little bit of
> Eternity dropped in your hands – and who knows what to do with
> it? (p. 173)

It seems quite clear what Blanche would like to do with rainy after-
noons in New Orleans. She is not content with flirtation, however, and
tells him that she wants to kiss him softly and sweetly, and she does,
without waiting for him to accept. But the reality of her situation is all
too clear, and the Blanche of Laurel becomes visible to us as she
dismisses the boy, lamenting that it would be nice to keep him, 'but I've
got to be good and keep my hands off children.' (p. 174).

Whatever she may be, this Blanche seems to be neither a prude nor
delicate to the point of weakness or passivity. As the young man from
the *Evening Star* leaves, Mitch arrives for their date: as effortlessly as she
drew the boy to the edge of seduction, so Blanche now effects appropriate decorum towards the man she wants, needs, for a husband.

> *Blanche*: Looks who's coming! My Rosenkavalier! Bow to me first! Now
> present them. [He does so. She curtsies low.] Ahhh! Merciiii! (p. 174)

This contrast between Blanche's encounter with the young man and
Mitch's subsequent entrance, is a deliberate and considerable shift
between sexual and courtship modes that in its abruptness and apparent self-consciousness enables a denaturalization of the role Blanche
projects for men, which is her negotiation of (their) power. Blanche is
able to express herself freely with the young man because she is situated
more strongly than he is: she has greater social power than the youth,
whom she clearly intimidates, by virtue of her sex, class, maturity and
sophistication. But in relation to Mitch, from whom she wishes to elicit
a proposal of marriage, her propriety and the condition of her acquiescence to that institution oblige her to be more circumspect. She must
not threaten Mitch, nor give him cause to take her sexual favours for
granted, they are to come later, when sanctified by his ownership of her
in the marriage contract: all her coquetry may illicit sexual desire, while
axiomatically maintaining its constraint. Later, when they have
returned from their date, Blanche asserts the roles for both of them, she
reminds them who they are supposed to be; unlike Stanley who con-
ducts his relationships with women on his terms, Mitch invites Blanche
to adjudicate his behaviour – the discourse of courtship into which they
have entered is one in which she remains confident, as a function of

her class experience. When Mitch attempts to grope her, she effortlessly keeps him at bay, reminding him that just because Stanley and Stella aren't at home, he shouldn't forget to behave like a gentleman. He defers to her, but does not understand the irony in her presentation of such sexual formality (p. 179).

Just in case we have not understood the irony of her self-presenta-tion, Williams adds a stage direction for Blanche to roll her eyes, in the knowledge that Mitch cannot see her face (p. 179). Her performance of feminine propriety admits her artifice to the audience. When Blanche suggests that Stanley and Stella's absence is not an excuse for Mitch to behave ungentlemanly, it is her assertion of what his gentlemanly behaviour should be like that he manifests – he, clearly, is supposed to have no idea how he should behave ('Huh?') and she controls the terms of their interaction. However, as Blanche makes clear, this is dependent on Stanley and Stella not being home – were they to be, what has been established in this play as normal heterosexual behaviour would be in evidence – a subordination of women through violence sublimated as animalistic and magnetic sexuality (this is represented by Stanley and Stella, and secured as normality by the similar behaviour of Steve and Eunice upstairs).

If Blanche is weak, flimsy or delicate it is because as an unmarried woman she has no material access to power, only to the privilege of her ethnic and class experience. Arriving in New Orleans at the house of her sister on the streetcar named desire, Blanche is in a desperate situation: she has lost her job, her husband, her home and the class status it rep-resented. As she tells Stanley, 'Everything that I own is in that trunk', and the trunk is full of faded glamour, romantic memories (love letters) and superfluous papers that are the only remaining tangible artefact of the 'place with the columns'. Whatever its cause, we should feel the serious-ness of Stanley's enmity towards Blanche, and the threat that he repres-ents to her: she has nowhere else to go. If Blanche's relationship with Mitch is tinged with nervousness, this is not the pathological mani-festation of her neuroses, but an index of her precariousness: she needs a husband.

Blanche's vanity always appears related to the presence of a man, as in the scene when she and Stella return from having supper at Gala-toires while the men play poker. Stella realizes that the game is still going on and Blanche's realization that the men are still in the house causes her immediate anxiety: she asks Stella how she looks and bids her sister wait until she's powdered her nose before opening the door (p. 144). Again, this vanity is a function of her anxiety, and not of pure 'calculation',[83] nor of 'denial',[84] or indeed of 'helplessness'.[85] Williams makes it very clear that he intends us to understand Blanche's self-awareness. Stella asks her sister why she is so sensitive about her age and Blanche replies explicitly that it is because of her vulnerability, her need to be wanted:

> *Stella*: Blanche, do you want *him*?
> *Blanche*: I want to *rest*! I want to breathe quietly again! Yes – I *want* Mitch . . . *very badly*! Just think! If it happens! I can leave here and not be anyone's problem . . . (p. 171)

It is significant that when Blanche asks Stella if she has been listening to her fears about her precarious position, Stella replies 'I don't listen to you when you are being morbid!' – Stella cannot accept knowledge about this gender structure and disavows her position within it by pathologising Blanche's fears as 'morbid' – a personal paranoia, rather than a structural inequality.

The brutal reality of Blanche's situation makes it easy to see why Kauffman and Taubman find *Streetcar*'s depiction of relations between men and women so troublesome. The structure of heterosexuality rests upon maintaining the ideological integrity of gender performance: the unquestioning acceptance of knowledge about the essential complementarity of gender roles, which naturalizes the power differential between them. Blanche is such a powerful representation because her performances of her gender are so openly depicted as functions of her material insecurity. Blanche's class experience, and her whiteness, gives the commodity that is her femininity added value, which it is clear she must utilise: the precariousness of her position, and the emotional toll this is taking on her, make it necessary.

Blanche first meets Mitch in Scene 3 when she and Stella have returned from Gallatoires. Stanley's Saturday night poker game is still in progress, a paradigm of homosocial intimacy. When the sisters return, Mitch is in the bathroom and emerges into the bedroom after the women have been exiled there: Stanley whacks his wife's thigh, to the edification of his confidants, to ensure her subordination to the homosocial ritual fronted by the poker game. Mitch returns to the game, but is distracted when Blanche puts on the radio. The other men don't mind the women enjoying the music, but this is Stanley's house, and he reacts to the competition for his buddies' attention angrily. He jumps up and turns off the radio. The stage description here bears notice:

[He stops short at the sight of Blanche in the chair. *She returns his look without flinching.*][86]

Again, this does not seem to be the behaviour of a woman passively strung up on the torments of a neurotic disposition. When Blanche continues to prove a distraction for Mitch, Stanley reacts with what can only be described as jealous anger: it is clear that he resents the competition for his friend's attention. Not only is Stella increasingly displaying attitudes towards her husband which are a function of Blanche's supremacist and class bound view of him, but now Blanche's 'enchantment' is displacing Stanley's homosocial intimacy with Mitch. As Blanche waltzes to the music 'with romantic gestures' and Mitch delightedly 'moves in awkward imitation' Stanley's demands for attention become more insistent; finally he interrupts the alternative bonding ritual enacted by the sisters and Mitch: he throws the radio out of the window, performing his violent masculinity in an assertion of his power. Stanley is threatened by the power Blanche has accumulated through her seduction of Mitch and of Stella, with her southern upper-class femme behaviour. He must either accept a position of aspirational subordination (as Mitch has) in relation to Blanche's privileged space or rebel against it: his class and ethnic identity (we have seen how his ethnic difference has been coded at different points as working-class ignorant East European, and as black Afro-Caribbean) gives him no other option: as a man he cannot acquiesce to her. He must exert his own working class authority – his physicality, violence and brutish sexuality are structurally threatened by virtue of their ethnic coding in relation to Blanche's cultured whiteness.

Blanche tells Stella that 'The only way to live with such a man is to go to bed with him', but Blanche's presence on the other side of the curtains is preventing the married couple from having sex (or at least the kind of unrestrained, noisy sex they usually have), and her challenge to Stanley's 'animalism' threatens Stella's security. To take Blanche's view is to end up as insecure as Blanche. Enchanted by the romantic and genteel space Blanche conjures to displace the poker game, Stella reacts disgustedly to Stanley's violence. Stella attempts to assert herself within her marriage and home, and is physically overcome: Stanley hits her. He is restrained by his buddies, lest the violence of his heterosexual passion over reach patriarchal normality and invite judicial intervention. He is grateful for this, 'They speak quietly and lovingly to him and he leans his face on one of their shoulders' (p. 152) and their homosocial bond is secured: they have entered into ritual competition with each other in the poker game, and are now mutually supportive of their status as men, men who control and desire women. Once his violent physicality is restored to an equilibrium it can then find its conventional outlet in his libido and he calls Stella to him. As the passion of violence and confrontation passes, to be replaced by more conventional, safer passions, the material reality of Stella's position reasserts itself. As she explains to Blanche the next day 'there are things that happen between a man and a woman in the dark – that sort of make everything else seem – unimportant' (p. 162), and they need to. Her desire for Stanley needs to overcome her knowledge of his power over her, and the displays he makes of this to her, and to his homosocial affiliates: if it doesn't, there is nothing to separate her from the vulnerability and paranoia of her sister. Sublimating her subordination in eroticism and her physical desire allows her to maintain some material security by virtue of her relationship with Stanley, a sublimation made all the more necessary by her pregnancy and its attendant pressures. Clearly there is the juxtaposition here of the imminent arrival of the final member of the normative family against the idea of Blanche's unnatural and disruptive imposition on that family.

Later we see more evidence of how Blanche's presence and defiance compromise Stella. In the discussion of astrological signs Blanche is attempting to assert some influence over the evening with feminine passive-aggression that punishes Stanley's uncouth maleness (p. 168), but he retaliates not just with the threat of knowledge he has about Blanche's past, but he refuses to kiss Stella in front of her; by withholding his affections and his sexuality from Stella he is exercising his primary method of control, for that sexuality and passion always has the connotation or threat of the violence of which it is a sublimation, and of the pleasure and fear that is Stella's experience of it.

When Stella protests about Stanley's treatment of her sister, judging him for his uncouth table manners, he reacts violently, hurling his plate to the floor and grabbing his wife. He rails against how they have both been judging him to be a vulgar and greasy Polack, and again the use of his name, Mr Kowalski is invoked as a sign of his ethnic difference. Stella begins to cry 'weakly' (p. 194), but as ever, his violence comes with eroticism:

> *Stanley*: Stell, it's gonna be all right after she goes and after you've had the baby. It's gonna be all right again between you and me the way that it was. You remember that way that it was? Them nights we had together? God, honey, it's gonna be sweet when we can

make noise in the night the way that we used to and get the coloured lights going with nobody's sister behind the curtains to hear us! (p. 195)

And we have little doubt that he is right – it will be better for Stella when Blanche has gone – the ambiguity of her position will not be so evident and they can return to an eroticization of the subordination she endures, and which makes the powerlessness not only tolerable, but exciting. There seems to be a strong indication here of the idea that the power relations within gender arrangements are inscribed with sexuality – that sex is the coercive mechanism by which domination can proceed within a consensual arrangement, almost an imperative of desire: Stella must endure because she must desire Stanley, and she must have him.

Despite the fact that she proved to be the catalyst for his suicide, Blanche's marriage to the homosexual Allan, as well as her structural opposition to Stanley's homosocial authority, offers her as a preferred location for gay identification, as we have seen. Indeed, her attitude to Allan's death is so remorseful that she almost comes to stand in for the tragic notion of homosexuality his death represents. She tells Mitch of her dead husband with a great poignancy which seems to seal their intentions: 'Could it be – you and me, Blanche?' (p. 184). Despite the heterosexual mannerisms of their relationship, we may choose to read Blanche's beau as homosexual. Mitch's character is not coherent throughout the play, and indeed he performs different structural functions in relation to the others at different points. In this he is like Stella: they are both required by the drama to lubricate the complex power dynamic established between Stanley and Blanche. Mitch is a man, but one who is not threatened by Blanche's display of her class experience; he associates with Stanley (is in fact, his side kick) and operates within a homosocial matrix with him and yet is at least partially identified in codes that signal a Freudian model of homosexuality. He lives with, and maintains a touching affection for his dying mother: the mummy's boy was a substantial signifier of homosexuality for popular postwar American Freudian ideology. Unlike Stanley, Mitch is conscious of the need actively to present and perform an image that asserts his gender identity. He is self-conscious around Blanche, unsure of his role; and he is ashamed of the way he perspires (p. 178) and aware that he may look clumsy. He goes on to attempt to play out the animal, physical and sexual role that the play establishes (around Stanley) as the necessary way in which (heterosexual) men occupy space, in positions of domination.

But he talks about his physique to Blanche, rather than simply manifest it; he describes his body rather than having it eroticised in the stage descriptions, and tells of how he acquired his physique by going to the gym. Mitch represents safety to Blanche by virtue of his social position as a man and by the fact that he does not threaten her with his position, indeed, he acknowledges and enjoys her manifestations of the privileges of her class experience. The basis of their romantic bonding is their shared experience of insecurity and loneliness, rather than sexual passion. Mitch needs Blanche to gain the heterosexual credentials he requires to function within the homosocial network which Stanley emanates, as she needs him to protect her from her exclusion from, and subjugation to, such networks of power.

Although Blanche talks to Mitch about Stanley hating her, and her finding him common, power relations and their proximity in physical terms make it impossible for the tension between them to be even conceptually contained by the idea of a purely personal enmity; they are both enmeshed in cultural tensions around race and national identity, class and gender:

> *Blanche*: ... Of course there is such a thing as the hostility of –
> perhaps in some perverse kind of way he – No! To think of it
> makes me ... [She makes a gesture of revulsion ...] (p. 181)

What she is speaking of is the 'hostility of' desire. Stanley desires Blanche, because in this play sexuality, predicated in terms of power, violence and sublimation, provides the medium through which gender power is asserted and contested. Blanche (on p. 161) and Stanley (on p. 196) are both concerned with what goes on behind the curtains – Blanche cannot bear to sleep with Stanley in such close proximity, Stanley wants to be able to make as much noise as he wants in sex without Blanche overhearing – this shows that both are supposed to be sexually aware of the other, and self-conscious about the physical and conceptual barriers (symbolized by the flimsiness of the curtain) that separate their desires from reality. The subtextual desire which organizes their interaction is anxiously policed by them both.

Stanley's commonness and class identity, his lack of breeding, and refusal to acknowledge the feminine southern gentility that Blanche produces, not to say anything of his brutal physicality, make him an obstacle to the security and haven she sought in coming to her sister's following her inauspicious departure from Laurel. Blanche invokes the inequality and rupture around class and ethnicity that the marriage of

Stanley and Stella represents, and she embodies the possibility of a consolidation of Stella's class authority – that Stanley becomes more the brutal Polack for Stella through Blanche's gaze. Blanche's education, class position and her relationship to Stella, along with her perform-ance of femininity, make her a threat to Stanley, especially as the mech-anisms by which he subordinates women are not available to him – he can't fuck her into acquiescent adoration, because he is married to Stella. Stanley desires Blanche because he wishes to dominate her. If Blanche does desire Stanley she cannot admit to her desires because that would mean an abdication of her autonomy, her authority; we know that Blanche is libidinous, but her desires are for men who have some degree of powerlessness or vulnerability in relation to her (the homosexual Allan, lower class soldiers, young boys from her school, the newspaper boy, Mitch), so we cannot presume that Stanley's threatening presence is erotically appealing to her.

Stanley is able to destroy Blanche by virtue of his homosocial power, which she has threatened on two fronts. Her presence in his home and her intimacy with her sister, his wife, undermines the cultural credibil-ity of his variously encoded aspirant working-class identity by refracting it through her aristocratic and colonial snobbery and gentility. Her rela-tionship with Mitch is specifically constructed as a distraction from the rigours of homosocial celebration, a romantic, cultured alternative to crude phallicism. Stanley's discovery of Blanche's past provides the justification of his violent mistreatment of her. If Blanche initially provided Mitch with the promise of heterosexual credibility, the disclosure of her past betrays his homosocial affiliations. If Blanche's chastely enacted decorum constituted respectability and passivity, the revelation of her promiscuity connotes her as dangerously knowing, deceitful and masculine: too threatening to give men homosocial cred-ibility. If a woman has had many men, she may be a cheap object of exchange, but she has also been exchanging men herself. There is a strong contrast between Mitch's naivety during his dates with Blanche and his later anger at the recognition of her apparent duplicity. Homosocially empowered, or impelled, by Stanley and his knowledge, Mitch attempts to force himself upon Blanche, in what appears to be a spineless anticipation of Stanley's later rape, but typically his perform-ance of brutishness is no match for Blanche's privileged poise, and he flees into the night, unsatisfied. Once she is no longer in control of the truth about her sexual identity, Blanche's facade and status as a prospecive wife are lost, and she suffers the plight of sexually active women in a social system that gives men status for sexual excess and sends women into asylums for similar behaviour.[87] To maintain the dominance of men in the play, Stanley must withdraw the privileges through which Blanche negotiates male power. As he tells Stella: he could not let his best friend 'get caught'. It is preferable that Mitch remain a mummy's boy than marry a woman with sufficient cultural privilege to hoodwink a member of Stanley's homosocial network. Stella's material security and social authority is dependent on her deference, her submission to Stanley's male power (she accepts and forgives his hitting of her, and comes down from Eunice's – *she* comes to *him*), a selling out of her class and ethnic identity. Blanche refuses to submit, refuses to use her status and culture to collude with Stanley's masculine pride, his arrogant expectation of an acknowledgement of his superiority. As a function of her material insecurity, Blanche should perform her femininity in such a way as to show her recognition of Stanley's power and her need for his benevolent patronage. As a single woman, she should constantly produce deferral to the conceptually superior marital arrangements of her sister; instead she incites Stella to leave her husband. As a woman, Blanche should display her recognition of Stanley's authority as a man; instead she presents his masculinity as a bestial reflection of her own 'pure white blood of the South'.[88] As a guest in his house, Blanche should reproduce the grudging deference shown by Stanley's wife to his homosocial relationships; instead Blanche creates autonomous spaces of her own 'enchantment' that are not only *not* feminine negotiations of Stanley's power, but which actually seduce his homosocial partner into forming 'adulterous' bonds with her.

Blanche has gone out of her way not to enact behaviour which recognizes Stanley's authority, despite manifesting a debilitating nervousness which betrays her relative powerlessness in relation to that authority; therefore, just getting her out of his house may enable Stanley to realize Blanche's fears of material deprivation, but will not neutralize her assaults upon his masculinity. Indeed, marrying Mitch will confirm the success of her determinedly privileged performances of femininity by awarding her with the material security she needs, and permanently inscribe her into Stanley's homosocial network as the wife of his best buddy. Stanley has not forgotten 'all that I took off her' (p. 198); when she meets his gaze, squirts jasmine perfume in his face, incites his wife to leave him; when she uses her breeding to humiliate him and seduce his buddy into an engagement, Blanche is committing acts of homosocial defiance. It is not adequate just to put a woman capable of such dissidence on the street, from where she may gain the romantic approval of a man less homosocially rigorous than Stanley and marry him, attaining

the cultural standing available to women who acquiesce to that institution.

In the 1995 CBS television version of *A Streetcar Named Desire* Stanley's rape of Blanche has little dramatic force. Jessica Lange's Blanche
has fluttered way beyond the realms of rationality by the time Stanley
returns from the hospital: Stanley's assault has little impact because this
Blanche does not exhibit any remnant of a gender performance that
acknowledges an awareness about material conditions and power.
Baldwin's Stanley is exuberant with virility about his impending fatherhood: she is available, unaware, easily overcome. This Blanche has been
so intrusive, so ineffectual, that one almost welcomes her dramatic
demise. This film is a reactionary appropriation of *Streetcar*. Williams's
text makes it clear that Blanche is drunk and emotionally distraught at
this point, not mad. This evening has seen her exposure, rejection by
her would-be husband and saviour, attempted rape by that saviour and
the consumption of considerable amounts of Stanley's whisky. Her
fantasies of safety, grandeur and Shep Huntleigh are the escapism of a
frightened and drunk woman. The poise and assurance that are functions of her experience, which we see displayed in her manipulation of
Mitch, her seduction of the young man, and in her earlier resistance of
Stanley, Blanche manifests as real struggle against her attacker.

Although the outcome is inevitable as an expression of Stanley's
gender superiority, the rape of Blanche, Southern White Goddess, in its
evocation of supremacist myth, also secures Stanley's conceptual inferiority by inferring his 'blackness'. If Blanche does exhibit madness in
this play, that madness comes in the final scene, and then this seems
the justified response of a woman whose reality is being invalidated,
rather than some neurotic self-indulgence or pathological illness. Stella
and Eunice collude in a denial of Blanche's accusation of Stanley:

Stella: I couldn't believe her story and go on living with Stanley.
Eunice: Don't ever believe it. Life has got to go on. No matter what
    happens, you've got to keep on going. (p. 217)

They must sacrifice her to maintain the plausibility of their own
relationships with men, on whom they depend for material security
and social privilege. To believe Blanche is to accept her exclusion from
male homosocial power for themselves; for Blanche, this has led to her
dispatch to a mental asylum. As Blanche leaves, Stella gives in to 'luxurious sobs' (p. 226), Stanley puts his hand into his wife's blouse and
the poker players deal another hand. Howard Taubman would no doubt

see this as a happy resolution of wholesome heterosexuality following the expulsion of the 'baneful female'. Thankfully, Gore Vidal offers an anecdote that allows us to pervert such hegemonic nonsense. In *Palimpsest*, Vidal recounts a meeting between Williams, his 'Glorious Bird', and the actress Claire Bloom, who was about to play Blanche:

> The Bird looked at her suspiciously; then he said, 'Do you have any questions about the play?'
> 'Yes.' Claire pulled herself together. 'What happens *after* the final curtain?'
> The Bird sat back in his chair, narrowed his eyes. 'No actress has ever asked me that question.' He shut his eyes; thought. 'She will enjoy her time in the bin. She will seduce one or two of the more comely young doctors. Then she will be let free to open an attractive boutique in the French Quarter . . .'
> 'She wins?'
> 'Oh, yes,' said the Bird. 'Blanche wins.'[89]

Vidal goes on to describe Bloom's performance, strengthened by her conversation with the Glorious Bird, as being 'splendid' and which culminated in Blanche leaving for the asylum 'as for a coronation'.

Inversionism has proved a useful strategy for hegemonically containing Williams's work. Even though the *content* of inversionist narratives, through which the playwright's pathologisation is effected, are themselves a function of gender, the *effect* of that pathologisation is his exclusion from the normative sex–gender system. This exclusion enables critics like Taubman and Kauffman, as we have seen, to render the troubling accounts of heterosexuality offered in works like *A Streetcar Named Desire* safe: they are not a comment on heterosexuality, but a perverse vengeance upon it. Thus, Blanche is understood as a twisted refraction of a freakishly abnormal sensibility and not a dangerously revealing, ideologically exposed portrait of heterosexual femininity. Inversionist knowledge is but one strand in a tapestry of competing ideological narratives through which we gain an understanding of our identities. Inversion remains operative in contemporary accounts of gay culture and identity because we are part of a wider system which handles differential gender power. If Blanche really is queer, it is not because she does not signify as a woman: the challenge she poses to Stanley and his responses are only intelligible coming from a textual position of 'womanhood'. Blanche's queerness is a function of her troublesome presence, which not only destabilizes normative masculine power, but produces this destabilization out of a critique of heterosexuality itself, and women's place within it, as subjects of male homosociality. Taubman and Kauffman's hegemonic narrative of Williams's inversion not only perverts the commentary *Streetcar* enacts in Blanche, but it conceals the operation of their homosocial masculinity. This homosociality keeps homosexuality right at the centre of the sex–gender system as a means of reproducing the natural balance of male power. Blanche DuBois is a heterosocial heroine, unleashed by Williams as queer dissent upon homosocial subjectivity. I shall be mapping out the terms of heterosociality in subsequent chapters.

2
Heterosocial Tendencies

A case of sexuality or gender? Feminism and queer theory

In order to understand more fully the nature of the fascination much gay male culture has with women, I want to explore the relationship between homosexuality and gender, and the conditions through which discourses of sex and sexuality relate to discourses of gender and feminism. Although the rhetoric and ideology of gay liberation has been deeply indebted to that of the developing women's movement during the late 1960s and 1970s, and indeed, continues to be influenced by feminist agendas, there is something of a discontinuity between epistemologies of gender and those of sexuality. This discontinuity is itself played out in conflicts among diversely situated feminists, many of whom have themselves been influenced by the political and cultural trajectories of gay politics: this is particularly the case in the area of lesbian feminism, which from the birth of the contemporary women's movement has been positioned ambiguously in relation to heterosexual feminism and gay male politics; of late this ambiguity has become manifest as tensions between so-called libertarian and radical feminists, which have become polarised around differing agendas: one which privileges sexuality and the other which privileges gender.[1]

All politics of sexuality, whether they be radical or libertarian, feminist, Foucauldian, feminist-Foucauldian, queer, essentialist or constructionist privilege some system of erotic desire and sexual practice and pleasure (whether strategically, historically, theoretically, biologically or culturally instated) as the terms through which identities and individuals are controlled and constituted within discourse, or through which individuals, subcultures and dissident activities may reconstitute or transgress social organization. Such a politics of sexuality came into an ascendancy through the feminist 'sex wars' of the 1970s and 1980s and has of late gained institutional authority through the virtual ubiquity of the work of Foucault, himself a gay male sado-masochist. These developments have enriched the field of radical politics, but have had the effect of throwing feminism into a series of theoretical deadlocks that have precipitated activist stasis, and enabled the dispersed Queer politics to become a somewhat aimless prescription of radical individualism and apolitical pleasure-seeking, because it has not been able to address the tensions of which it is a product.

Gayle Rubin's essay 'Thinking Sex' has become something of a land-mark in the evolution of these debates, particularly as it has been inter-preted as a retraction of her earlier, and seminal, work, 'The Traffic in Women'.[2] In the later work Rubin writes: 'feminist thought simply lacks angles of vision which can encompass the social organizations of sexu-ality.'[3] This later position Teresa de Lauretis characterizes as one con-cerned with a *non-gendered* notion of sexuality, centred around 'the sensations of the body, the quality of pleasures, and the nature of impressions.'[4] Such work has found expression in debates that cut across earlier allegiances of gender and sexual preference: in work on porno-graphy, sadomasochism, perversion, drag, performativity, promiscuity, trans-gender, camp, role-playing, bisexuality, and gay and lesbian history, so-called libertarian and radical positions have become entrenched, but all the while foregrounding sexuality – desire – based analysis.[5] There is, as ever, a problem with making assertions about such culturally-loaded terms. The notion of desire that has arisen through the ascendancy of a politics of sexuality is one specifically concerned with desire as pleasure, rather than desire as the means for reproduction; it is a politics which sees, in other words, pleasure as the *point* of desire, rather than repro-duction – which is perhaps the governing principle of Freudian accounts of sexuality: reproduction is the purpose, pleasure the perversion. Multi-gender, diversely practising, diversely identified constituencies that emerged out of these debates coalesced for what now appears to be a brief (and highly mythologised) time in the activist Queer politics of the early 1990s, which emerged, particularly in America, as the second wave of gay cultural responses to the urgency of the HIV/AIDS epidemic.[6]

Even those feminists for whom Foucault is a fruitful, but *carefully* deployed theorist, the terms of discussion remain embedded in eroticism and sexual practice,[7] or lead to assertions of the body as but a function of the axes along and through which sexuality and sex are theorized: 'Bodies are understood in relation to the production, transmission, reception and legitimation of knowledge about sexuality and sex.'[8] This seems somewhat at odds with Caroline Ramazanoglu and Janet Holland's assertion of the body as the site of feminism's struggle to attain some measure of control for women (from men) – a gender based struggle encompassing a range of conflicts upon material grounds where women are oppressed, including (but not encompassing) their sexual desire.[9] Feminist theorists such as Ramazanoglu and Holland, Jana Sawicki and others[10] identify Foucault's usefulness in conceiving of power in sophisticated ways that transcend totalizing notions of patriarchy or capital. Foucauldian conceptualizations have facilitated analyses of how identities and bodies are effects of power, of discourse; but as Sandra Lee Bartky points out:

> Foucault treats the body throughout as if it were one, as if the bodily experiences of men and women did not differ and as if men and women bore the same relationship to the characteristic institutions of modern life. Where is the account of the disciplinary practices that engender the 'docile bodies' of women, more docile than the bodies of men? Women, like men, are subject to many of the disciplinary practices Foucault describes. But he is blind to those disciplines which produce a modality of embodiment which is peculiarly feminine.[11]

For all the familiarity, even ubiquity, of such criticism of Foucault, that gender blindness has nevertheless continued to influence the trajectory of sexual and gender politics and theory. Domna Stanton's introduction to the collection *Discourses of Sexuality* sets out comprehensively the emergence and evolution of studies of sexuality, and its relation to feminism, history and literary studies.[12] In a discursive terrain which does not facilitate differentiation of the category of woman – in order to identify clusters of power through which that category is experienced as oppressive – gender becomes meaningless, and it is thus understandable how sexual politics has become sublimated to the politics of sexuality – of *desires*, perverse or otherwise. Yet clearly it is insufficient to ascribe the material oppression of women to the results of their perverseness *as women*. This is the epistemological tendency endemic in the drive towards privileging sexuality as the preeminent genealogical frame of reference in work on power, identity and the body.[13] Reinscribing authoritative structures within camp rhetoric, flouting the category of normality by reversing its terms and celebrating perversity, has very different effects for gay men than for lesbians or heterosexual women;

even for gay men, such strategies of transgression limit the scope of our potential political effectiveness. If we want to understand the attraction women and female identification hold for gay men, categories of knowledge that are limited to sexuality and desire as eroticism and the concomitant idea of perversity, are insufficient; what such relationships express are the formation of subcultural understanding, history and identities through patterns of bonding, association and identification that are, of course, structured by the terms of sexual practice (and are in turn constrained and controlled through them), but are not entirely circumscribed in terms of that sexual practice alone, whether deviant, celebrated or perverse.

It is my contention that the extent to which the very plausibility of gay male identity has become utterly dependent on these diverse politics of sexuality as eroticism is inhibiting to the continuing dissident potential of those possible gay male identities. In his recent book, *Homos*, Leo Bersani assesses the radical possibilities in gay identity. He asks:

> Should a homosexual be a good citizen? It would be difficult to imagine a less gay-affirmative question at a time when gay men and lesbians have been strenuously trying to persuade straight society that they can be good parents, good soldiers, good priests.[14]

Bersani cruises through an emerging alternative canon of gay male literary immoralists in a search for figures to inspire and question gay identity: Gide, Proust, Genet.[15] It is in Genet that Bersani's search culminates, in a fascinating and subtle analysis of Nazi erotics, aestheticism, rimming and anal intercourse in the novel *Funeral Rites*. The figures in whom Genet symbolises the radical nihilism that Bersani celebrates in *Funeral Rites*, a couple who apparently renounce intimacy as the precondition for an identity between the penetrator and the penetrated, uncover 'a fundamental sameness between them – as if they were relay points in a single burst of erotic energy toward the world. Relationality here takes place only within sameness' (p. 170). This is an idea not dissimilar to Sue-Ellen Case's butch–femme lesbian couple who, she argues, inhabit the same subject position. Bersani offers the symmetricality of gay sex as what Jonathan Dollimore would call a 'transgressive reinscription' of fertility and reproduction, as the German soldier Erik fucks the young collaborator Riton from behind (crucially not completing the 'perfect oval of a merely copulative or familial intimacy' p. 165), they come 'not with each other but, as it were, *to the world*, and in so doing they have the strange yet empowering impression of looking at the night as one looks at the future.' (p. 166) as, Bersani notes, does Genet's Hitler, discharging onto his enemies' territory millions of young German males, 'with his stomach striking their backs and his knees in the hollows of theirs.' (p. 167) For Bersani, the radicalism of Genet's text is that in the solipsistic circulation of jouissance through the medium of a Führer,

> absolute narcissism . . . opens a path onto the world, a world emptied of relations but where relationality has to be reinvented if the dangerously overloaded self is to escape the fatally orgasmic implosions of Hitler's soldiers. (p. 171)

As Bersani acknowledges, this is territory which is politically precarious, at the very least.[16] In terms of the particular concerns under discussion here, it is the vision of the buggering couple as an undifferentiated sameness, a symbolisation of potential mutuality, that I am concerned with. This sameness, a very phallic sameness, could be said to embody the realm of those very authorities beyond which transgression seeks to articulate, to imagine. The reinforcement of such sameness represents the same terms through which the security of gender hierarchies are maintained. Genet's transgressive buggers, Erik and Riton, are exalted through phallic terms (emissions, penetrations, ejaculations) which identify Erik's penis, the penetrat*or*, as symbolically central and not the penetrat*ed* anus of Riton: whatever nihilistic reimaginings the couple enable are represented through Riton's subjection to Erik's penetration: it is from this point of masculinism that 'absolute narcissism' offers a doubling that will 'open a path onto the world . . . emptied of relations'. However glorified the intercourse, it is still intelligible – for Bersani, radical even – in phallic terms; the value of the buggery lies in the penetrating activity of the penis: the buggered arse is merely a vehicle for the performance of that penetration.

It seems that the kind of gay man Bersani wishes to constitute and wishes to celebrate as transgressive resistance lines up with what Teresa de Lauretis, borrowing from Irigaray, has described as the hommo-sexual.[17] In her authoritative essay 'Sexual Indifference and Lesbian Representation' de Lauretis attempts to constitute the discursive knots which inhibit the elaboration of lesbian representation. In order to facilitate this project she takes up Luce Irigaray's understanding of sexual difference as a patriarchal formulation. Sexual difference, she argues, does not describe or constitute gender, but rather inscribes maleness and measures womanhood as the distance from that maleness and as a function of it. De Lauretis posits hommo-sexuality as the representation made of unified phallic power by this system of sexual (in)difference. She wants to

> remark the conceptual distance between the former term, homosexuality, by which I mean lesbian (or gay) sexuality, and the diacritically marked hommo-sexuality, which is the term of sexual indifference, the term (in fact) of heterosexuality.[18]

For all Bersani's resistance of good citizenship, his notion of a political male homosexuality ('absolute narcissism') elides the kinds of understandings of gender and homosexuality lesbian feminists like de Lauretis offer, and in doing so he posits that resistance as both masculinist (hommo-sexual) in its phallicism, and counter-intuitive, oppositional even, to feminist agendas apparently adjacent to our own. Bersani's refusal of good citizenship is in principle highly laudable, but the terms of this refusal collapse the distance de Lauretis opens between hommo-sexuality and homosexuality: the path to sameness and equivalence is one forged through an even more intense fixation upon our masculinity, our ability to penetrate. Queerness is no longer a dissident negotiation of hetero-patriarchal representational systems, but a virile embracing of them. These kinds of celebratedly penile, penetrating formulations which Bersani makes are at odds with the many gay male identities which make the performance of effeminacy the basis for a refusal of good citizenship and which make that refusal a gender dissent. While Bersani's version of the gay man clearly has strong currency in the iconography and practice of much gay male sexuality and identification, that currency is a function of his figure's incorporative manifestation of hommo-sexuality: as the ventriloquism of a powerful, patriarchal formation we should expect such practices to remain residual and attractive. As a radical sex terrorist Bersani's hommo-sexual queer is not only elusive because of his alignment with the very centres of Western political authority (militarism, phallicism, Fascism) but is an obstacle to the opportunities gay men have for engaging with political projects, such as feminism, symmetrical to our own in their diverse attempts to resist good citizenship.

One of the central problems contemporary feminist theory has returned to is a post-Foucauldian tendency for models of power and ideology to become so elaborate as to inhibit the possibility of being able to imagine resistant subject positions. Sue-Ellen Case cites de Lauretis's essay 'The Technology of Gender' as a perceptive illumination of the entrapment dilemma. Case suggests that the lesbian butch–femme couple is a resistant position that eludes entrapment in both theoretical and practical terms; her principle example being the theatrical work of Lois Weaver and Peggy Shaw in Split Britches, whose collaboration with Bloolips in *Belle Reprieve*, was discussed in the previous chapter.

Case argues that the lesbian butch–femme couple inhabit one subject position. Her intervention, characterized by a kind of performative campy panache, attempts to imagine gender roles in lesbian relations as eluding the structural iniquity of heterosexual ones. Case asserts that lesbian butch–femme is outside ideology, but however daring such a strategic announcement is, it ultimately reanticipates the entrapment it attempts to circumvent. None of us can conceive of ourselves outside ideology. Indeed, we might suggest that all subject positions are relational; for example, as depicted in *A Streetcar Named Desire*, heterosexual femininity is a function of masculine authority and the need to illicit male desire and to signal an appropriate passivity so as to gain affirmation and heterosexual privilege. This is something that de Lauretis's term sexual (in)difference recognizes, that cultural authorities produce one kind of identity, in relation to which all others are complementary, supplementary, functional. Yet clearly Case has a point: lesbianism has a fundamentally ambiguous relationship to phallic patriarchal authority, where that authority is often symbolically valuable (erotically and emotionally) while remaining structurally absent. As with any other dissident arrangement the possibilities of breakthrough are momentary, precarious – not all butch–femme arrangements can be radical in their effect – particularly given the weight of *internal* and external homophobia they must bear; that homophobia itself being an instrument of the patriarchal constitution of gender roles.[19]

Bersani's attempts to develop a gay identity that refuses good citizenship fail because his sense of queerness collapses back into hommo-sexuality. His opportunity for imagining oppositional gay maleness is already foreclosed by his naturalization of that maleness as a function of a very penile-centred, penetrating subjectivity. It would seem that we need an alternative model through which to appreciate gay men's place within wider systems of gender and with which we can find political promise. Despite the potential Bersani reveals for gay male identities to merely reproduce sexual indifference, gay male gender identifications do seem to have a potential to align themselves with women against hommo-sexual authority. Tennessee Williams's work in *A Streetcar Named Desire* illuminates that potential. Yet we lack a model for understanding the conditions through which such identification may take place and with which we may judge the effectiveness of such a relation.

In the critical culture with which Williams's work has been surrounded we can see how far gay male interventions rest on a terrain vigorously policed by ideological mechanisms whose effect is continually to fragment marginal affiliations or reposition them in order to reproduce already powerful formations. While many representations effected by gay men are misogynistic, the recuperative way in which many critics have shielded their patriarchal interests and displaced their own misogynistic agendas by hurling such accusations at gay material, such as *Streetcar*, makes the concept an insufficiently sophisticated tool with which to gain critical access to the axes of gender (sexual indifference) and sexuality at the same time. Sue-Ellen Case's work shows us how crucial it is that we resist slippage into entrapment, but it also shows us that we cannot escape ideology, however difficult it may be to simultaneously come to terms with the complexity and contradiction of cultural formation and maintain a commitment to uncovering dissident potential in the midst of such an imbroglio.

As indicated in the title of this book, I want to introduce the notion of *hetero*social bonding to describe gay male[20] gender identification; that heterosociality constituting a strategic negotiation of hetero-patriarchal male *homo*sociality as theorised by Eve Sedgwick. In choosing such a term I want to recognize the structural nature of affiliations made between women and gay men so as to foreclose purely frivolous understandings of our relations and to validate the institutional difficulties such bonds endure, as well as the dissent potential they hold. The distinction of *hetero*social is intended not only to indicate that such bonds are operative between different sexes, but that for each party they take place under literally heterogeneous conditions produced as these bonds are formed across the opposed axes of sexuality and gender. As I shall discuss in some detail, male homosocial relationships exist as a function of what de Lauretis calls sexual indifference and they serve to uphold the integrity of hommo-sexuality, the identification with masculinity as sameness, unity, subjectivity. Bonds between women and gay men not only work to offset the authority of such patriarchal sameness, but in their very enaction they make negotiations of difference. The choice of the term heterosocial is important in part because it enables a differentiation between the role of women in the arrangement of hetero-normative male bonds (which are an expression of hommo-sexuality and work to enforce sexual indifference) and the role of women in gay male–female identifications, the circulation of which may embody hommo-sexual potential, but which attempt a resistance of the phallic unification of sexual indifference and which enact dissent upon the inevitability of hommo-sexual maleness. Would it be fair to say that all men circulate images of women and associate with them in the same way? Are the purposes of each transaction the same? How are gay male identities embedded in patriarchal power and how can we disrupt such relations? In order to begin to propose the possibility of heterosocial bonding, it is clearly crucial to first examine in detail the constitution of homosocial bonds and how these may relate to notions of gay male identity, 'hommo-sexuality', penetration and sameness.

Homosocial regimes, male power and not getting fucked

In her ground-breaking work *Between Men: English Literature and Male Homosocial Desire*, Eve Sedgwick suggests ways of understanding the proximity between sexual and social desire between men. She offers a model in the form of a continuum with men loving men at one end and men promoting the interests of men at the other. In her approach gay men, and the possibility of homosexual desire, lie at the heart of male patriarchal authority: the proximity of homosexual desire acting as a constantly invoked abjection from which men must flee at all costs. This desire acts as a 'prohibitive structural obstacle' that is strenuously suppressed through the demonization of faggottry and the exchange of women: which is the object of such structures. Sedgwick goes on to assert that, 'homophobia is a *necessary* consequence of such patriarchal institutions as heterosexual marriage.'[21] Part of Sedgwick's breakthrough is her suggestion that the homophobia of patriarchy does not merely have a regulatory imperative for homosexual desires, but that it potentially facilitates dominant 'definitional leverage over the whole range of male bonds that shape the social constitution.' (BM p. 86) Homophobic anxieties about where particular men may have cause to position their bonds on the homosocial continuum render them vulnerable and bind them into structures of patriarchal authority.

Informed by the work of Foucault, and emerging at a point of intersection between academic feminism and gay politics, Sedgwick's work suggests terms through which the structural importance of male homosexuality within patriarchal authority lies not in the fact of homosexual desire itself, but in the terms through which the meanings of such desire are embedded in the functioning of gender authority. Sedgwick's point is that male heterosexuality is produced through discursive mechanisms that are inherently paradoxical, in that they express a double bind: 'For a man to be a man's man is separated only by an invisible, carefully blurred, always-already-crossed line from being "interested in men".' (BM p. 89) In other words, men's relationships with each other are enacted from within an understanding of the proximity of the dangerous realm of same-sex passion – the negotiations, suppressions and disavowals of that understanding are constitutive of men's mannish relations with other mannish men.

Sedgwick's thesis is useful not only for the conceptualization of masculinity that it offers (as has been pointed out, its conceptualization of a female continuum is much less satisfying)[22] but for the strategic importance it credits to gay male negotiation and intervention, for the confidence with which she is able to suggest that the material effects of such dominant discursive processes are not inevitable, but sites of struggle (BM p. 90). Sedgwick's further innovation, of course, was to show how homophobic structures work to police, and to *constitute*, the entire spectrum of male relations and not merely those of an apparent sexual minority. Women are instruments of male power and functional in allaying homosocial anxiety: the sharing of, or competition for, sexual conquest of women, the sharing of the action of subordinating, being the glue of homosociality at the same time as procuring homophobic reassurance that the crossing of the always-already crossed line has been resisted. In this she rendered new terms to connect anti-homophobia and feminism – not as a corollary, but as an alliance 'most fruitful if it is analytic and unpresuming' (BM p. 20).

This progression has historically been a key intervention. As Craig Owens argues, work by some second wave heterosexual feminists – such as Elaine Showalter and Luce Irigaray, among others – before the emergence of contemporary lesbian and gay theoretical work, has been repositioned and represented to form a trend that can be interpreted as suggesting that philosophy, fascism and capitalism itself are driven through homoerotic formations.[23] This proposition was clearly a strategically attractive one, in that it identifies the strength of the bonds through which men act in the interests of men, to the exclusion of women; however such suggestions collapse all men's bonds with each other into structural transactions, and efface the particularity of homosexual desire or cultural dissent: they cannot account for the possibility of male same-sex passion, or the production of homophobia (which would be unnecessary if men acting in the interests of men was functionally secure) nor can they theorise the importance of *exchanging*, rather than merely excluding, women.[24] Owens credits Sedgwick with a

definitive insistence against the tendency to assume patriarchal institutions to be hotbeds of homosexuality; actually they are mechanisms for
the production of homo*phobia*. (p. 230) Such mechanisms require the
suppression of male same-sex passion through the material exchange,
the exploitation, of women. Owens argues that the Freudian proposition that homophobia is caused by the repression of homosexuality
elides the active production of homophobia, the fear of homosexuality
which necessitates the control of relations with women as the mediation of such fear. Sedgwick's work has also enabled formulations
which resist the post-Freudian tendency to collapse the blame for
homophobia into (repressed) homosexuality.

Thus we can see that within homosocial structures (heterosexual)
women and homosexual men are instruments that enable the constitution of a powerful, homogenous male heterosexuality. Power is retained
within the structure by securing bonds of common interest between
men, while the whole matrix serves the necessity of economic reproduction through the importance of fatherhood and heterosexual pro-
creation. Masculine homosociality is then a coercive mechanism
through which men acquire cultural and social power and the patriarchy is reproduced in the interests of capital. The threat of breaking
ranks is managed through the active production of misogyny and the
requirement of constant *display*. In order to participate in dominant
power men must continuously represent their credentials, and more
importantly, represent distance between themselves and the always-
already present possibility that they will act discontinuously with their
own gender interests, and not display their dominance over women.
Just in case the impediment of dominant faction membership is not
sufficient motivation, *not* continuously displaying power over women,
not redemonstrating the already implicit understanding of male
authority, is continuously conjured as latent homosexuality.

One can then imagine how the vicissitudes of the closet and the coercive power of homosociality conspire to make many homosexual men
behave in ways that attempt to display *their* dominance over women.
Retreating from the abjection of public homosexuality and aspiring
towards the authority of homosociality necessarily demands the reinforcement of misogyny, for such retreat and aspiration is never secure,
even in apparently heterosexual men, never mind co-opted homosexuals:
the need for reiteration, for reassurance that can never be absolute, is
the strength of homosocial mechanisms. Men who are not *seen* to act
in the interests of men are the always ever-present faggot-other, the
shadow cast over all male–male bonding. One of Sedgwick's strengths is

her theoretical insistence that male heterosexuality is a site of instability, panic and constant reproduction.

However, before going on to assess the extent to which gay male subcultural practice may offer the opportunity to resist homosociality by exploiting and amplifying these instabilities, it seems important to examine more closely the fabric of institutional fantasy upon which homosocial narratives rest. What is it that actually constitutes Sedgwick's 'always-already crossed line' – this circumscription of maleness by a continually conjured abhorrence that is homosexuality? Leo Bersani famously offers an answer when he conjures 'the infinitely... seductive and intolerable image of a grown man, legs high in the air, unable to refuse the suicidal ecstasy of being a woman.'[25] The always-already crossed line is the blurring of fantasy scenarios with which male power eroticises itself – in effect seduces itself into reproducing. Men are encouraged to identify with masculinity – with the ideal homosocial subject, one to whom the display of attractiveness to women is evident, even hyperbolised; a display through which the potential to subordinate and control women through sexual desire is made apparent. This display, the characteristics which manifest this display, are a man's thing for other men – as a generation of feminist writers have pointed out (unlike femininity, which is for others). Bersani recognizes this:

> Unfortunately, the dismissal of penis envy as a male fantasy rather than a psychological truth about women doesn't really do anything to change the assumptions behind that fantasy. For the idea of penis envy describes how men feel about having one, and, as long as there are sexual relations between men and women, this can't help but be an important fact *for women*. (p. 216)

The gap produced in homosocial formations between the necessity of continually conjuring and aspiring to the efficacy of masculinity, to the trappings of its power and between over-investing in this fantasy, is the gap in which homosexual-as-abject becomes deeply functional. The difference, for example, between admiring another man because of the largeness of his penis (penis envy) which more fully lives up to the authority of phallicism, and desiring his large penis for yourself so that you may make a more powerful symbolization of male power and therefore more powerfully dominate women, is conceptually slight for homosocially constituted insiders (straight men) and outsiders (gay man) alike. The ever-present, ever needing to be repressed erotic–abject of male penetration is a consequence of the reliance on the notion of men acquiring power through penetrating others, and of the need to make an identification with the body image with which that penetration can be effected. Bersani concludes that the transgressive potential of gay sexuality is that it makes material this erotic–abject that he calls a 'self-shattering *jouissance*', male penetration. It is this loss of self that men fear and for which gay men are punished through an association embedded in phallocentrism.

Yet, as Tania Modleski has pointed out, this transgression, the self-shattering sexual moment is 'surprisingly individualistic'.[26] As Modleski shows in her reading of *Lethal Weapon*, much mainstream male culture flirts with the notion of masochistic release: in terms of gender power it isn't much of a transgressive manoeuvre. As part of its ideological matrix, 'phallocentrism has, of course, sought *continually* to instil in women a sense of the value – for them – of powerlessness and of masochism' (pp. 148–9); furthermore, 'masochism in the *guise* of powerlessness is . . . frequently the luxury of empowered beings . . . social power and sexual humiliation may coexist quite easily.' (p. 149) What Modleski is suggesting is that homosocial structures fracture no more easily around the image of a man with his legs in the air waiting for his self-shattering penetration by another man's penis, than they do when faced with a parodic performance of leather motorcycle drag, as Bersani himself points out (p. 207). Bersani's argument, following a Freudian paradigm, carries an ahistorical notion of processes and fears – it offers male behaviour and fantasy as a developmental given, a move that is ultimately inappropriate for the purposes of my argument here. Nevertheless, Bersani's contention about the fear of anal penetration for men is clearly an insight into a significant point of rupture and disquiet for homosocial structures. The particular processes through which the fear of penetration is conjured as a consequence of male homosocial activity, and managed through the exchange and positioning of others, remains a fertile ground for the exploitation of faultlines available for subcultural manipulation.

Pulp Fiction: fucking butch

This obsessive return to the dangerous possibility of male anal penetration that is a consequence of clashing dominant fantasies of homosociality remains operative in contemporary popular culture and is nowhere more dramatically apparent than in the massive commercial cult-crossover hit that is Quentin Tarantino's *Pulp Fiction*. What is extraordinary about the reception and discussion of this film, aside from a lemming-like consensus over its apparent brilliance, is the hegemonic way in which its obsessive return to the motif of male anal penetration has remained unidentified. This is all the more notable when, as we shall see, these motifs are not exactly represented half-heartedly.

There are two scenes in *Pulp Fiction* when the hectic, cartoonish pace of the breakneck dialogue and grotesque black comic violence becomes fractured. The first is the flashback scene when Captain Koons (Christopher Walken) visits a small child, who transpires later to be the boxer, Butch (Bruce Willis). Koons' lengthy monologue deliberately slows the narrative pace and acts as a disconcerting segue between two of the four disparate dramas that comprise the film's construction. Koons is returning a gold watch to the child, Butch, which belonged to his father and grandfather. Koons fought in Vietnam with Butch's father and was later imprisoned in the same POW camp with him. Butch's father held on to the gold watch, a present from his own father, by keeping it in his anus, despite, Koons tells the boy, having dysentery. When Butch's father died he entreated Koons to keep the watch and after the war to find his son and give it to him. Koons was able to hang on to the watch himself, and deliver it, despite being held a prisoner of war, by putting it up his arse. Thus the anus of his father and that of his father's closest friend proves to be the medium for a bonding Butch is able to enact with his father and grandfather through the totem of the watch.

Next we see the narrative purpose of this strange scene, which despite its comic intentions, appears to be too graphic and unbalancing, too protracted and contemplative to actually draw laughs. We return to the present: Butch has won a fight he was paid to lose and is on the run with his girlfriend, Fabienne. They are in a motel room, and Butch has just realized that Fabienne did not pack his father's gold watch. His fury with her eclipses their earlier romanticism and he dangerously decides to return home to retrieve his watch, leaving Fabienne frightened and in tears. At home Butch encounters his boss's hitman, Vincent, sat on the toilet with his trousers round his ankles, and has to kill him in order to escape with the watch. Butch is driving back to Fabienne and the motel, when he comes across Marsellus, the black gangster boss who paid him to throw the fight. Marsellus is crossing the road and Butch unsuccessfully tries to run him over, crashing the car in the process. Marsellus, intent on murder, chases Butch into a pawn shop where both are captured and held hostage at gunpoint by a couple of sado-masochistic gay men. Marsellus is being raped by the men when Butch, who will be raped next, escapes. However, in the midst of his escape

Butch hesitates, before considering an array of weapons hung on the wall with which to enact and enforce his return (hammer, baseball bat and chainsaw). These phallic symbols, conveniently placed for Butch, belong to the abject queer rapists; as displayed, inactive objects they would seem to represent the hysterical attempt by the queers to display masculinity: Butch/Willis, as a real man is able to activate them, to release them from passive display. Butch selects a samurai sword, ritualistically displayed on a lacquered stand, which immediately imbues his return to free Marsellus with intense romantic symbolism. Such nobility is particularly striking as Butch and the man he has chosen to liberate (when he could quite easily leave him there: indeed, this would logically suit the boxer) were but a few moments earlier vigorously intent on killing each other. Homosocial integrity is restored as Butch wields the sword at one cowering faggot who is watching the other raping the gangster. As the first man is cut down, Butch steps aside to allow Marsellus to shoot his rapist between the legs, turning the faggot's groin into a bloody pulp, thus representing his castrated non-man queerness and disavowing the rape.

This bizarre and graphic chain of events is rendered in a much more realistic tone than the earlier hectic dialogue or trendy violence. (One of the most blackly comic scenes in the film, which appears to draw substantial laughter from audiences, shows Vincent the hitman accidentally blowing the back of a man's head off in a car, and his subsequent adventures in cleaning up the car and disposing of what is left of the corpse. This scene is dominated by the charismatic and powerful figure of Mr Wolf, the fixer (Harvey Keitel) and by a cameo from Tarantino himself – despite its violence and danger then, a scene reassuring enough for the *auteur* to dramatize himself in.) The predicament of our anti-hero appears much more serious and less exhilarating than his earlier adventures. The possibility of being anally penetrated is so inimical that not only must Butch/Willis himself escape, but the empathic fear such an act engenders leads him to rescue his erstwhile foe, embodying an intense romantic symbolism as he does so. The residual power of the homosocial bond, through which men are attached by a suppression of the possibility of becoming womanly, becoming queer, becoming penetrated, overrides Butch's enmity towards Marsellus – expressed earlier in the very same scene by his trying to run over the gangster in a car. Getting run over by a car is better than being buggered. Here the contradictory narratives through which gay male identities are seen to occupy abjection functionally reinforce one another. On the one hand the inimical threat that drives the force of the scene depends not only on the unpleasantness of being raped, being taken against one's will, but being penetrated, as a man, by another man. Submission not only to rape, but to penetration enforces a relation to queerness – it is to have that negation forced upon you. Here the notion of homosexuality, of abjection, is secured through the idea of passivity, womanliness.

On the other hand however, the actual queers in this scene *are the rapists*, they are the aggressors, upon whom the heterosexual hero and villain have innocently stumbled in the course of their entertaining and quite legitimate duel. Here the queer threat is plausible in the same way in which it is meaningful when incited by the religious right as a potential aggressive conversion of the 'innocence' of children: as something predatory, conniving and lurking in the dark recesses, always ready to entrap. Such is the agility of patriarchal hegemony that both narratives produce functional effects within homosocial structures. The distasteful nature of penetration reminds us that identities which eroticise male penetration are truly queer, truly execrable: the boundary between heterosexuality and otherness is necessary, real. But this is a real and tangible threat (so runs the homosocial logic), because those queers who eroticise anal penetration aren't just passive, they're after yours, they want to inflict it on you too, so you must constantly be on guard, and constantly display that you have a healthy fear of the penetration: you must re-represent the abject nature of it. Backs to the wall, boys.

This rescue of a man, whose death would be convenient for Butch, from the process of becoming abject before his (and the audience's) very eyes, is a passionate, even romantic, act unlike any other in the film, underscored by the use of the iconographically charged samurai sword as object of the liberation. Furthermore, it is an act only necessary because Butch must recover the totem of his father, a totem that has acquired its poignancy by being kept in the anus of his father and his father's best friend. (It is, of course, also an act which displays Butch's recognition that male penetration is an anathema.) Moreover, the possibility of Butch's rape, of his abjection, is brought about in the first place by the ineptitude of Fabienne, which necessitates Butch's return for the gold watch. This circuit of homosocial bonding, from Butch through Koons to his father and grandfather, is secured by the eroticised abjection of anal penetration, by the stupidity and consequent exclusion of the girlfriend Fabienne, and by the scapegoating of the black gangster, whose abjection at the hands of the queers is tolerable because he's black and because it is preferable to the spectacle of our white everyman-hero, *Die Hard*'s John McLane, spread-eagle over a table being buggered. Representations of black male sexuality exhibit the same degree of contradiction and conflict inherent in dominant accounts of homosexuality. Yet the ability of racist hegemonies to thrive on such contradictions makes such hostile representational modes difficult to locate; however we could identify several modes, including a hyper virilisation, a feminizing objectification, a suggestion of exotic primitivism and an infantilising gender indeterminacy as being particularly prevalent. Marsellus's rape by the queers in *Pulp Fiction* neatly dovetails these conditions of racist representation with homosocial homophobia. The image of the huge black gangster bent over the table being buggered by one of the queers secures a reassuring sense for white male audiences of both his objectification before our gaze (thereby quelling fears of his excessively active black male sexuality through the scene of his abjection – feminization – by a faggot) and, in turn a fixing of the demonization of gay men as culpable predators rather than the victims of homophobic regimes. Marsellus's exoticism (size, racial identification, mysterious underworld connotations) neatly trades with his maleness to at once raise the threat queers pose to manliness and keep it at a safe distance from an imputed white male audience.

In *Pulp Fiction* there is a richness and complexity to the bonds, relationships and experience of men with and for men that does not exist for the women characters, of whom there are few and who exist in solitary narrative circumstances: they relate to, and facilitate the men, but not each other; nor do the men really relate to them, but humour and tolerate them. Mia Wallace (Uma Thurman) is taken on a date by Vincent the hit man, under the instructions of Marsellus, her husband and his boss: their episode leads to a compelling scene in which Mia has overdosed on Vincent's heroin and must be resuscitated with a terrifying adrenaline injection into her heart. Here the film acquires its dramatic *frisson* because of the authority of the absent Marsellus and his relationship with Vincent – if she dies the hit man will be in big trouble: Mia is the decorative vehicle for a more profound relationship between the men. The foot-long needle Vincent plunges into Mia's chest is a phallically symbolic violation that punishes her for threatening the relation between Vincent and Marsellus. Similarly *Pulp Fiction*'s other women – Jody (Rosanna Arquette), Honey Bunny (Amanda Plummer), and Fabienne (Maria de Medeiros) do not even coexist in the same narrative strand, never mind have the opportunity to enact meaningful bonds with each other: their purpose is to provide the (hetero)sexual credentials of their men, and facilitate (as Fabienne does) the opportunity for the men to recover dangerous, usually life-threatening scenarios and thus display their masculine credentials for the edification of homosociality. In recovering his watch, an act necessitated by Fabienne's ineptitude, Butch is able to display his credentials to Vincent (he kills him), Marsellus (he saves him) and – of course – *prevent* them from being *displayed* to the hostile, raping, faggot-others.

In her discussion of the action film *Top Gun*, Tania Modleski notes Klauss Theweleit's discussion of the proximity of violence and sex with women for heterosexual men. This violence stems from 'a fear of dissolution through union with a woman', and this fear 'propels man – or, to use Julia Kristeva's terms, abjects him – into a homosocial relation with other men.'[27] The penetration of women, that which is to be penetrated, enables the possibility of other penetrations, penetration of men, the unthinkable yet always-present possibility, the leverage that constitutes homosocial relations and renders them interminably unstable. The proximity of such possibilities must be excised through violence – through masculine display – preferably for the spectatorship of homosocial comrades, and through the identification and demonization of others, those who are homosexuals, the apparently always-penetrated not-men. Similar themes are self-consciously handled in the stunning film *L.A. Confidential*, with its fastidiously gendered male leads (touchingly, one is bookish, bespectacled and feminized, while the other is all Brando poses and snarling butchness). Their powerful romantic affiliation is cemented through a common disgust for corruption, the pomposity of their moral purpose, and the homosocial exchange of a hooker who looks like Veronica Lake (*pur-lease!*) who is a conduit for their barely repressed passions for each other.

We can thus summarize the deployment of homosocial relations. The bonding of men requires the constitution of an inside group from which power can be mobilized. The security of that inside group depends upon the manifestation of outsider-others. Within patriarchal homosociality women are the principal outsiders, the oppression of whom is a necessary condition for the succession of property rights: women are the bearers of children and the opportunity for sexual pleasure, to be exchanged as symbols of potency and value as currency between men; they are also the bearers of future generations through which to secure the ownership of capital, to control in proximate nuclear arrangements, and crucially to facilitate class and racial reproduction. Homosexual men are conjured as the treacherous and barren ever present insider-other through whom the exchange of women breaks down; their existence also blurs the boundaries between who exhibits phallic power and who bears it: they are demonized and represented as the inimical possibility of male anal phallic penetration.[28] *Pulp Fiction* also shows us that within such homosocial regimes constructions of black male sexuality operate as both the inside manifestation of a masculine virility which spills over into excess and threat when mapped onto the racially charged homosocial commodification of white women and thus also operates as outsider-other as well, particularly in the context of white propagation, and attendant fears of miscegenation and racial impurity.

Homosocial dissent, female bonding

The terms of possible dissenting and alternative interventions are diverse – necessarily so given that not only are functionally marginal identities produced and discursively controlled in different ways, but in ways which actively precipitate conflict and disunity *within* those margins. The key problem in Sedgwick's work on homosociality is that she does not 'take responsibility for enunciating'[29] the shape of female homosocial bonds, thereby effacing lesbianism, which is an effect of her assertion that there is a greater continuity between women who act in the interests of women and women who desire women. This may be the case and the shape and effects of a female homosocial continuum would certainly be different from the male one that Sedgwick theorises. The gap in Sedgwick's work lies in her failure to suggest that some heterosexual women may actually act in the interests of men, that is, act against the interests of other women (politically, sexually, culturally, emotionally, psychologically) and thus may functionally require homophobia against lesbianism to naturalise a radical *dis*continuity between women who act in the interests of women and women who desire women. Furthermore, Sedgwick does not accept the significance of substantial lesbian subcultural and political activity which has attempted to open up distance between acquiescence to heterosexual institutions (which have been characterized as precisely not serving the interests of women) and woman-identified cultural assertions as a political intervention in order to resist hetero-patriarchy. The very possibility of Sedgwick's enunciation, in terms of both content and the existence of the space from which to speak, is in no small measure the result of lesbian political and academic intervention. Given the potential that feminist and/or lesbian interventions realize – that women may politically organize in ways that disrupt their functional complicity with male homosocial formations (by refusing and disrupting the authority of masculine sexuality and corresponding social subordination) – it does not seem too bold to suggest that there would need to be a corresponding hegemonic production of a radical discontinuity between the appropriation of feminine-heterosexual acquiescence and lesbian-other.

If lesbianism promises the refusal of patriarchal control it must be sufficiently reorganized within male hegemonic narratives in a manner that would turn its potentially appealing radical-refusal into a homosocially constituted abjection from which women, in order to properly occupy feminine heterosexuality, must flee and repress, the more to display reassuring obedience and of course to benefit from the cultural capital feminine passivity accrues. Heterosexual female homophobia – towards lesbians – is a functional and necessary component of male homosocial formations. As Julia Penelope points out in her intervention into a debate which found articulacy in *Lesbian Ethics* in the late 1980s (and which had probably begun in 1970 at the Second Congress to Unite Women when twenty women calling themselves 'Lavender Menace' – later to become Radicalesbians – interrupted the proceedings to protest at homophobia within the feminist movement): 'Lesbians who are committed to personal and social change must not only rid ourselves of the HS [heteropatriarchal semantics] dichotomy, but the HP [heteropatriarchal] misogyny that values femininity as a female attribute.'[30]

There are antecedents who could have offered Sedgwick the means to broaden the scope of her homosocial system. It was in order precisely to address the patriarchal context in which women are actively impelled to act in the interests of men that radical feminism so powerfully advocated the notion of sisterhood and female bonding. In *Gyn/Ecology* Mary Daly resituates the notion of the Great (world) War as the binary deadlock of patriarchy, in which it is all men, whatever side on which they fight, who oppose women: 'The secret bond that binds the warriors together, energizing them, is the violation of women, acted out physically and constantly replayed on the level of language and of shared fantasies', and 'the male who is not willing to go forward blindly on the march of massive destruction is a "female".... Such fear is also called fear of being "effeminate".'[31]

Daly's work draws on a radical essentialism through which she blazes against male authority and female subordination, invoking the possibilities of the discovery of sisterhood as both a refusal of dependency within male structures and a subversive reinvisioning of bonding relationships which differ 'radically from male comradeship/brotherhood, which functions to perpetuate the State of War' (G/E p. 369).

Daly's argument feeds into a second-wave tendency to collapse infatuated and adoring masculine bonds into homosexual desire. Daly looks
at accounts of brotherhood and bonding written by (heterosexual) men
and theorises their tremulous and hysterical eroticism of brotherhood
as equivalent to passionate same-sex desire, a 'diseased State of Fratern-
ity' from which 'radically Lesbian loving is totally Other' (G/E p. 372).
She quotes from military accounts in which men swoon over the profundity of their bonding with comrades by simultaneously effacing
homosexual desire and relegating the importance or pleasure of bonds
with 'mere' women (one account Daly quotes reads: 'the communion
between men is as profound as any between lovers. Actually it is more
so. It does not demand for its sustenance the reciprocity, the pledges of
affection, the endless reassurances required by the love of men and
women' G/E p. 372.) Daly rightly pours scorn on such accounts, but
fails to differentiate between men acting in the interests of men and
men desiring men, thereby collapsing homophobia into homosexuality:

> Male-defined erotic love involves loss of identity and is inherently
> transitory. It involves hierarchies, ranking roles – like the military –
> on the model of S and M. While male erotic love is seen as similar to
> comradeship in these respects, it is experienced as weaker in intens-
> ity and depth [compared to the 'gynaesthetic experience'] (G/E
> p. 372)

Clearly it is an imperative of Daly's separatism that she strategically
insist upon as much distance as possible between Lesbian Loving and
all structures of romanticized affiliation constituted by and through
men. Historically speaking, the integrity of radical lesbianism depended
upon a rejection of all accommodations of men precisely so as to enable
the conceptualization of relations between women that would not
reproduce women's subjugation to hommo-sexual subjectivity. Indeed,
such bonding, 'The Fire of Female Friendship', is the political corner-
stone of Daly's programme as prescribed in *Gyn/Ecology*.

It is my intention here to theorise forms of gay male subjectivity which
are themselves resistant to homosocial terms of maleness, in which
homosexuality is always an abjection. The force of Daly's work in the
context of my argument here is to show the importance of an analysis
that foregrounds gender as the system through which masculinity and
femininity are meaningful, and which recognizes sexuality as the tool
through which the integrity of masculinity and femininity are policed,
producing homophobia as the legislative force of that policing. This is

not merely intellectual preciousness, necessitating 'trivial' semantic quibbling in emphasizing one category over another. The degree of investment made by gay men – beyond the specificities of same-sex desire and sexual activity – *against* mannish cultural concerns and practice, and with women and so-called 'female' interests and modes of expression, suggests that intellectual methodologies formulated in order to understand gay male practice and to anticipate the success of such interventions which reference only rigidly Foucauldian terms of sexuality will only be able to anticipate shifts and meanings in the realm of sexual desire, that is, the erotic – and I would argue that homosexuality is meaningful in terms way beyond those alone. In order to be able to precipitate advances in gay male cultural practice – that is, to elicit greater political gains – intellectual inquiry must engage with the enormous subcultural investment gay men make with women, that is, with identification and thus with gender, and attempt to understand what this means. Not to engage with gender in work that attempts to enquire into gay male identity is to naturalize gender difference and invite complicity with homosocial mechanisms; for it is the foregrounding of desire, of heterosexuality, that demonises homosexuality and reinforces misogyny. Heteropatriarchal hegemony continually resecures notions of masculinity and femininity in order to maintain its control of women through the continuously repetitive invocation of homosexual abjection.

A characteristic effect of Sedgwick's theorisation of conditions in which gay male identities and (heterosexual) women's identities are produced as functional effects of heteropatriarchal power, is a tendency towards entrapment. While Sedgwick's breakthrough is in part to illuminate the precariousness of male authority, and to locate homophobia and sexism as effects of that precariousness, heterosexual male identities remain central in her model. The activities of either gay men, or heterosexual women within those male homosocial bonds, are conducted through a functional association with hetero-male power. The possibility of male homosexuality lies on one side of the homosocial arrangement, policing the terms of the bonding – protecting the conditions of intimacy, while women lie on the other side, the currency of exchange with which men effect their transactions with each other. Straight men remain the central term across and through whom gay men and heterosexual women would appear to be prevented from associating with each other.

Despite the currency female identification has in gay culture, we have seen in the previous chapter how a key strategy through which gay men have negotiated the production of their own sissified abjection remains the aspirational celebration of masculinity; it is a tendency that characterizes Bersani's particular refusal of good citizenship. We could suggest then, that the entrapment which is an effect of Sedgwick's theorization of male homosocial relations actually does record a material condition of gay male marginalization. Gay male identities are circumscribed in relation to homosocial masculinity, such that empowerment is often seen as a function of ventriloquizing the terms of that homosociality in a quasi-denial of queer abjection. Similarly, within heterosexuality not only is female agency denied, but mutual recognition between women is made conceptually implausible, beyond the passive contemplation and complaint of generic difficulties (domestic or sexual squabbles, and so on): these denials are enforced by the commodification and objectification of women through relations of male alliance, something that may explain the oblivious popularity of *Pulp Fiction*. As I shall go on to discuss in relation to a significant critic of Sedgwick, the material effects of the proximity that both gay men and straight women have to the functioning of male homosociality, and their consequent diversity of resistant manoeuvres, have often resulted in an endlessly exploited breach in parity between them. Conflicts of desire, cultural legitimation and political agenda have produced tensions and discontinuities between gay men and straight women, particularly in subcultures which have adopted essentialist agendas, or where there has been a direct conflict of interests caused by the limitation of exploitable faultline possibilities. These conflicts are particularly crucial in a contemporary political landscape in which the idea of activist feminism has little credibility, being continually portrayed as opposing pleasure and choice.

The dangers of such conflicts can be seen in the kind of position elaborated by one of Sedgwick's most shrill critics. In 'The Beast of the Closet', David Van Leer holds Sedgwick responsible for the production of categories of the homosexual within homosociality, in the process of which he argues she underwrites a 'homophobic thematics'.[32] The underlying nature of Van Leer's anger towards Sedgwick becomes clearer in the dialogue that emerged between the two in the pages of *Critical Inquiry* in 1989. He resents the intrusion into the subcultural ghetto of an outsider, a woman apparently occupying a heterosexual identity. In order to effect this rejection of Sedgwick, and her attempt to fashion a coalition between gay male politics and feminism, Van Leer naturalizes gender difference, foreclosing the conceptual space from which feminism speaks, in his desire to effect closer union with heterosexual men, imputedly because gay men have more in common with heterosexual men that we do with women. In this we can see the fag-end of clone culture and what would now appear to be its hysterical need to assert the butchness of homosexual men, as a resistance to earlier notions of stereotypical effeminacy, which we have seen in the previous section to be caused by the strength of inversionist models of homosexuality and the attendant dominance of heteropatriarchal structures. Thus the conjuring of homosexual men as an abject through which heterosexuality retains virility is resisted by homosexual men by consigning women to the otherness of *true* feminine abjection, and consequently the internal logic of homosocial structures retains intact – bolstered even – by the very groups that are its anathema. Van Leer's hostility is understandable given the urgent political and material necessity of resisting homosexual pathologisation through feminization, yet his strategy precisely reproduces, recirculates the conditions of heterosocial hegemony by corroborating the function of women as subjugated objects of exchange.

Van Leer's discomfort produces contradictory effects. What is clear from his arguments is that his project is assimilationist. Van Leer evades naming himself as a gay man and his precious prevarications over his own queer self-identification collude with oppressive secrecy mechanisms through the privileging of naturalised male heterosexuality – his silence about his identity produces an indeterminacy of identification only valuable through its homophobia. On the one hand Van Leer wants to sanctify his minority status and exclude Sedgwick (women) from such domains: 'unable to speak from within the minority, Sedgwick must perforce speak from within the majority' (p. 603). On the other hand, he berates her for apparently attempting to *disallow* him an alignment with men, 'real' men. The effect of both manoeuvres is to anticipate and recommodify the very conditions Sedgwick's model elaborates: namely that heterosexual, homosocial masculinity identifies real men, who are kept in place by the production of an execrable second term – un-real, perverse, but necessary – desiring and striving towards that ever-elusive real manliness that is the very reassurance of the negation of womanliness. As I have suggested, because masculinity is structurally elusive and necessarily so, in order to reproduce the conditions of hegemony, such a performance is precarious, and precisely becomes visible through the distancing of other terms – women, queers.

Mapping heterosocial bonds

In the BFI series *Film Classics*, Richard Dyer says of *Brief Encounter*:

A bar in London, popular with well dressed, worked-out gay men, is called 'Brief Encounter'; I once suggested meeting my friend Hugh

there, but he said he couldn't bear it, it was so very 'Brief Encounter',
if I knew what that meant, and for some reason I did. For years
I wanted to do a remake of it, starring Jane Fonda as Laura and
Barbra Streisand as the lover . . .

A few paragraphs later, Dyer tells of how he once watched the film with
a group of Australian and Canadian gay men who were unfamiliar with
it, and his mother who:

> I could see . . . was uncomfortable with my doing Laura's lines over
> Celia Johnson, because it was mocking a lovely film. It was also
> mocking, or at any rate pastiching, a woman. Yet, like many gay
> men, I ardently identify with women characters in 'women's films', I
> prefer the company of women to that of men and I think of myself
> as pro-feminist.[33]

Dyer appears to be professing a form of bonding, an association, an
identification with women, not shared by his friend Hugh, for whom it
seems the proximity of up front gay men and the campy overtones of
'Brief Encounter' are uncomfortable (but does the archly epicene
'couldn't bear it' protest too much?) and not understood by his mother;
we may infer that this is because she is unfamiliar with the codes of
camp in gay male subculture, or because for her such identificatory
practice is 'mocking' or 'pastiching' her gender. For the Australian and
Canadian gay men Dyer's induction of them into the campy British
repression that is the splendour of *Brief Encounter* is an act of subcultural
affiliation undertaken through a sign of female identification and in the
presence of the mother (Freud's mummy's boys again). The meanings
here are located in the shared bonding across and over the barrier of
sexual (in)difference, a barrier naturalized by homosocial structures and
policed by homophobia.

I would contend that this subcultural and shared act of identity
formation could be described as heterosocial, in that it addresses the
efficacy of masculine homosocial structures and yet attempts to denaturalize the sameness secured by homosocial policing of gender normativity and consequent intra-male allegiances. In the case of Richard Dyer's
friend who will not rendezvous at 'Brief Encounter' the refusal to identify
with the subcultural space is a refusal of Dyer's position (whom we
already understand to identify with women) stated through a rejection
of the gayness of the bar (which he can't 'bear'). Here the anxiety is precisely one of sameness: Hugh wishes to retain an allegiance with his

gender, wishes to preserve his masculinity – his refusal is a homosocial act – his allegiance is with the maleness that comes into articulation precisely through a suppression of the heterosocial identification (identification with feminine spaces *against* naturalized heteropatriarchal gender orders) represented in 'Brief Encounter'/*Brief Encounter*, a suppression and rejection of Richard Dyer's female identification.

As Theweleit and Daly, among others, have shown, maleness is established through the suppression of any bonding (identification) with women – this is what misogyny and homophobia police – women are beneath reason, (literally) beneath masculinity. The principal identification required for the maintenance of patriarchy is with other men, with the potency of phallic authority through the elaboration of homosocial bonds. Appropriate heterosexual masculinity is achieved in male subjects by an hysterical over-identification with the promise of phallic authority. The continued repetition and restatement of this over-identification is necessitated, as we have seen, by the threat of homosexuality – this is an effect, a purpose of homosocial structures. Thus I would argue that hysterical anxiety over the display of appropriate manliness (such as not wanting to associate with inappropriate displays, such as the campiness of *Brief Encounter*) is to accede to the power of patriarchal identification – it is to aspire to the sameness of male identity, a sameness secured through misogyny and homophobia. Clearly gay men elaborate and enact many forms of dissent, many ways of alleviating and remodelling the particular circumstances in which they find themselves; it is not my purpose to lambast others who are making the best of whatever faultline conditions they can identify and exploit. However, it is appropriate here to identify the contingency of the practices under discussion. As in the discussion of David Van Leer's rejection of Eve Sedgwick's heterosocial overtures, it is worth identifying the allegiances of Richard Dyer's friend Hugh as being counter-intuitive to the female identification Dyer himself enacts and which I am attempting to formulate.

Heterosocial bonding with women is a reversal of the discourse of homosociality – in which appropriate masculinity is achieved through a suppression of women that *a priori* instates a faggot-other disavowed through misogyny. In a review of Ronald Hayman's biography of Tennessee Williams Andy Medhurst comments on the identification Richard Dyer describes in his negotiations of *Brief Encounter*, a relationship gay men have with many iconic texts:

The complex question of how Williams' female protagonists are related to his homosexuality again demands far more sophisticated and sensitive thinking than Hayman brings to bear. Referring to *Sweet Bird of Youth*, Williams claimed in a fine flourish of camp rhetoric that 'I was Alexandra del Lago from start to finish' – and there are many comparable examples in gay male culture: think of Tony Warren and Elsie Tanner, Pedro Almodóvar and Carmen Maura, the Richard Dyer/Celia Johnson interface revealed in the former's recent book on *Brief Encounter*, and what happens to me whenever I watch *Meet Me in St Louis* (I am Esther Smith from start to finish).[34]

Heterosocial bonds between women and gay men need not express mutuality; indeed, given the complexly different conditions through which gay male, and heterosexual female identities are discursively produced and contested, claims towards such mutuality would embody a power relation in themselves. Bonds gay men enact with women often circumvent people, women themselves, in favour of iconography, scales of gesture and performance, fragments of dialogue – bitchy epithets, semiotics of glamour, femininity, divinity even: dislocated and endlessly refracted representations, objectifications, enacted as a parodic refusal of homosocial masculine unification, a defiant celebration of the abjection that pivots around the display of possession, or denial, of masculine (phallic) authority, as Paula Graham has noted:

> traditionally, gay male camp takes the fetishized Hollywood female star as its focus – not just any female star, but the 'strong', highly sexualized feminine images, the sirens, vamps and femmes fatales; in other words, what psychoanalytic language would designate as the fetishized phallic feminine. Camp pleasure – that most refined and ecstatic sexual pleasure – lies in a fetishistic tease of presence/absence of phallic control: power and the threat of its loss. Camp expresses the relation of gay men *to* male authority, *mediated by* a relationship to representations of 'the feminine'.[35]

Camp practices structure representational negotiations gay men make with the feminine, political interventions that have resistant or transgressive effects in terms of the conditions through which gay male identities are experienced as problematic. Camp interventions may not necessarily be effective as strategies for lesbians in the same ways that they are for gay men, as Graham argues:

> gay men usually seem to identify with the feminine excess *and parody of authority* embodied in the mad-bad-pervert-witch or repressed

but sexually seething boss-woman. Lesbians, on the other hand, seem to prefer the cross-dressing Amazon or tart – even though she is heterosexualised and defeats a female order to restore a patriarchal one. This difference is probably due principally to a characteristic feeling on the part of gay men that their sexuality is repressed by masculine authority; as against a characteristic feeling on the part of lesbians that they are excluded from authoritative action by passive sexualization (as spectacle) for men.[36]

This could in part account for a greater symmetricality in heterosocial relations between gay men and straight women than between gay men and lesbians. Clearly there is a powerful and ongoing history of identification with lesbians, which may be structured by equivalences in gender identifications, as I suggested in the discussion of Sue-Ellen Case's butch–femme aesthetic. In terms of heterosexual women, despite their similar subjection to the passive sexualization of lesbians, in the way that Graham describes above, there is also a disparity in such experiences. Clearly most women must experience such specular control as oppressive, but within heterosexual arrangements straight women at least have the opportunity to trade such objectification as social capital, attaining a measure of legitimacy and institutionalization in the process, unlike lesbians whose identity is precisely predicated on the resistance of such arrangements, and ostracism from them as a consequence. I will go on to map the intricacies of these dynamics in the next chapter, which considers the American television sitcom, *Roseanne*.

Whatever the appeal of camp for gay men, however promising the heterosocial bonding I identify at work in the writings of Dyer and Medhurst, such strategies are not necessarily dominant ones in gay subculture. We have already seen how Leo Bersani's notion of gay radicalism is tied into highly masculinized poses, and how David Van Leer's rejection of Sedgwick's attempts at heterosocial affiliation embody the seduction of male identification for gay men. The celebrated British gay writer Mark Simpson approaches questions of masculine display that I have been analyzing here. However, rather than accepting that it is a defining condition of patriarchy that masculine display is performance for other men, as I have done, Simpson suggests that the male inducement towards narcissistic consumption of masculinity is a recent popular cultural phenomenon that spells the end of manliness as we know it. He says:

Men's bodies are on display everywhere. . . . Traditional male heterosexuality, which insists that it is always active, sadistic and desiring, is now inundated with images of men's bodies as passive, masochistic and desired. . . . Sexual difference no longer calls the shots, 'active' no longer maps onto 'masculine', nor 'passive' onto feminine. Traditional heterosexuality *cannot survive this reversal*, particularly because it brings masculinity into perilously close contact with that which must always be disavowed: homosexuality.[37]

Clearly the move Simpson is making here is attractive strategically, particularly if we ourselves wish to revel in popular culture's infatuated gaze upon the libidinous male body – suggesting that masculine display through the advertisement of jeans, aftershave, football and the like, sets up a homosexual gaze is a cheeky, not to say camp, whimsy. But of course, in order to effect this manoeuvre, Simpson actually has to collapse both ends of the male homosocial continuum into one another, making men acting in the interests of men the same as men desiring other men erotically; and, more insidiously, once again offering a gay male intervention which exalts, in its straining voyeurism, the efficacy of the butch hetero-male as the apex of desire – anybody's desire, including other butch males. It may be true to say that traditional heterosexuality cannot survive the current conditions in which the male body is represented: clearly popular feminist gains and the increasing visibility of gay male influence over popular cultural tastes have effected changes, but as we know to our cost, dominant arrangements do not stand still: dissident interventions are continuously assimilated, neutralized, reversed and ignored in the rolling repetitions of hegemonic reformation. As Lynne Segal has noted of Simpson's hopeful assertions: 'Sadly, however, sex and gender hierarchies seem to manage to thrive on their own contradictions.'[38]

Precisely so: given the instability of manly masculinity *and* its necessity to the reproduction of patriarchal conditions, there are weaknesses, faultlines to be exploited; however, we cannot imagine that male authority, like any other dominant formation, is not able to assimilate and process its own contradictions, and moreover, use our dissenting interventions as the very means to do so. Of course it is necessary that men consume images of precisely how irresistible their manliness should be, how else could the patriarchy attempt to instil in all its male subjects the arrogance of power, an arrogance which needs must overcome the unmanly shortcomings of those men who may be variously oppressed and suppressed themselves within structures of economics, professionalism, race, class, disability, location, education and skill level, effeminacy and so on?[39]

The 'undifferentiated' gaze upon the passive figure of the hetero-male body which Simpson identifies, a gaze which 'might be female *or* male, hetero *or* homo' (p. 4) does not disperse gender difference, it naturalizes it by precisely clarifying the status of the butch hetero-male as the most erotic spectacle of all, because he embodies power. The imagery Simpson discusses may proffer the notion of male passivity, but unless you have the material means and sufficient identificatory authority to conjur a subject position from which to enact your own *activity* and thus to enforce *his* passivity, then all that has been reinforced by that representation is his ability to be everywhere – to flirt with all subject positions as a demonstration of his power. What is concerning about Simpson's contentions is that they do seem to account for what is currently a dominant strain of affluent, cosmopolitan gay identity which is, ironically, understood as a kind of liberation: the liberation of the pink pound, a function of gay men's economic success.[40]

Thus far I have shown the inherent force of homosocial ideological mechanisms and the paradoxical instability through which those mechanisms are formed. To stress this uneven and necessary contradiction is not to suggest that resisting or supplanting such formations is a straightforward business – on the contrary, being aware of dominant contradiction in itself gets you nowhere, for we have seen the terrible power that homosocial formations exert in spite of their intrinsic instability. Indeed, in so far as any ideological matrix derives its effect from the way in which its subjects become complicit with its terms (Van Leer, 'Hugh', Simpson), the drive for a resolution of inherent contradiction ensures the need in those subjects for scapegoats through which unease can be temporarily and violently dissipated. However, this state of contradiction, if strategically exploited in agile and reflexive ways, does offer the opportunity for those residing in the functional margins of dominant ideologies to reformulate in dysfunctional arrangements. I want to suggest that the understandings produced by particular subcultures of gay men (those affiliated in similar ways to Richard Dyer and Andy Medhurst, as opposed to Dyer's friend Hugh) through bondings and identification with women, produce a particular set of arrangements that I refer to as heterosocial. Heterosociality rejects the unification of patriarchal sameness sustained through the manifestation and abjection of others; rather, the possibility of heterosocial bonds acknowledges the violence of such sameness and attempts to act discontinuously with the hegemonic unity of interests expressed in manliness as an instrument of authority. Rather than suppress bonds with women, displaying domination of them through public institutions of romance and courtship and the display of rigorous, penile male power, gay male–female identification opens the possibility of a denaturalization of gender difference, an attempt therefore to re-imagine gender power.

Straight talking: get some *Attitude*

In Britain in May 1994 a new queer magazine appeared called *Attitude* which advertised itself as being 'aimed primarily but not exclusively at gay men' which was 'really not interested in policing boundaries'.[41] *Attitude* was one of a number of new queer publications that appeared at the time and one of only two that survived, the other being a lesbian 'lifestyle' magazine published by the owners of the long-running *Gay Times*, yet it appears to have perceptively addressed the gay male subject as consumer, and has set the standard for gay publications in this country, much as *Out* has done in the US.[42]

In accordance with its insistence on a post-queer integration of groovy heterosexuality, *Attitude* has a column called 'Straight Talking' in which mainly female heterosexual journalists enact a commentary on gay male culture. Thus we have had articles on how boring identity politics is because it is cool to flirt with kd lang even if you're a straight woman who enjoys the missionary position and likes hairy backs;[43] we have had consideration of media obsessions with reproductivity and about the relationship between pleasure and masculinity by way of musings on spunk;[44] how serial monogamy, double incomes and childless heterosexual couples are making the differences between gay and straight more insignificant;[45] and, of course we have had (in the very first issue, no less) the manifesto of a 'theoretical fag hag' on relations between women and gay men.[46] Suzanne Moore says: 'I fail to see how anyone remotely interested in sexual politics could be anything but a theoretical fag-hag'; this is because 'while much in straight culture settles for the appearance of truth, what gay culture continually questions is the truth of appearances.'[47]

One of the reasons why I have suggested that gender is a more illuminating epistemic category than sexuality in attempting to elaborate heterosocial bonds is that even though straight women and gay men both desire men, the structural manifestations of that desire are different. Women's desire for men, and pleasure with them, is naturalized, that functionality conferring a degree of cultural legitimation, while gay men's equivalent erotic desire of men is perverse. Enacting bonding on the grounds of mutually shared desire alone, then, would require women to embrace perversion positively, in a reverse discourse, as gay men do; but this would be compromising for women, who would have to negotiate away the cultural capital they accrue through their hetero-sexuality, their 'normality'. This is one of the unspoken terms through which gay male and straight female relationships are structured. Heterosexual women are agents of cultural reproduction, in terms of parenthood, partnership, citizenship, social and cultural presence. Straight women may have to suffer parochial and constrained identities in the course of responsibility, caring, nurturing, providing, in roles performed for families, husbands and institutions of the state, but in all of those areas they are entitled to trade on their cultural capital as women. Occupying lesbian identity, or attempting to trade on that cultural capital without the licence of male respectability – self-determining behaviour not enacted for scopofilic consumption by patriarchy, or as subservi-ence to its material needs – is ruthlessly punished by the withdrawal of those privileges of cultural capital. As we can note from the continu-ingly vicious war waged upon single mothers by politicians and the media, attempting to assume responsibility for cultural reproduction without male authority makes women scapegoats of that authority.

Thus, in accounts by straight women of how valuable their bonds with gay men are, the disavowed term is always the possibility of the writer's own potential lesbianism. Not only could this possibly compromise the very authority through which fag-hags, theoretical or otherwise, trade cultural currency in their relationships with gay men, it also raises the thorny question of the constitution of female homo-sociality through homophobia, or more accurately, lesbophobia. In what amounts to an incoherent corrective to Suzanne Moore's celebra-tion of fag-haggery, Suzi Feay suggests that there's a conspiracy of gay male misogyny.[48] She argues that gay male drag parties, and gay male designers have conspired to produce an unrealistic image of femininity which real women have difficulty living up to. Yet this dismay at gay men's power to make de-naturalized representations of femininity that apparently compels women to conform, naturalizes Feay's heterosexu-ality: her idea of a realistic femininity is a function of homosocial auth-ority more constraining than any Parisian excesses.

There are significant claims to be made upon gay male misogyny, even within those constituencies of the subculture which do identify in some way with women, let alone those for whom assimilationism and masculine identification are productive moves.[49] But there is a danger in making such claims for gay male misogyny from a position of naturalized heterosexuality which refuses to acknowledge its cultural privilege: Feay notes, 'I've ... become all too familiar with what seems a widespread horror of female secretions. Though why a group of people whose sexual lubricant is a mixture of shit and Vaseline should find a bit of mucus so objectionable is baffling.'[50] Slinging around such bitchiness (however accurate or amusing) suggests that Feay is more than capable of engaging her cultural capital in order to resecure her own naturalization.

While this may be a reciprocal relationship, it is sustained by the suppression of the unspeakable term of lesbianism: 'In fact some of us [straight women] are so gay-friendly we feel as if we *are* gay ... men, that is.' The qualification exclaims the structuring absence. Such resistance, even though it is conducted in the name of breaking the barriers down ('It's time for rigid sexualities to be dissolved in a solution of mutual tolerance. No more fear and sneering; no more imprisoning definitions.') precisely reinstates a naturalising boundary between queer and straight. Feay shreds gay men for camply inferring that all men are queer, or can be had if pushed, suggesting that 'underlying all such attitudes is the assumption that homosexuality is more authentic than straightness'. Such shrill resistance to a standard camp rhetorical device indicates the underlying struggles over power, identity and autonomy that must necessarily characterize heterosocial bonds, given the resistant terms of their constitution. The reciprocal, or uneven exchange within heterosocial bonding is not based on (and therefore upheld by) sexual domination, domestic or maternal dependency, or heterosexual imperative, although it might well be based on an economic exchange, in which gay men trade economic power for stigma – straight women representing a cultural legitimation.

Indeed, as Suzanne Moore notes of some gay men who are 'conservative little gits' because they don't draw connections between all those who fall short of straight white male ideals,

> believe me it's these connections that matter, not whether people enjoy fucking each other with eighteen-inch dildos or not. What you get up to in bed may make you extremely happy, but please don't kid yourself it's about to change the world.[51]

Here bonds, affiliations and identifications across what is a homosocial void of sexual (in)difference, for women and gay men, constitute acts of political growth and cultural dissent. Within the authority of homosocial domains female and homosexual identities are negated. Substantive gains won against these terms are produced within the faultline cracks in those very mechanisms. These identities may not only offer women the best advice 'on the right shade of lipstick'[52] or gay men an appropriation of cultural capital, but point out possibilities for resisting the security of hierarchical gender authority and offer profitable strategies for the acquisition of subjectivity.

Slash fantasies/heterosocial bonds

Yet it is crucial to recognize that dissident opportunities will necessarily cluster around points of tension within hegemonic formations. A fascinating example of this comes in the subcultural fan literature known as slash fiction, which appropriates dominant homosocial pairings from popular television texts and inscribes them within explicitly homosexual romantic narratives. The genre, which predominantly works within science fiction, gets its name from stories written in the 1970s about Kirk and Spock from *Star Trek*, which were designated K/S (Kirk–slash–Spock). With the advent of easy internet access in the mid- and late 1990s, and the growth in popularity of science fiction television, slash has become a substantial fan culture. Slash writers appropriate a wide range of pairings and texts, which include Chakotay/Paris (*Star Trek: Voyager*), Blake/Avon (*Blake's 7*), Picard/Q (*Star Trek: The Next Generation*), Bodie/Doyle (*The Professionals*), Vecchio/Fraser (*Due South*), and Mulder/Krycek (*The X Files*), as well as pairings from *Highlander*, *Hercules: The Legendary Journeys*, *The Sentinel* and *Stargate SG-1*. Henry Jenkins and Constance Penley have been foremost among those academics who have written about slash fiction.[53] Both approach the genre as one written by heterosexual women about ostensibly heterosexual male characters who are 'slashed' into homoerotic encounters or relationships which offer 'insights into female sexual fantasy'.[54] However, over the last couple of years there has been a growing body of slash work written by women, heterosexual and lesbian, which slashes ostensibly heterosexual female characters, such as Captain Janeway and B'Elanna Torres from *Star Trek: Voyager*, and Xena and Gabrielle from *Xena: Warrior Princess* into lesbian sexual relationships; while a growing number of gay male authors have joined their female counterparts in slashing male characters.[55] The question of who is appropriating whom when straight women write about apparently 'gay' relationships and sexuality in their own terms and when gay men write in 'women's' slash genres has been debated online.[56]

How is the heterosocial dynamic working in these slash narratives? As fan fiction, slash narratives already contest the transnational corporate ownership of texts and scenarios which acquire particular significance in the emotional imaginary of audiences. Jenkins refers to such contestation as 'textual poaching' in order to legitimate fan practices and repudiate conventional understandings of fans as immature, obsessive and culturally unsophisticated. In what ways does this already resistant space handle affiliations between women and gay men? How do slash authors situate their fantastical imaginings?

A particularly prolific slash author is Britta Matthews, who has written a series of stories which are serialized on her website; they include *The Taming of Tom Paris, In Dreams, Undaunted, Bored in the Delta Quadrant*, and *Susurrations*.[57] *The Taming of Tom Paris* won three Golden Orgasm awards in 1998: best *Voyager* story, best corporal punishment story and best overall story, on ASCEM (L), a major web newsgroup devoted to 'Treksmut'.[58] *Taming* follows a familiar slash narrative. Its logic is derived from the *Star Trek* series produced and owned by Paramount, and is situated aboard the starship Voyager, stranded in the delta quadrant seventy years from home after an encounter with an omnipotent being. It depicts the burgeoning sexual relationship between the ship's first officer, Commander Chakotay, a mature, big built Native American and the ship's helmsman, Tom Paris, a cute, boyish, blond WASP. *Taming* is told in the first person voice of Chakotay, through whom Matthews makes the nature of the attraction between the men clear:

> I wanted him to submit to me, totally, unconditionally. But he had to do it willingly. His surrender to my will had to be complete but he had to make the decision. When the day came that he offered himself to me, I would accept with the greatest joy. His submission would be the most precious gift I would ever receive and I would cherish him forever for giving it to me.[59]

Two points seem immediately clear. First that the interchange between the two men is gendered, with the butch Chakotay positioned as a dominant, active protector of the more feminine, passive Paris. Second it is striking that the author's own identification is with the dominant male in his sexual subjugation of the other. In Paramount's text *Star Trek: Voyager*, Tom Paris is portrayed as being a charming, confident womanizer, whose roguish past and winning smile produce a striking level of heterosexual charisma, which is utilized in a number of different episodes of the series. One of the many pleasures of *The Taming of Tom Paris* is its depictions of this stud-like character on his back being fucked by his butch, well-hung superior officer, or being bent over Chakotay's knee begging to be punished. We could perhaps suggest that here the slash scenario enables Britta Matthews to locate her own sadistic orientation to cocky, stud-like men, in a way that might otherwise be difficult to do within conventional heterosexuality. Particularly so given that the unfolding narrative of the two men's relationship is rendered in distinctly romantic terms, with a high emphasis given to the open negotiation of feelings, rather than to the more pornographic elements. Slash enables Matthews to circumvent the rather conventional terms of heterosexual romance, and formulate a cross-gendered identi-fication that facilitates a sexual and social authority in her alignment with Chakotay that would be much more contorted were she to identify with a woman, such as B'Elanna Torres in a sadistic relationship with Paris. Clearly heterosexuality can accommodate female sadism in rela-tion to male masochism, but inevitably such scenarios are always an inversion of more predictable arrangements, and thereby they retain the necessity for some narrative negotiation of the anticipated hetero-sexual gender roles in order to facilitate a convincing inversion.

Chakotay and Paris may be gendered, but we anticipate that both men occupy full subjectivity; queering the men enables the depiction of gender difference while maintaining the ability to locate both subjects convincingly in such a way that power play between them doesn't imply the negation of the identity of either. This identification with a sadistic male 'top' is offset by locating this fantasy through Chakotay, who despite his size, maturity, ranking and phallic prowess is ethnically represented as Native American 'other'. In as much as *Star Trek*'s liberal universe is populated with aliens who represent ethnic and racial differ-ence, slash fiction retains an investment in ethno-centric racial fetish-ism. Traditionally Kirk/Spock slash maps ethnic difference onto gender, depicting Spock in terms which connote exoticism through quasi-mystical, religious trappings that alternately feminize him in the logic of white racist fantasies of orientalism and masculinize him as a func-tion his logic and intellectualism: Spock in his dispassion represents the mind, Kirk in his vanity represents the body. In *Voyager* slash, the other most popular top is Harry Kim, who is Asian, and whose gender ethnic-ally signifies in similar ways to Chakotay's. Chakotay's ethnicity is heavily fetishised in Paramount's *Voyager*: he is frequently to be found communing with his spirit guide, or meditating on his ancestral hered-itary, while his facial tattoo stands as a constant signifier of ethnic difference; representationally these acts are made to signify his general sensitivity and emotional depth and thus feminize him in a way that contrasts with his butch authority and physical size. Furthermore, Chakotay's membership of the rebel Maquis group who are fighting Federation and Cardassian colonialism, instates his political and moral righteousness. These elements work to offset Chakotay's sadism and dominance in *The Taming of Tom Paris*, making him a safer, more acceptably liberal place through which to locate sexual and social power.

We could perhaps suggest then, that slash expresses a heterosocial dynamic in terms of providing women with the opportunity to appropriate homoeroticism as the means to enact an empowering identification with a subject position through which they may exhibit power (such as Chakotay), while being able to avoid such an identification slipping into a ventriloquism of patriarchal dominance. The fact that Britta Matthews's object of identification is expressing homosexual desires positions him ambiguously within homosocial power systems, and yet he remains a man, with access to the privileges of his gender, and his position as second in command on the ship, yet still manifesting both cultural integrity (as an 'oppressed minority' ethnically connoting passivity and femininity, and with a heritage richly commodified within *Star Trek* culture) and emotional dexterity.

Here homosexuality is functioning as a means of enacting gender dissent for female slash authors, who are resisting their alignment as feminised objects of heterosexuality and enacting queer sistership through an identification with male homosexuality. There are problems with such identifications, however.

It is telling that *Taming*, as with the majority of such fiction, locates its idealised vision of a more egalitarian sexuality in men, and thus simultaneously retains female heterosexual identification towards men (and it is a common motif in slash that the homosexual encounter occurs for the first and only time, arising out of extraordinary circumstances in a narrative in which both participants continue to manifest heterosexuality) and expresses a homosocial counter-identification with the notion of lesbianism. Slash often preserves the potential for female heterosexual specular pleasure in male physicality, while inherently rejecting the possibility of lesbian alternatives, which could potentially exhibit the same range of metaphors of more egalitarian sexual relations that are exploited in the male homoeroticism most narratives toy with.

Slash erotisim of gay sex acts tends to follow rather formulaic patterns which detail the mechanical aspects of, for example, anal sex, whereby narrative time is spent explaining how the top will use his fingers to relax his partner's anal musculature, and introduce lubrication. Such fastidious attention to detail (and it is striking how relentlessly and repetitively slash authors dwell on such matters) works to denaturalize gay sex acts in a way that doesn't occur in gay pornography written by gay men. Similarly, if slash enables a degree of narrative punishment of 'straight' men, like Tom Paris, as the fucking tables are turned on them, then this makes an unfortunate correlation between 'passive' gay sexuality and humiliation, that is out of step with our expectations of heterosocial affiliation. In practice such correlations remain largely subtextual: in *The Taming of Tom Paris*, Britta Matthews is careful to introduce a degree of versatility into the sexual and emotional role playing that takes place between Tom and Chakotay. Indeed, if the relationship merely ends up replicating the more demeaning connotations of gender difference, slash would lose its dissident potential for authors like Matthews, when its very appeal seems to lie in constituting sexual partners both of whom have access to full subjectivity within gender systems.

Nevertheless, both slash fiction and the 'theoretical fag-hags' of *Attitude* demonstrate that gender dissent and heterosocial bonds, like any other radical manoeuvre, hold no guarantee of political breakthrough. Our opportunities for cultural change or leverage arise out of knowledge, language, relationships and artefacts appended to potentially oppressive hegemonic regimes of power.

3
Roseanne: Domestic Goddess as Heterosocial Heroine?

Given the extent to which gay men and straight women do bond and affiliate through a diverse range of cultural discourses despite the resistance any such relation must encounter, because of the extent to which both gay male identities and heterosexual women's identities are circumscribed through homosocial mechanisms, it would seem that these relationships may illuminate both the faultlines within the homosocial matrix and important structural negotiations of homosocial entrapment. I refer to these negotiations as heterosocial relationships. We have already seen some of the blockages such relationships need to negotiate in the writing of the 'theoretical fag-hags' in *Attitude*.

There have been some other striking representations of heterosocial affiliation recently. The Hollywood films *My Best Friend's Wedding* and *The Object of My Affection* have respectively been significant star vehicles for Julia Roberts and Jennifer Aniston (the latter still struggling to establish herself as a big screen star beyond her enormous popularity in the US sitcom *Friends*). Each film represents heterosexual romance as inherently problematic for its central, female, character. For both women intense, but confused relationships with gay men are seen as the space through which the intolerable paradoxes of heterosexuality can be resolved. When marriage eludes (and fails) Julia Roberts' character in *My Best Friend's Wedding* all she has left is her dashing gay male side kick, played with career-redefining bravura by Rupert Everett. *The Object of My Affection* represents Aniston's character falling in love with a gay male stranger who gives her unsolicited support in the face of straight male beastliness. Both films almost seem to take it as axiomatic that heterosexual men are to a greater or lesser degree unworkable for women, and that they will inevitably have greater emotional, intellectual and sexual synergy with gay men. Both films, however, are relatively incoherent in their attempts to make sense of the repercussions for wider social and sexual relations that such a synergy may precipitate. *The Opposite of Sex* is less reverential about relations between fags and hags, relishing the wickedness of the Christina Ricci character, and asks trickier questions before capitulating into a cosy resolution. Similar heterosocially intriguing representations have been offered in the US sitcom *Will and Grace* and the UK sitcom *Gimme Gimme Gimme*, both of which depict domestic 'romances' of fag and hag co-habitation. *Roseanne* predates all of these heterosocially promising texts. However, I have chosen to focus on it here, because as I shall go on to show, it offers representations not only from the point of view of a heterosexual woman, but understood to be a product of that woman's perspective. More interesting still, unlike *My Best Friend's Wedding* or *The Object of My Affection*, *Roseanne* situates heterosocial bonds in wider contexts of heterosexual marriage, domestic nuclearity and patriarchal networks, and over a relatively long narrative period.

Straight women and gay men are positioned in radically different, if symmetrical, spaces within matrices of power. Women are generally disempowered in relation to gender identities organised through capitalist patriarchies, being subject to men's superior power in relation to the family, economic systems and institutions of the state. Gay men are generally understood to be disempowered in relation to sexual identities organised through patriarchal heterosexuality, and are therefore acknowledged to be economically and institutionally powerful as men and socially and institutionally oppressed as perverts. Theories of homosociality have provided us with an alternative framework for conceptualizing gay men's oppression and the proximity of such experiences to those of women within systems of gender power. As I have suggested, conceptualizing gay men as sexual outlaws and transgressive perverts may re-empower us erotically, but underestimates both the extent to which our identities express negotiations of gender, and how far our oppression is the result not just of sexual marginalization, but of organizational *functionality* within homosocial patriarchy. In other words, the homosocial narrative portrays gay men as perverse in such unpleasant and unspeakable ways that our very connotation forecloses the possibility of male–male bonds becoming so infatuated as to displace the erotic subjection and control of women. To put it another way, gay men's *sexual* perversion is functionally reproduced within *gender* systems. Furthermore, the adherence to political and cultural agendas which see gay men as only erotic or perverse subjects makes it hard to fashion relationships across the structures in which our identities operate.

Subcultural affiliation and strength may be the precondition of any enlightened or grounded cultural or political activity by gay men, but queerness figures variously and in many places within structures of power: to remain located and active in gay subculture *alone* not only forecloses the complexity of our identities and experiences, but leaves us potentially complicit with regimes of power other than the heterosexual. Metropolitan gay subculture may express our erotic marginalization and resultant political and cultural empowerment, but many of us in that enclave are middle-class, or white, or able-bodied, or men, or antibody negative, many of us don't have children, many of us are well paid and institutionally or corporately powerful. Certainly the conceptualization of gay subculture as the shared experience of sexual perversity privileges gay *male* experience, and at the very least compromises strategic visions of lesbian and gay male affiliation.[1] So, the complexity of our identities as gay men – internally, and in terms of how gayness is manifested across a terrain of other contexts, necessitates our constant mediation between micro and macro subcultural engagement.

Heterosexual women may make 'positive' or refreshing representations of gay men, as gay men may make similarly helpful representations of women. But what kind of manoeuvres are involved in staking a powerful and empowering claim to your own representation, from a position of oppression, and offering helpful representations of other identities implicated in the systems of that oppression? This is the question we pose by attempting to assess the opportunity for heterosocial bonding in work authored by women, or by gay men. How can gay men make a claim for self-authority *without* instating themselves within homosocial regimes which subject women? How can straight women manifest privilege without invoking their heterosexuality in such a way as to re-demonize and disempower queers? This chapter considers dissident affiliations made from a position of heterosexual womanhood; the next one assesses similar affiliations made by a gay man.

An illuminating illustration of this problematic dynamic appears in the form of the American sitcom *Roseanne*, which was first aired on ABC in 1988. The series enjoyed enormous popularity in America: the season which ended in the later part of 1995 generated the fourth highest advertising rates on the ABC network, after the Super Bowl, the Academy Awards and *Home Improvement*.[2] The popularity of the show, along with Roseanne's own transgressive behaviour, has made her a darling of the tabloid and sensationalist press, such as *The National Enquirer*. However, latterly Roseanne and *Roseanne* became popular and celebrated with self-consciously credible and intellectually precocious audiences.

In Britain *Roseanne* was scheduled on Channel 4 in the context of late night 'quality' situation comedies and up-market alternative cabaret. In the press, Roseanne was celebrated as a serious and troubled artist: the watershed moment being a substantial and gritty piece by John Lahr in *The New Yorker*, but earlier profiles in *Vanity Fair* and then in *Spin* gave Roseanne middle-class intellectual credibility.[3] This graduation from being interesting because of the vicissitudes of her personal life, to being considered a serious artist can be attributed to a perception of *Roseanne* as a political vehicle for social commentary:

> ...in these puritanical, politically correct times, nothing is more welcome than a voice that pierces dull notions of what should be with barbs of what is. *Roseanne* has made history by tackling everything from marital ennui, to 'maternal ambivalence,' to poverty, menstruation, homophobia, and mental illness in a medium that once reflected only the most sanitized versions of American family life.[4]

If there is one issue for which Roseanne has been vilified by her critics and adored by her fans it is the representation of homosexuality in her series. In February 1996, in a special issue on the up-coming Presidential primaries, America's *Out* magazine put Roseanne on the cover with the caption: 'Primary Special: Dole, Clinton & the rest: Their positions on our issues. Our choice? ROSEANNE FOR PREZ! For Gay Marriage, Lesbian Kisses & Real-World Feminism'.[5] The same magazine named her an honorary gay person the year before,[6] while she was named Person of the Year in January 1995 by *The Advocate*, for whom Peter Galvin writes:

> Gays and lesbians have been waiting a long time for someone like Roseanne to come along. Blasting stereotypes, flouting convention, transcending ignorance, the star's landmark sitcom, *Roseanne*, is that rare network television program that dares to treat homosexuality as nonchalantly and inconsequentially as heterosexuality....She is a rare person who, perhaps because of her own differences with the mainstream, identifies with the struggles of gays and lesbians *completely*.[7]

This sentiment is shared by Tim Allis of *Out*, when he says:

> [*Roseanne's*] gay characters were eye-opening – not because they were played as heroes, but because they were just as cranky and dysfunctional as everybody else in the manners-free Conner household.[8]

It is clear that Roseanne is perceived by these voices of American gay subculture as enacting a bonding with them through the representation she makes of gay characters in *Roseanne*. Roseanne herself confirms the affiliation: in *Out* magazine, Sue Carswell notes that Roseanne has promised that before *Roseanne* is finished for good, one of the series' co-stars, 'a character we never would have presumed to be queer, will be revealed as gay or lesbian'; Roseanne is quoted as saying, 'It's a real shocker, and I'm doing it for all you kids out there.'[9] It is clear that *Roseanne* is understood to make a feminist appropriation of the domestic sitcom; it is also clear that the show is understood within the queer subculture to be making helpful lesbian and gay representations. What I want to do here is to assess the extent to which *Roseanne* successfully enables the opportunity for heterosocial bonding and determine the terms in which such a relationship negotiates larger structures of homosociality.

Roseanne and political credibility

It is not difficult to see why gay men might love Roseanne; aside from the explicit visibility and humour *Roseanne* has offered in its representation of homosexuality, there are many features of the star's public persona that resonate with gay male subcultural practices around female star icons. The very cradle of Roseanne's popularity, her eponymous sitcom, turns many conventional understandings about representing family life on its head. Even though the Conner family appears structurally normative and nuclear: mum, dad, three children living together, sister and mother living in extended familial proximity, they are firmly placed in the working-class: specifically the Conners are what the series flags self-referentially as 'white trash'.[10] Becky, the eldest child, is married and for the penultimate season lived at home with her husband; Darlene is at college by the time of the strong queer presence in the programme, but her boyfriend David lives with Roseanne and Dan, rather than with his abusive mother, who Roseanne Conner accused of 'giving respectable white trash a bad name'. This family is also meaningful in dramatic terms as conflicted and dysfunctional, not especially or pathologically, but routinely and necessarily. This dysfunction is normalized in two ways: it is either located in the structures in which family life exists, or is attributable to the rebellious disposition of particular characters. Most often, both strategies co-exist; for example, the character of Jackie, Roseanne Conner's sister, is portrayed as somewhat hysterical and as promiscuous and unable to commit herself to long term relationships. These character attributes are rendered endearingly as transgressive but confused and eccentric, and as the behaviours of a woman damaged by an abusive father and by badly behaved boy-friends: crucially each is presented as the attempt to heal, to improve herself and make herself more self-sufficient and less dependent on the affirmation of abusive men. The progression of these narratives necessarily involves the representation of conflict and it is in this that *Roseanne* really achieves its distinctiveness. Its comedy arises out of the deadpan ironic engagement of the characters with a series of conflicts not rooted in trivial domestic misunderstandings and sight-gags, but in economic pressures, gender disputes, power struggles and other natural-istic oppressive conditions. As John Lahr puts it:

> Roseanne's neurotic TV family was the first one to put America in contact with something resembling real life in the working-class world – a place where children are difficult, parents have real emo-tional and financial problems, and there's a discrepancy between what American society promises and what it delivers.[11]

The question of Roseanne's authorship of *Roseanne* is complex, but it is an important one if we are to make a claim for the programme's hetero-social value on the basis of Roseanne Barr/Pentland/Arnold/Thomas's manipulation of her feminism, her heterosexuality and her commitment to queer affiliation.

In her autobiography, *My Lives*, Roseanne details her move from stand-up comic to being cast in her own show through a multitude of struggles with ABC, the television network which commissioned it, and Carsey-Werner the production company which owned Matt Williams' original concept and which produced the original series.[12] By the time of the 1995 season *Roseanne* was produced by Roseanne's own com-pany, Full Moon & High Tide, with a contract for four more seasons with the network, and she has been executive producer of the show for the last four years, two of them jointly with her ex-husband, Tom Arnold. Lahr's substantial and considered portrait of the star pays con-siderable attention to the power struggles Roseanne has won to wrest control of *Roseanne* from Carsey-Werner, Matt Williams and the writing teams originally in place. Firing people is one of the principle constitu-ents of Roseanne mythology, and like the speculations that Roseanne doesn't write the series (and her furious refusal of these claims), such material is principally valuable in the extent to which audiences find that mythology meaningful. Lahr's comment, after much prevarication, is:

In any case, the argument about creative ownership of the show is academic: Roseanne owns the mill and the charisma. And she treats the writers as extensions of herself.[13]

Whatever the complex and mediated reality of Roseanne's authorship, and of her circumscription in the context of American network television, she seems to be able to muster enough performative authority to make her claims for ownership convincing. A celebratory interview in *Entertainment Weekly* opens: 'You've got to understand the ground rules: *Roseanne* is Roseanne's show, and Roseanne rules' the piece continues, 'By the way, do you understand that Roseanne calls the shots? Just in case you don't, she says something like this: "There's no room for anybody but me anywhere in the f---in' world."'[14]

Whatever the intricacies and constantly shifting conditions of the corporate environment, this bombastic, no-nonsense, and brazenly powerful Roseanne is the one which sells magazines and propels *Roseanne* to such high ratings success. Given the popularity of *Roseanne*, and the attendantly high advertising revenue it generates, Roseanne herself occupies a relatively powerful position within the complex of media corporations in which she works. From this position of complicity, of being embedded in powerful structures, Roseanne is perceived as being resistant and challenging. Peter Galvin suggests that:

> although her vision of a 'politic of humanity' as she calls it, has sometimes been clouded by the ever-present – and occasionally self-created – media sensationalism surrounding her personal life, her commitment to exposing hypocrisy and fostering tolerance has never wavered.[15]

Roseanne herself makes characteristically modest claims for her politics:

> *Entertainment Weekly*: *Roseanne* has made greater strides for including homosexuality as a part of life that any other show on television.
> *Roseanne*: We're the only ones, too.
> *EW*: Well, now we see it on other sitcoms.
> *Roseanne*: But they all do it badly. And I know, because I'm a homosexual! I just like the message of humanity for everybody. I know everything on *Roseanne*'s revolutionary. And I know that people aren't gonna get half of it for 50 years.
> *EW*: Can you get in trouble for anything anymore?

Roseanne: Oh, they let me do everythin' now and it's no fun. I'm pretty bored. I've covered all the bases.[16]

Clearly one of the 'bases' covered by *Roseanne* is homosexuality: that is one of the major 'issues' that the series is associated with.

One of the things that makes *Roseanne*'s treatment of political issues distinctive is that at its best the show does not seem to shy away from implicating its principal, and highly identifiable, characters in unflattering or ideologically damning ways. Perhaps the most powerful example of this is an episode from the 1994 season which Roseanne herself has called 'the best show we've ever done'.[17] The storyline concerns Roseanne and Dan Conner's son DJ not wanting to kiss Geena, a girl in the school play, because she is black. From here the plot progresses to Roseanne Conner accusing her husband of fostering racism in her children, to Dan seeking exoneration from his black friend, Chuck, who then challenges Dan's assumptions, to Roseanne being confronted by DJ's teacher as a racist parent, to finally being confronted by the girl's father, Mr Williams. This final scene of the narrative is characteristic and representative of the treatment given to the whole episode. In it Roseanne Conner and her sister Jackie are cashing up a busy late night shift at the diner they jointly own. A black man appears at the door asking to be admitted. Roseanne refuses, turning the sign on the door to indicate that they are closed. After the man slams his hands against the door and storms off, Roseanne and Jackie agree that the incident was 'scary', and when he appears at the door again, Jackie reacts by shoving the cash draw back into the till and the women panic until the man identifies himself as Geena Williams' father. Roseanne lets him in, asking him why he didn't just tell her who he was. Mr Williams replies by asking her if she needs to know who all her customers are before she lets them into her restaurant. Roseanne defends herself by suggesting that for two women working late at night, safety is a priority. Jackie intercedes, attempting to placate the situation, but she inflames it further with anxious liberalism, by suggesting that Roseanne didn't refuse him entry because he is 'African-American', but because he is a man. Roseanne follows through with one of the show's standard comic lines about how she hates *all* men equally: the line receives the only laugh of the scene from the studio audience, and from the soundtrack it is clear that it is an anxious, relieved sound, rather than the fulsome and ecstatic response usually audibly forthcoming in response to one of Roseanne's trademark deadpan statements. Roseanne Conner then makes the conflict explicit: she says that late at night, with their safety at stake, women alone must act on their instincts to protect themselves. Williams replies that he guesses that her son inherited Roseanne's instincts, before angrily leaving the restaurant. There is a moment of awkward stillness in the women, before Jackie attempts to comfort Roseanne: she suggests that Williams overreacted, and that most people would have behaved exactly as Roseanne had. As Jackie walks off, the tension behind her, Roseanne contemplates her sister's words and says, 'Well isn't that great?', her delivery uncomfortable and her tone ironic. The credits then roll over an unrelated and unreservedly comic scene in which neither Roseanne nor Dan are present.

What stands out about the scene with Mr Williams is not only its specificity and the explicit nature of its conflict, but the direction and delivery, which for a comedy show is unflinchingly dramatic and disquieting, stretching its generic conventions seemingly beyond breaking until comedy is restored and there is a delivery from the tension in the over-credit sequence, which is particularly funny, but also innocuous. Mick Bowes offers an indication of the distinctiveness of this lack of resolution:

> the most characteristic feature of the 'classic' situation comedy is narrative closure. In other words, each story is resolved within the 30 minutes of the programme. In addition this closure is generally circular – it returns the characters to the positions they occupied at the start, thus allowing the next week's programme to start afresh. This circular narrative closure allows little room for progression . . . [18]

Leaving the principal and eponymous character of *Roseanne* compromised and morally unsure about her behaviour at the end of the narrative is a fairly powerful statement. The fact that this disquiet arises out of a recognition that Roseanne's behaviour is typical, that she clearly thinks she reacted in a racist manner and that most people – that is, most of us – would have reacted in the same way, leaves the challenge, the culpability, not only with Roseanne Conner herself, but with a white audience generally.

The impression given by the episode is that racism is a subtle and pervasive part of attitudinal responses, even concerned and anxious ones, and that this is a serious issue worthy of sober reflection. At the end of the narrative, completion is withheld and our principal sources of identification remain uncomfortable and implicated, their unwitting and self-identified racism refusing a cosy restabilising of domestic and ideological harmony, and furthermore, left to pervade and inform future narratives and our perception of our favourite characters. The narrative processing of the 'issue' of racism, and the presence in the ensemble of the black characters of Chuck, Geena and Mr Williams, do not function to illustrate the further coolness and daring of the Conner household: they are not reassuringly integrated into the deadpan dissent that we gleefully anticipate from Roseanne and her family. In this narrative race functions precisely to fracture the angrily comic, and often cosily including, experience of oppression we share with the Conners by identifying them as white, culpable and sufficiently institutionally interior to actually be in a position to oppress others who might be more excluded than they are.

Roseanne and homosociality: the queer challenge

It is not difficult to see why such an ironic, conflictual and woman-centred representation of family life as *Roseanne* usually offers might be popular with a constituency whose identities are constantly being reproduced in homophobic culture as antithetical to the concerns of the family, even though we are all products and members of families in complex symbolic and emotional relationships. Roseanne herself has very publicly spoken out about her own abuse by her parents and how this produced self-loathing behaviour in relation to her body image; again there are resonances here for identities historically associated with images of sickness and physical deformity.[19] Principally, however, it seems that it is the mythology around her control and power as a woman that has the most allure for Roseanne's queer constituency, and an indication of the extent of the belief in this mythology is the unquestioning way in which lesbian and gay journalists unmediatedly attribute the apparent gay-friendliness of *Roseanne* to its star. *Out* magazine has called this authority from a woman like Roseanne 'real world feminism'.[20] Roseanne herself has suggested that she dislikes the label 'feminist' and prefers the title 'killer bitch' and she has been called, quite fabulously, a 'Goddess of Retribution'.[21] This ambiguity in relation to questions of feminism is complex: on the one hand in interviews and public statements Roseanne enacts a scathing, class-based attack on academic feminism and on so-called feminist Hollywood actresses like Meryl Streep and Jodie Foster, on the other hand she employs male writers on *Roseanne* because women have apparently learned how to ventriloquise men too effectively and are less able to produce empowering dialogue for women than men are.[22] Yet whatever the vicissitudes of Roseanne's strategic performance of her feminism, her vocalised commitment to some kind of pro-women politics appears unequivocal: 'Everything I do is from a commitment to feminism.'[23] It would seem then that there are abundant conditions here for the proliferation of heterosocial bonding: a powerfully situated and politicized heterosexual woman directly courting queer constituencies both in her affirmative personal statements, and in the public work that she is understood to author, where she offers gay representation apparently unfettered by the 'unreal' demands of positive images and politically correct liberalisation. How effective a basis for heterosocial bonding are the queer representations *Roseanne* makes?

There are two long running queer characters resident in the repertory company of *Roseanne*, these are Nancy, Roseanne Conner's friend and co-owner of the diner, and Leon, her old boss and now another co-owner of the diner, with whom she has shared a long-running and often hilarious enmity. One key element in both characterisations that has been celebrated by the American lesbian and gay press is that they are 'just as cranky and dysfunctional as everybody else in the manners-free Conner household.'[24] The most famous and controversial 'queer' episode of *Roseanne* follows our eponymous heroine and her sister Jackie on a night out with Nancy and her girlfriend Sharon to a gay bar in the nearby town of Elgin. The principal tension that organises the narrative of the episode lies in the disparity between how 'cool' Roseanne Conner thinks she is and how cool she is perceived to be by Nancy and Leon.

The episode opens in the diner, and Roseanne and Jackie are moaning to Nancy that she hasn't yet introduced them to her new girlfriend, and they suggest that Nancy is uncomfortable with their heterosexuality; Roseanne Conner says:

> ...because you've never been able to accept our alternate lifestyle. It isn't a choice you know!

Before the discussion can continue, the door opens and Nancy's girlfriend Sharon comes in. She is played by the actress and model Mariel Hemmingway. Nancy has not always been a lesbian in *Roseanne* and was previously married to Arnie Thomas, a friend of Dan's, played by Tom Arnold, Roseanne's real life husband at the time, and co-executive producer of the programme. As Sharon sits down at the counter, Roseanne asks Nancy why it is that when she dates men they look like Arnie and when she dates women they look like Sharon. The studio audience pick up the joke and respond uproariously, acknowledging Mariel Hemmingway's beauty and the bitchy reference to Roseanne's actual husband.

The effect is complex: at an ideological level the joke seems to reference the stereotypical notion that lesbians are mannish women and therefore 'unattractive' in heterosexual terms, and subverts this idea with a mutual recognition of Mariel Hemmingway's credentials as a typically heterosexualized blond beauty and the fact that she's playing a lesbian role. At an intra-textual level Roseanne's dry witticism inserts the figure of her own husband, and Nancy's fictional ex-husband, into the representational frame in a direct comparison with Nancy's current lesbian lover. Arnie/Tom loses the contest on looks, but then we would expect him to: men are not supposed to justify their occupation of cultural space on the basis of their appearance – Arnie was not judged in his worthiness as Nancy's husband on the basis of his beauty. The humour is sharp and incisive, but its effect is to render the spectacle of Sharon, and the lesbianism she represents, as little more than an object for visual consumption.

Clearly this has multiple effects, depending on the audience constituency we are considering. *Roseanne*'s deft acknowledgement that lesbians are not supposed to be attractive in conventional feminine terms, and then its transgression of this expectation with the fetishised display of Sharon shows how lesbians can be just as beautifully feminine as straight women, women like Mariel Hemmingway.[25] Queer constituencies familiar with lesbian diversity and with the alluring glamour of lipstick lesbian femmes might well appreciate such a stalling of homophobic stereotyping. Yet the display of a familiar, heterosexual icon of feminine beauty, along with the narrative label of 'lesbian' has the effect of neutralizing the cultural impact of lesbianism on ideologies of gender, collapsing the difference between straight and queer women, even in the most banal physical and visual ways, and confirming that both can be equally understood as displaying the markers of heterosexual femininity for men. Nancy was introduced as a lesbian on *Roseanne* in a similar fashion when she brought her first girlfriend, Marla, to the diner and literally presented her to Roseanne and Jackie, and of course, to the audience. Marla was played by Morgan Fairchild, another iconic manifestation of blond, big-haired, glamorous heterosexual beauty. Part of the effect is to render Nancy's lesbianism as meaningful and rational for a straight audience: of course she would rather choose to sleep with women when they are as attractive as Mariel Hemmingway – wouldn't you? Lesbianism thus becomes an issue of desire, and the difference between heterosexuality and homosexuality a matter of a simple choice between desiring women or desiring men. Within this framework, manifestations of homophobia are a function of the toleration of erotic difference, rather than an integral part of the constitution of hetero-sexuality and men's authority within it.

After Roseanne's acknowledgement of Sharon's looks, the two women bond and Sharon invites Roseanne and her sister to come dancing with her and Nancy. Nancy appears uncomfortable with this idea, as does Jackie when she realizes that they will be going to a gay bar. At this point Leon comes into the restaurant from the kitchen, and acknowledges Sharon and Nancy by saying, 'Hiya fellas'. Again there is ambiguity here: *Roseanne* is clearly displaying an awareness of queer subcultural codes, and Leon's line is camply deadpanned in such a way as to suggest an immediate sisterly solidarity between him and Sharon and Nancy, that excludes Roseanne and Jackie, instating a recognition of their shared cultural difference. Referring to the women, whatever the status of their performance of femininity, ironically as 'fellas' recognizes their lesbianism from a fellow position of gender dissent. Yet at the same time, for an audience not conversant with queer subcultural vernacular, putting these words into the mouth of the gay male character scapegoats him as enunciating the mannish lesbian stereotype: an archetypal heterosexual construction in itself, and an insult only meaningful as such within a heterosexual context. In this reading, queerness homophobically victimizes itself, leaving the tolerant and comfortable straight folks unassailably 'cool'. To decisively conclude which meaning the text prefers is difficult and I think that it would be a little mean-spirited to suggest that it is the latter reading, in which the gay male character is the bearer of the homophobia, that *Roseanne* ultimately favours; its intentions are ideologically honourable. Nevertheless the script does embody the ambiguity, unwittingly privileging heterosexuality. The scene ends with Leon approaching Roseanne and telling her that the evening in prospect should prove to be quite entertaining. When she asks why, he replies that 'a gay bar is like a size twelve dress: you just won't fit in.' The treatment of homosexuality here suggests a sincere attempt not only to represent, but speak to, a queer subcultural constituency: it is unclear, however, what kind of homosexuality is being spoken of in the name of *Roseanne*'s daring and political sophistication, let alone how queer constituencies are to interpret such ambiguity in the context of the mainstream, mass appeal of a top rated network sitcom.

The next scene opens at home with David, Darlene's boyfriend and the Conner's unofficially adopted son, and his brother Mark, who is Becky's husband, sat together on the sofa, sparring as to which is the more successfully masculine. There is a complex history of interactions that informs this sibling rivalry. The character of Darlene Conner, played by Sara Gilbert, is a tomboy, and has been widely subculturally interpreted as a lesbian: she has never been interested in boys that much, she went through a long period of depression during which her tastes and demeanour became quite gothic. For years she was only seen to wear black, she has always been politically outspoken and independent, she is a militant vegetarian and once staged an action outside the family's loose meat restaurant, she is interested in science fiction and writes comic books with her boyfriend. One of the main ways in which Darlene's relationship with David has been comically meaningful throughout its history on *Roseanne* has been in how it transgresses our traditional expectations of the representation of power relations in heterosexual teenage romance. As an expression of *Roseanne*'s pro-feminism, Darlene has always been shown to be the more powerful and less dependent one in the relationship, while David has been shown to be passive, emotional and artistic. On the other hand, Darlene's sister Becky has always been shown to be much more traditionally feminine and girlie, always being interested in boys, mortally depressed if she didn't have a boyfriend, and eventually so committed to her relationship with Mark that she dropped out of school and a successful academic career to elope with him at the age of 17. Mark has been similarly shown to be suspicious of any emotional expression, and as Roseanne once remarked of him, he has a 'dangerous, sexual thing going on'. For Dan and Roseanne, Mark has always been a threat to their daughter's sexuality, while David has been so lacking in sexual threat that he can be moved into the house to live with Darlene when they are both still 16.

We could say that the relationship between Darlene and David is a feminist representation in that it shows that women need not remain embedded in subordinated positions in relation to men in heterosexual relationships. To some extent, in Darlene and David, *Roseanne* is taking the patriarchal stereotype of the shrewish wife and hen-pecked husband so beloved of much television situation comedy and turning it inside-out by showing that women need not be stridently and unsympathetically represented as scapegoats to be empowered, and men in relationships with empowered women need not be continuously and impotently chafing against the shackles of shrewishness. In relation to Darlene and Mrs Conner, David is a sympathetically drawn and viable characterization: adorably malleable, expressive and funny, unthreatening and sensitive about women's issues without being condescending. It is in relation to the male characters in *Roseanne* that David's characterization becomes more problematic. In an earlier episode Mark has referred to

David as an 'art femme'. In the present scene with David and Mark sat on the couch, Mark grunts derisively and accuses his brother of being 'pathetic' because Darlene bosses him around and he does her laundry: rather than exchanging his girlfriend homosocially for masculine credibility, David is, quite literally, serving her. David makes a lame denial of the accusation of castration, but within the framework Mark embodies, a framework authorised and validated by the dominance of homosocial structures and the absent but towering masculinity of their symbolic father, Dan Conner, he cannot answer the insult because it is true: David is an inadequate male in homosocial terms. The interaction reproduces the homosocial matrix so completely and authentically that the character of David has little option but to attempt to regain ground within it: the narrative cohesion of *Roseanne* demands that David's heterosexuality remain textually plausible.

Mark's wife Becky has taken a job at a local restaurant, and her uniform consists of an extremely brief cropped top and a miniscule pair of hot pants, with the restaurant's name, Bunz, stitched across the buttocks. Becky comes home from work, in her uniform, just after Mark has conjured the inadequacy of David's homosocial credentials. After she has greeted her husband and gone upstairs to change, David apes Mark's derisive grunt and says that he wouldn't let his wife go out dressed in the Bunz uniform, because 'it gives other guys ideas'. Mark sneers in reply and with a knowing leer tells David that he can keep Becky satisfied. The remark at once conjures Mark's sexual potency and challenges David's: a man who cannot 'satisfy' his woman cannot guarantee that she is his to display and exchange. David shifts uncomfortably and defensively replies that he can keep Darlene satisfied. At that moment Darlene passes through the room angrily shouting at David for not having used fabric softener in her washing. Here *Roseanne* is itself exchanging Darlene and her washing in a confirmation of the homosocial network, using her dissatisfaction with David (and he can't even do her laundry, let alone keep her happy sexually) in the same way as it uses Becky's lasciviously displayed rump: to validate the masculinity of Mark and feminize David.

Because of his modestly political refusal to exchange women, or actively display his masculine credentials, David signifies queerly in relation to both Mark and Dan – it could be argued that David functions as the third queer regular on *Roseanne* in spite, or indeed, because, of his relationship with Darlene and his relative inability to function homosocially within it. Other episodes of *Roseanne* have addressed Dan's discomfort at David's overt displays of emotion: in one memorable example when Darlene had broken up with him, David bursts into tears at regular intervals, while Dan blunders around, bereft of any homosocial script with which to conduct his interaction with his adopted son. The effect is to illuminate how far outside Mr Conner's ambit of masculinity David is. Another *Roseanne* dealt with the problem of DJ getting bullied at school and his inability to fight off his attackers; Dan is unable to teach the 13-year-old to fight, who, to his father's exasperation chooses to cry or curl up on the floor in a ball when confronted. DJ eventually overcomes this 'problem' by beating up David, an elder but more ineffectual foe, much to the amusement of Mark and the embarrassment of Dan, to say nothing of David's humiliation. What seems crucial about this episode is that all the male characters, even the 13-year-old DJ find common ground which isolates and 'queers' David: even a child can function within homosocial bonds more successfully than David.

We might suggest that if *Roseanne* was more fully committed to being pro-queer David's lack of masculine credentials would not end up isolating and punishing him within the narrative framework, but Roseanne Conner's heterosexuality enforces a relationship between David and her husband. Ultimately the need to situate David heterosexually (that is, within the homosocial matrix that Dan emanates) compromises *Roseanne*'s heterosocial potential, by making him the repository of homosocial anxiety the show so carefully shields and transfers away from its self-consciously out and labelled queer characters. We may conclude that here *Roseanne* is effectively collusive with a metropolitan liberal circulation of homosexuality; this issue will be discussed in greater detail in the next chapter, in relation to Pedro Almodóvar. Homosexuality circulates through the text in such a way as to reassure the participants and the audience how cool and trendy they are: homosexuality is continually conjured in enlightened and frank ways, but continually reframed within structures of heterosexuality and homosociality that representationally reproduce the conditions of our oppression and powerlessness.

This scene of David's homosocial humiliation within the infamous 'lesbian kiss' episode of *Roseanne* reaches its climax when Dean Bates arrives at the door. David lets him in, announcing to both the audience and his brother Mark, that Dean, who is a jock-type football player, once dated Becky. In an aside between the brothers, David tells Mark that Dean is much better looking: his purpose is to threaten Mark by conjuring Dean's apparently superior homosocial credentials, but the strategy backfires, and Mark replies, 'Why don't you go and give him a big kiss?'. Here David becomes the corporeal embodiment of the double bind inherent within the homosocial system: 'For a man to be a man's man is separated only by an invisible, carefully blurred, always-already-crossed line from being "interested in men".'[26]

David's already disempowered position enables Mark to exert definitional leverage upon his brother's remarks, drawing on a commonly understood rhetoric of homosexual panic to effortlessly repel David's homosocial challenge and rewrite it as an erotic interest. The scenario may be humorous, but the effects are unfortunate in the light of *Roseanne*'s apparent queer friendliness. Even if we were to reject the notion of David's nominal queerness, the effect of his homosocial exclusion is to constitute a powerfully interior and cohesive masculinity within the textual confines of *Roseanne*, a masculinity signifying sufficiently aggressively – and hegemonically – as to be able to exert definitional control upon gender behaviour. David's failure and Mark's success at deploying their masculinity are brought into visibility by the text through the connotation of a demonized and inexplicitly unpleasant homosexual outside that is meaningful only in the extent to which *Roseanne* upholds a homophobic consensus. David may remain nominally understood within the text as a heterosexual characterization, but his indeterminate performance of this in relation to other men is used to luridly constitute a homosocial system of homophobia which goes spectacularly unchallenged by the show's non-homosocially powerful female figures, such as Darlene or Roseanne Conner herself.

Indeed, as the scene with Mark, David and Dean Bates continues, we see that Darlene's autonomous feminism can actually function to collude in David's homophobic exclusion. It transpires that Dean has arrived at the house to give Darlene a lift back to school: this prompts an argument because Becky resents Darlene using her old boyfriends to get rides. Mark challenges Becky, asking her why she cares if she is now married to him, and Becky flounces out of the room. Dean is loading the car and David gloats to Darlene about Mark's jealousy. Darlene is at the door, about to leave and she agrees with David, but says: 'Yeah, Becky's not the one who's going to have to think of some way to pay Dean back for the ride. See ya, David.' Here Darlene's refusal to cosset David's masculinity seems to be less about her need for autonomy, than it is about her collusion with David's homosocial abjection: not only can he not trade on his relationship with Darlene to inflate his masculine credibility in public exchanges with men, but in private, Darlene refuses to indulge his insecurities and indeed exploits them under the gaze of the audience so that the scene may end with a laugh.

The next scene opens at Lips, the gay bar in Elgin, with the arrival of Roseanne and her entourage. Several comic exchanges illuminate

Roseanne's progressive intent, and its ease around a queer subcultural environment. Jackie is still uncomfortable about being in a gay space, she tells Roseanne that she is uneasy about people thinking that she's gay: Roseanne replies that she can think that they are gay right back at them. Jackie is pregnant and loudly proclaims, 'Anybody can see that I'm *conventional*.' A little later, Jackie spots the woman who delivers her mail standing at the bar. The woman comes over and Roseanne embraces her sister as if they were lovers, she says: 'Now, now, you don't have to hide our love.' The woman is pleased to see Jackie and tells her that she had a feeling about her being a lesbian. As the woman walks off, Jackie is thrown into confused panic and she asks, 'Why, what did I do?' Later at the bar Roseanne flirts with the woman serving drinks: she introduces herself, and tells the woman that she is the father of Jackie's baby. Jackie angrily shrugs off Roseanne's show of affection, calling her 'psychotic' and reacting incredulously to her sister's flirtation with the woman behind the bar. Roseanne tells her that she is doing what she would do in any bar: scoring free drinks. Here it seems that the joke is on Jackie and her lack of coolness in the queer environment: she is comically scapegoated to illustrate Roseanne's comparative ease and familiarity.

This is enjoyable stuff for a queer constituency, making the uptight heterosexual woman alienated and unattractive in the clenched anxiety of her behaviour, normalizing the queer space through her amusing but abnormal reaction. The action then moves ahead a little: Roseanne, Nancy and Sharon have been dancing, Roseanne and Sharon take a break and sit at a table together, and Roseanne says, 'Can you believe that Nancy doesn't think I'm cool enough for this place?' Sharon confirms that Roseanne has disproved the slur by teaching 40 people to dance the monkey. Both women agree that they should hang out more often and Roseanne suggests that next time they should leave the 'wives' at home, gesturing towards where Jackie is sat at the bar. Sharon's body language and tone inflect her reply with a collusive sexual intimacy as she says, 'you read my mind'. Roseanne blanks the assumed collusion, registering some confusion that ruptures her normal deadpan stubbornness, the only reply she manages is 'Huh?'. As we are registering the confusion on Roseanne's face, the back of Sharon's head moves into the shot, and we get a brief glimpse of Roseanne's widening eyes before Sharon closes up and we assume that she kisses Roseanne. As Sharon pulls away from the kiss she hugs Roseanne, whose face we can now see over Sharon's shoulder. Roseanne wipes her mouth on Sharon's sleeve, her face twisted into an expression of distaste.

It is interesting to note the account *Out* magazine offers of this 'lesbian kiss':

> mainstream America – for a single moment in time – watched a woman kiss another woman *without flinching*. The press made it sensational; Roseanne made it ordinary.[27]

It would be quite difficult to speculate on the cause of the disparity in accounts here, but whatever the strategic reason for Carswell's emphatic applause of the kiss, her interpretation is extraordinary. Pedantically speaking Carswell is correct, Roseanne does not flinch away from the kiss we may assume is forthcoming from Sharon, although it is more of a connotation of a kiss than the real thing, given that we only see the back of Sharon's head moving in front of Roseanne's, inclining slightly and resting there for a second or two. Roseanne may not flinch, but wiping your mouth on somebody's sleeve with your face screwed up is a fairly substantial expression of at least ambiguity, if not out and out loathing. What seems clear is that this display of distaste is only representationally meaningful, and certainly only comic, in the context of a heterosexual gaze. Roseanne's disgust at the homosexual act she has just been involved in is collusively displayed for the edification of a straight audience: sure, Mariel Hemmingway might be great to look at, but kissing her makes you into a dyke and we all know how distasteful that is. Roseanne refers to this episode as the 'homophobia show':

> I think homophobia is something everybody has, and on that night Roseanne Conner dealt with her own homophobia. I don't see it as the big lesbian kiss show, but lesbians do, and I give them that.[28]

Implicating the character of Roseanne Conner in homophobic attitudes and behaviour, as *Roseanne* implicated her in racism, as we saw earlier, would be a significant piece of political commentary by the programme, even an instance of heterosocial affiliation. Clearly we can read the representation *Roseanne* makes of Roseanne's reaction to Sharon's connotated kiss in this way, in that it displays her culpability. However, notwithstanding the distinct ways in which race and sexuality are differently mobilized within structures of power, we could also argue that *Roseanne* deals with the two issues quite differently, according the racism substantially more seriousness.

As we saw earlier in the episode of *Roseanne* where DJ refused to kiss a girl because she was black, Roseanne and Dan Conner's culpability was represented so unsettlingly as to invite a rupture in the expected generic conventions of the programme. Roseanne's racism was not displayed for the comic edification of the audience, but to challenge us about our own potential complicity with systems of racism. If Roseanne Conner's reaction to the 'lesbian kiss' is homophobic, then that homophobia is upheld by the programme itself, as the opportunity for an audience to identify with her discomfort and share relieved laughter that the kiss, and the lesbianism it represents, was not enjoyed. For it seems clear that Roseanne's distasteful reaction, displaying homophobia, does not invite a challenge to dominant attitudes ventriloquizing liberalism; it does not invite us to distance ourselves from her politically unacceptable reaction: rather it panders to it, inviting voyeuristic collusion. You can gaze upon daring and weird queerness, and share disgust with it at the same time. The studio audience's reaction to this scene, embedded in the text on the soundtrack, expresses shocked titillation at the extraordinariness of the kiss, which is greeted with a loud chorus of 'oohs', while Roseanne's mouth-wiping and grimace, signs of her robust heterosexuality, and of her homophobia – which the programme is of course supposed to be apparently condemning – are marked with increasingly raucous and enthusiastic applause and laughter.

The next day, post-queer trauma, Roseanne offers her sister and subsequently Nancy, a number of accounts of her unease. At the diner, we know that something is amiss because Roseanne is cleaning: Jackie tells her that it is a shame that Sharon didn't 'slip her the tongue', because they might have been able to get the place up to code. Roseanne describes the kiss as the kind that Dan used to give her before they were married: this makes Dan look unromantic, but in as much as these kinds of expression are the realm of women, such a remark actually reminds us of the status of Dan's masculinity. At first Roseanne denies that she is bothered because she has been kissed by a woman. She tells Jackie that she is upset for Nancy: she feels that Nancy will jealously regard the kiss as adulterous. When Nancy arrives at work, it transpires that she already knows about the kiss and has expressed reservations to Sharon about her having done it: she anticipated that Roseanne would 'freak out'. Roseanne denies this, but Nancy speculates that Roseanne actually enjoyed the kiss and notes that sexuality 'isn't all black and white'. Roseanne replies that she knows all about the grey area and isn't bothered by some tiny percentage of her gayness. Nancy is now angry: she tells Roseanne that she is a hypocrite and that this is exactly why she was uncomfortable about taking her to a gay bar in the first place. Roseanne replies:

> R: Oh yeah? A hypocrite doesn't go to a gay bar and teach forty gay people how to do the monkey!
> N: Oh, and we're supposed to admire you because you went to a gay bar? I'm supposed to think you're cool because you have gay friends?
> R: I don't care if you think I'm cool at all, because I know that I'm cool, baby. I'm probably the coolest chick you've ever met, and for your information I have friends that are way gayer than you!

Before the argument can continue, the narrative side-steps to a brief scene between Dan and DJ, which makes an interesting reflection on the ideological struggle underway at the diner. DJ asks his father whether it is wrong for his mother to go dancing with other women. Dan's answer is delivered as a litany, he says, 'No, and anybody who tells you otherwise is wrong.' DJ then asks Dan if he dances with other men: at first Dan stays within his self-consciously insincere liberalism and says that he does, immediately retracting: 'no, never, ever, not once'. DJ says that he is glad, because he doesn't want to dance with men either. As his son walks away, Dan heaves a sigh of relief, saying 'hallelujah'. This scene is played straightforwardly comically, the laughter arising out of Dan's well meaning (but unfelt) attempt at liberal parenting. This humour is a function of an assumed consensus about maintaining a successful liberal ventriloquism of progressiveness while keeping homosexuality an abject: remaining clear that a son with homosexual tendencies or curiosity is a bad thing. Such humour seems to be saying that despite *Roseanne*'s high queer content, audiences can be assured that their normative heterosexual world-view will remain intact. Given that this scene breaks another, larger one, which is debating the limits of heterosexual progressiveness in challenging ways, the interlude's effect on potential heterosocial spectatorship is pretty depressing, using the humour to once again delineate included and excluded audience constituencies.

Back at the diner Roseanne is still cleaning, so we know her anxieties are unresolved. Jackie attempts to placate her, 'It's not so bad that the kiss freaked you out, you're just not as cool as you thought you were'. But Roseanne is not ready to concede yet: she incinerates her sister, reminding her of how totally uncool *she* was at the bar. Roseanne now suggests that she is upset because Dan will be jealous, but her delivery of the proposition is becoming less convincing. She reminds Jackie of how threatened Dan got in high school when another boy kissed her, and how Dan beat him up. Jackie remembers, and asks Roseanne if she thinks Dan will beat up Sharon, because Dan will feel threatened by her. Jackie's tone here is incredulous, while Roseanne's confirmation betrays the implausibility of her fear. Again, the studio audience is having a good time with this: it seems preposterous that Sharon would have sufficient homosocial credibility to threaten Dan in this way. As we have seen, Sharon is so scopically heterosexual and alluring that she cannot even elicit the threat conjured by the mannish butch dyke. Jackie finishes her account of Roseanne's fear by suggesting that she will end up sleeping with Sharon. Unseen by the sisters, Nancy has come into the kitchen. Roseanne is the goddess of retribution: 'Of course not! I am NOT GAY!' At this, they turn to Nancy as she slams out of the kitchen. Roseanne follows her,

> R: I just don't like people calling me things that I'm not, like a hypocrite, or gay, you know, because I'm not. I wouldn't like anybody to call me an astronaut because it's fine to be an astronaut, but I'm not an astronaut. I'm not going to admit I was wrong or anything, but I just don't wanna fight with you anymore, so, I was wrong.
> N: Thank you.
> R: I'm still pretty cool, you know, for a forty year old mother of three who lives in Lanford, Illinois. I like that Snoopy Dog Dog.

Despite the indeterminacy of Roseanne's apology (what is she actually apologising for? is she admitting her homophobia?) Nancy reassures Roseanne that she does not have to be cool to be her friend. She says that she feels sick every time she pictures Roseanne and Dan in bed together and Roseanne says that she does too. Here, once again, the idea of Dan and the masculinity he represents, is used to frame the discussion. The friends are acknowledging Dan's place within Roseanne's heterosexuality, recognizing that she is his to homosocially exchange. Indeed, *Roseanne* itself is exchanging her in the name of Dan's masculine credibility at this point. It does not really matter that he is portrayed unflatteringly: notwithstanding how secure and invested we know the Conner's marriage to be, his absence is structuring and women do not necessarily have to like men to be subject to them in homosocial exchange, nor do men have to please women sexually to acquire them as homosocial currency.

'I now pronounce you men': Queer marriage and the domestic goddess

The other significant episode of *Roseanne* infamous for its homosexual content portrays Leon's gay wedding. As the show opens a man is leaving the diner and complaining to Roseanne about the food; he is quite insulting. He leaves a cheque for the bill and no tip. There is another man sat at the counter. He sympathizes with Roseanne and tells her how he used to work in a restaurant and that she should not have to put up with such bad behaviour. The second man, who we learn is called Scott, asks for the phone, and uses the details printed on the cheque to ring the man's wife. He pretends to be the desk clerk at the Come and Go motel in Elgin and tells the woman that he has some underwear that she must have left the last time she stayed.[29] The man's wife obviously does not know what he is talking about and he says, 'Oh, you're not a busty twenty year old blonde? Woops, my mistake'. Roseanne is thrilled to have found another queen of retribution, and the incident bonds them in its delicious maliciousness, as it bonds the audience to this stranger:

> *R:* Wow! He stiffs me for a tip and you destroy his marriage – that's awesome.
> *S:* I thought that you'd enjoy that. You look like you've ruined a few lives in your day.
> *R:* I think I should tell you I'm a married woman. But I'm not a fanatic about it.

The nature of this bond, its shared currency, is the punishment of an abusive heterosexual man by invoking a stereotypical homosocial narrative against him. The errant customer's identity as a heterosexual man is constituted through a system that constantly exchanges women, the blonder, bustier and younger they are the more rigorous the heterosexuality and the more distance he is able to open up between himself and the queer abject. The nature of the bond here is all the more profound for its indexical relationship to the homosocial debility of Roseanne as a middle-aged brunette who may be busty, but who is also militantly fat, and of Scott as a gay man. We could describe their relationship as heterosocial.

It transpires that Scott is in town to meet up with the person who he is about to marry, the person who jilted him at the altar five years ago. Roseanne is defensive on behalf of her new heterosocial partner, she asks: 'What kind of a horrible bitch would dump you?' at the exact moment the door opens and Leon walks in. Roseanne is incredulous that her new buddy could be marrying the subject of her long-term enmity: 'even in a small town like this one he is at the very bottom of the homosexual heap.' But Leon has the opportunity to return the blow. It transpires that the couple are having trouble putting their wedding together. Scott suggests that they ask Roseanne, and Leon replies, 'No, no, no, no. No. Roseanne is not to be trusted with anything that involves cake . . . I've always dreamed of a ceremony that would culminate in a hog-fry.' But of course, the last line is Roseanne's: 'I've always thought of you as the middle-aged, obnoxious gay son that I've never had.' Under pressure from Scott, Leon finally agrees to let Roseanne plan the ceremony.

The scene is now set at the Conner home and time has passed. David and Jackie are helping plan the wedding. Roseanne rings to check the seating plan and David tells her (to much studio laughter) that it's fine: 'Boy, girl. Boy, boy. Boy, boy. Boy, boy. And boy.' Having fetishised this marker of the occasion's strangeness, we move on to Jackie, who is checking a brochure of strippers: she doesn't know whether to choose Rod, Lance or Shaft. She calls to Dan to help her choose a stripper and he comes running, only to back off uncomfortably (to much applause) when he sees the brochure: 'Those aren't strippers, they're guys.' In Dan's experience it is only women who are prepared to consent to offering a display of their bodies for shared male consumption. He asks Jackie if Roseanne is planning Leon's stag party as well and she tells him that the strippers are for the wedding. Dan thinks that Roseanne is going over the top, and Jackie agrees, but neither will tell her.

Having got some idea of the occasion in prospect, we now move on in time and to the Lanford Women's Club, where Leon arrives to meet Roseanne. She takes him into the hall, which is decorated in a gaudy mix of pink garlands, large inverted pink triangles bearing the logo 'Gay Love – Gay Power', statues of Adonis and of David adorned with pink ribbon, portraits of Streisand, Bowie, Dietrich and others, topless beefcake hunks in bow ties and two drag performers, one impersonating Judy Garland, the other Liza Minnelli. Leon is somewhat perplexed:

L: What is all this?
R: It's a gay wedding.
L: This isn't a wedding, it's a circus. You have somehow managed to take every gay stereotype and just roll them up into one gigantic offensive, Roseanne-iacal bunch of *wrong!*

R: Relax, nobody gets the wedding they really want . . .
L: It's off.
R: What do you mean?
L: I said the wedding is off.
R: Well of course it's a little off, it's two guys, for god's sakes!

One of the principle virtues of the treatment of the gay wedding in this episode is that it is complex and raises a number of issues.

Whether or not gay people should be getting married is a vexed question for lesbians and gay men themselves, as much as it is for legislators, right-wing religious activists, good liberals, and other moral commentators. Fundamentally all groups see the question in the same way; they are trying to assert some idea about what queer people in our cultures are for. Are we merely the victims of ignorance, blighted by an accident of difference which needs greater understanding, equality and tolerance from those who would seek to oppress us, because they do not really know that we are the same as them, underneath it all? Or, are we already known by those who would oppress us as fundamental and structuring threats to the fabric of their identities and power? Are we, or can we, or should we, be good citizens? We have seen how this question is put by Leo Bersani:

> Should a homosexual be a good citizen? It would be difficult to imagine a less gay-affirmative question at a time when gay men and lesbians have been strenuously trying to persuade straight society that they can be good parents, good soldiers, good priests.[30]

We are all too familiar with how these issues are debated by heterosexual power groups: even the apparently super-liberal, gay friendly President Clinton told *The Advocate* that he does not believe that gay people should be allowed to marry.[31] More significantly, lesbian and gay writers and activists have themselves expressed a wide range of investments in this question. The much-feted Andrew Sullivan, ex-editor of *The New Republic* achieves perhaps the most considered and gay (male) affirmative example of assimilationism in his *Virtually Normal*; yet however considered there remains a chronic naiveté at the heart of his position:

> [marriage] would also be an unqualified social good for homosexuals. It provides role models for young gay people, who, after the exhilaration of coming out, can easily lapse into short-term relationships . . .[32]

Here the enemy scapegoated to bring about gay inclusion seems to be promiscuity, but however parochial, at least Sullivan is under no illusions about his position:

> Gay marriage is not a radical step; it is a profoundly humanizing, traditionalizing step. It is the first step in any resolution of the homosexual question – more important than any other institution, since it is the most central institution to the nature of the problem, which is to say, the emotional and sexual bond between one human being and another.... It is ultimately the only reform that truly matters.[33]

Such insistent pomposity is precisely a danger inherent within a politics that is insufficiently heterosocial: with the exception of his antibody status, Sullivan speaks from the relatively privileged position I spoke of earlier; in particular his whiteness and maleness, to say nothing of his corporate authority, education and money at best make his words hegemonic in their very ignorance, and at worst traitorous in their solipsism.

In the form of their work as much as in its content, the Homocult collective exhibit a radical difference from the liberal mewlings of Andrew Sullivan. Homocult's work takes the form of graphics, posters, graffiti, flyers and collages in mixed media, that have been collected in a book, but which are more generally to be found in urban spaces: the group was founded in Manchester. One montage says: 'Shame: Rich Gays play Dead, their language in conserving, stagnating, lingering, death'. Another reproduces an image from an advertisement for a national dating agency with the caption 'You must marry. Issued by Dept. of Social Order, in conjunction with Hetrolife Plc.'[34] For Homocult being a homosexual is not about becoming a good citizen; their 'ultimate plan' is 'the destruction of the "moral" state.' The homosexual politics of the Stonewall Group in Britain, and the queer politics of Outrage are an anathema: 'Now the Stonewall Group formed from our blood police our language, needs and lives. Outrage is a cosy sham. You can only be outraged by what surprises you. It's no surprise to common queers that there is no justice for us. We are not outraged, we are defiant.'[35]

Roseanne's treatment of Leon and Scott's gay wedding could potentially tap into this range of ideas that diverse and complex communities of gays and lesbians produce, side-stepping a problematic unification of queer cultures and making a more radical presentation as a result. Roseanne's camply overdetermined notion of what constitutes a gay wedding can be understood in several different ways. As a heterosexual character her delivery of the wedding and her unrepentant insistence upon Leon going through with it, can be read as an abusive appropriation of gay culture for the edification of Roseanne Conner's much-invested 'coolness', and for the voyeuristic consumption of *Roseanne*'s audience. Here, her statement that 'Well of course it's a little off, it's two guys, for god's sakes!' becomes the invocation of a gap between the strangeness of gay matrimony and the normality and dignity of heterosexual union. Gays can get married, but such ceremonies are a bit of camp fun, not profound and meaningful occasions. However, Roseanne's production of the gay wedding could also be seen as a parodic inversion of exactly such profundity, using the dissident place queerness inhabits within the mythologies of marriage to critique its conventions. Why should queers mimic ceremonies of commitment sanctioned by a hostile state, when we have a distinct culture of our own from which to draw ritualistic meanings? In this reading, Roseanne's suggestion of how 'off' the ceremony is becomes a recognition of the futility of Leon's aspiration for the public sanction of his partnership and a reminder to him of the difference of his queer identity. Yet even within this 'positive' reading of *Roseanne*'s gay wedding, one which gives her the benefit of queer doubt, Roseanne Conner is the arbiter of essential dissident queerness, a heterosexual woman who teaches overly liberal gay men how to regain their lost transgressive perversity.

The narrative continues after the passing of time. The wedding is now imminent and Roseanne has locked Leon in the bathroom so that he cannot escape. Leon's mother arrives, presenting an opportunity for more bitching. Roseanne's opening line seems to shore up the idea of her queer iconicity, as she references *The Wizard of Oz*: 'How wonderful it is that you were able to get that house off of you before the wedding!' While the retort of Leon's mother introduces another way of decoding Roseanne's wedding vision: 'Look at this place. Have you ever seen such a horrific display of blue collar tastelessness?' As Leon's mother flounces off, leaving her class critique unpursued, Dan finally plucks up the courage to intervene in the unfolding queer debacle:

> *D*: Honey I think you should tone down the wedding like he wanted.
> *R*: No! This is *my* wedding, and he is lucky I cast him in it.
> *D*: Roseanne, I know you wanted this wedding to be a certain way, but if you don't do something, there isn't going to be a wedding, it's going to be all your fault, and you know who's going to suffer? Me.

Here the balance seems to be shifting back towards Roseanne's oppress-ive appropriation of queerness and her heterosexually privileged authority: it's her wedding and we know that weddings are all about bridal desires: here it is Roseanne who is the bride, even though she is not getting married, she is the heterosexual princess at the centre of the occasion. Once again Dan is deferring to Roseanne's control in the manner that we expect and love, but his massively masculine, working-class pres-ence and our intra-textual familiarity with his utter lack of deference to anybody else, both infers Roseanne's relation to his masculinity and re-locates her within a heterosexual matrix that is often quite normative.

Roseanne then goes to the bathroom to persuade Leon to take part in her wedding. She tells him that she has toned down the gay kitsch, but he still wants to leave, not because she has turned his wedding into a 'circus', but because he is having second thoughts about marrying Scott. Any potential liberal guilt that may be amassing due to the impending fiasco now passes back to Leon: *she is* not domineering, *he* is just flaky and unreliable. Roseanne bullies Leon, telling him that he can't leave Scott at the altar again, that Scott is that best thing that has ever happened to him. Leon agrees, but he is scared of the commitment and the permanence. Leon suggests a whole range of stupid reasons why he cannot marry, giving Roseanne the opportunity to occupy a position of rationality and knowledge with increasing belligerence. Finally Leon says:

L: Okay, then how about this, ready? What if I'm not really gay?
R: You couldn't be any gayer if your name was Gay Gayerson.
L: Oh yeah? Well you just think about it, young lady. I hate to shop, I am absolutely insensitive, I detest Barbra Streisand, and for god's sake, I'm a Republican.
R: But do you like having sex with men?
L: Well, I . . .
R: GAY!!

Here the loud, accusative naming of gayness, within the context of *Roseanne*'s self-consciously gay-affirmative liberalism, transgresses our conventional expectations about screaming 'Gay!' at somebody. Queers are used to being named, abused and taunted by heterosexuals with the words with which we may identify ourselves. Here Leon's homosexual self-doubt conveniently vacates the space of queer articulacy, allowing the ultra 'cool' Roseanne to become the bearer, arbiter, originator, of confident, assertive and positive queer identification. Leon's deficiency in expressing the markers of gayness that *Roseanne* posits (shopping, Streisand, sensitivity, liberalism), only makes Roseanne herself even more successfully queer: she can speak it and she can do it, as we are supposed to deduce from her decoration of the wedding. Furthermore, it seems as though it is Roseanne's insistence on being in control, of knowing and determining Leon's doubts about the marriage that goads him into more and more outrageous retorts in order to gain some self-determination and leads him, eventually, to renounce his sexuality in the hope that she will leave him alone. His final retort challenges her expression of his sexual orientation. He says, 'Oh yeah?' and then grabs her and kisses her passionately on the mouth. He pulls back and shakes his head in a suggestion of revulsion, and strides for the door: 'I'm gay. Let's do it'. It would seem that there are dual causes of dismay for queer audiences here.

Any vestiges of identification we are supposed to have left with the self-confessed right-wing, insensitive, Streisand loathing (this confession is of course the absolute worst) Leon are scoured away by the script when it has him kiss Roseanne: using homosocial sexual objectification of women to regain his homosexuality is a pretty unsympathetic act, not only in its sexism but in its lack of queer pride – it humiliates him as a gay man, even more than his preceding renunciation. On another level, the kiss, like that between Roseanne and Sharon, is supposed to elicit revulsion out of fascination and progressive 'cool'; queerness here is once again the plaything of heterosexual voyeurism, and Roseanne is the unassailably heterosexual location for audience identification. Once again she gets a brief taste of the strange fruit (at least from the right gender this time), while the narrative meaning of the kiss depends upon *her* heterosexuality and *their* strangeness. For Leon's 'test' of his gayness, as much as for Sharon's desire of Roseanne, the fixed point from which resolution springs, is Roseanne's heterosexuality: her normativity proving Leon's homosexuality and displaying Sharon's kinky lesbianism. Neither of these interactions, as the epicentre of *Roseanne*'s queer narratives, troubles heterosexuality or problematizes normative gender roles as the source of homophobia. The wedding ceremony itself follows, conducted by an inept preacher who adds comic relief by twisting up his words. There are a few moments of apparently genuine celebration of queer partnership:

> *Scott*: I love you in a way that is mystical and eternal and illegal in twenty states.
> *Leon*: That's the most beautiful thing I've ever heard.

However, the overall tone is patronizing. The inept preacher is from Leon's home town and was brought to conduct the ceremony especially. The fact that he was chosen by Leon himself makes him partly responsible for the ceremony's comic illegitimacy, especially as the preacher's shortcomings mean that Scott and Leon have to make up and say their own vows.

> *Preacher*: Do you, Leon, take this Scott to be your awfully rabid husband?

Again this indication of the gay couple's distance outside conventional heterosexual matrimony has dual meanings: either their impromptu vows are a transgressive reinscription of patriarchal matrimony, or they are an indication of the couple's lack of normality or recognition by state or religion.

> *Preacher*: I now pronounce you man and . . . er . . . I now pronounce you men.

The preacher's indeterminacy about how to address the couple highlights the inadequacy and heterosexism of 'traditional' notions of marriage and the language used around sexual partnership; however, it also further highlights the couple's strangeness, especially as the preacher's function is precisely to recognize and authenticate the occasion, not to belittle it. As the newlyweds kiss, the camera quickly pans away to Dan and Roseanne. Dan is shifting in his seat, looking but not looking, mesmerized and shocked by the kiss:

> *Dan*: And there's the kiss. I was wondering if they were going to do it, and they're doing it. Look at them going at it.
> *Roseanne*: They are not 'going at it' Dan, it just happens to be two people of the same sex kissing, and there's nothing wrong with that.

At this moment, out of nowhere, Mariel Hemmingway (Sharon) appears over Roseanne's shoulder and says hello. Roseanne returns the greeting, with just a little too much enthusiasm, and the episode ends on a close up of her fixed and ever so slightly too wide grin.

Sharon's appearance, and the jog that it provides to our memories of Roseanne's discomfort with her own 'lesbian' kiss neatly dampens the ardour of her liberal superiority in relation to Dan, and the moment is very funny, providing us with a very satisfying and rare occasion of

Roseanne's silenced defeat. But of course, the cost of that humour is that both the wedding kiss of Leon and Scott, and the 'lesbian' kiss of Roseanne and Sharon from the preceding season, are displayed for voyeuristic heterosexual consumption: indeed given the rapidity with which the direction moves us from Leon and Scott's kiss (seen only from the back of Leon's head, of course) to Dan's reaction to it, we may conclude that the very point of the kiss is not its display of gay love, but its garnering of disgusted heterosexual titillation. Rather than circulating through *Roseanne* as a cultural threat, something that contextualises and denaturalises masculinity and the heterosexual power with which it dominates women, homosexuality becomes but an effect of a liberal world view ventriloquising progressiveness, based on diversity and inclusion, but always under the terms of existing power relations. Certain issues and identities can be run through this world view in a challenging way, as the confrontation with Mr Williams challenged Roseanne's racism. But in that episode, as with the current one, difference is not allowed to articulate for itself, but only as a testing and enlightening reflection of the oppressive term in each binary.

Homosexuality is liberally enshrined, and direct expressions of homophobia are not allowed to be directed at gays and lesbians themselves. It is only in relation to the quasi-queerness of David that *Roseanne* even begins to dare to examine the place of homosexual panic in the constitution of homosocial systems. Such questions are however kept at some distance from actually identified gay characters, who all circulate through the woman-centred ambit of Roseanne herself. But as we have seen, even here, Roseanne's heterosexuality remains the structuring condition of queer representation. Queerness signifies, often blatantly, but always as the opportunity for progressive, 'cool' assimilation rather as the occasion for a challenge to heterosexual authority, Roseanne's included. Specific and distinct cultural expressions of homosexuality are ultimately seen as in no way incompatible with 'cool' heterosexuality. Indeed such expressions are displayed for the edification of cool heterosexuals, both in political terms – by flattering the liberal ego and in voyeuristic terms – by always framing queerness as kinky and strange. Queerness rarely appears strange and weird to queers themselves.

Mary-come-lately or gay goddess?

What makes these limitations in the scope of *Roseanne*'s queerness so marked, is the extent to which the show invites lesbian and gay subcultural investment: and as we have seen from American publications, this is certainly forthcoming. However, it could be argued that the disparity between the tenor of the treatment accorded the 'issues' of racism and sexuality in *Roseanne* is due neither to the distinct and radically different nature of the questions themselves, nor to some ideological shortcoming on the part of the producers, but occurs because *Roseanne* is drawing performatively on a camp register that is characteristic of much queer cultural negotiation. This register, an attitude of *mise-en-scene*, timing, tone and irony, as well as the more substantial qualities of script and direction, can in itself be appealing to queer audiences as it elicits a way of reading well versed through a canon of appropriated camp classics. This is a quality of the material not highlighted in mandarin, formalized discourses of textual analysis, and I am aware of the need to do justice to the multiple and ironic layers through which *Roseanne* pitches its treatment of homosexual life. Features of the sitcom would make it highly valuable as a cultural resource for gay men regardless of its specific gay content, as most films and television in the subcultural queer canon attest.[36]

As I have tried to indicate, *Roseanne*'s scenes of dialogue have a distinctive performative quality that at its most successful manages to convey the weight and substance of experiences the show dramatises, yet at the same time inhibiting earnest, unengaged and complacently liberal empathy. Characters frequently get upset, angry, violent, but *Roseanne* frames such emotional outbursts within a structuring representational mode of deadpan, almost dispassionate irony that scours away any latent limp humanism our generic expectations may enshrine. The formal ideological terms through which *Roseanne* makes queer representations are thus in constant negotiation with the show's performative vernacular, which constantly frustrates suspension of disbelief, peeling away layers of textual authority. It is this quality of *Roseanne* which registers with queer audiences, the duality enforcing a recognition of the artfulness, the constructed nature of the text and what it represents. Alas it seems that this reflexivity begets continuing queer identification even as the ideological investments of the show betray and trample on such investment.

The ideological intent which drives the narrative and specular organization of the 'lesbian' kiss episode of *Roseanne* does seem to be genuinely based in an appreciation of the need to question the political authority, cultural uniformity and complacency of heterosexual society; this appreciation would appear to be derived from an allegiance and familiarity with queer subcultures. There are a sufficient number of in-jokes and subcultural references throughout the episode which suggest the presence of an 'authentic' queer subcultural voice within the dialogue that is intended to be recognized as such. These interventions have been interpreted by publications that speak from queer subculture, and by Roseanne herself, as having heterosocial effects; that is, that they enact bonding between women and queerness. Yet the failure of these affiliations lies in their inability to diegetically transcend homosocial ideological systems: this is something made all too apparent in the later gay wedding episode. It is these homosocial systems which in their dominance maintain the breaches between women and queerness: homosocial control produces the dissident need for a bonding that will enable us to re-envisage gender relations, to reconfigure patriarchal gender roles. Heterosocial interventions attempt to elude the homosocial functionality conferred upon homosexual and female identities within male homosocial structures. Heterosocial work requires a reflexive awareness of the complex matrix of power relations that maintain difference and sometimes enmity between diverse marginal identities: that must be the fundamental basis of any affiliation conducted on the grounds of that difference. We must see the conditions which shape the experiences of our potential allies and be able to perceive our complicity with systems that enforce their oppression, as we see their complicity in ours.

It is very striking that after the initial exuberant burst of heterosocial activity between Roseanne and Scott at the beginning of the gay wedding show, there is no further interaction between them at all. Given the terms of their bonding this isn't surprising: it would be difficult to sustain such a relationship in the light of the insistence with which the Roseanne character later maintains her control and superiority over gay men. This is to say nothing of the difficulty the producers of the show would have in reconciling the anti-homosocial nature of Roseanne and Scott's continuing interactions with Roseanne's heterosexuality and her relationship with Dan. What would the show do with Dan while his wife and Scott heterosocially challenged male bonding and power? We know that it is okay for Roseanne to disempower Dan, indeed this is a central component of *Roseanne's* distinctiveness. We are familiar with her fabulously bombastic rantings and we know that this does not castrate Dan or make him impotent in the overall representation of his character. There are always spaces in *Roseanne* for Dan to interact in manly homosocial terms with other men, often recognizing his wife's substantial material authority in the process and trading that for masculine credibility with others: on the roof fixing tiles with Mark, playing poker with his buddies, down at the bike shop with Mark, at the municipal garage where he is the boss, or down at the Lobo bar with Fred.

However, it would be a completely different proposition for Dan to be disempowered by an affiliation between Scott, a gay man, and his colluding wife. Such a direct challenge would be much more damaging to symbolic male power than Roseanne's 'domestic goddess' alone – precisely because her domestic goddess requires him to come home every night and demand his dinner on the table so that she can refuse him and they can then have a power struggle. *Roseanne* is carefully manipulated so as to preclude the writers having to find a way of reconciling the heterosocial queerness of Scott or Leon, with the progressive and queer-positive intent of the show, while retaining sufficient unchallenged throbbing virility in Dan Conner. Dan's homosocial credibility is maintained in that he never has to be positioned directly in the heterosocial discourses of his wife and her faggot associates and friends, a positioning that would either compromise him (and the show itself) politically, or would sacrifice some of the homosocial power he accrues through his relationships with Fred, Mark and others, and which is measured by his symbolic distance from David, the 'art femme'.[37] In close proximity and in discourse with the queer cohort, how could Dan maintain difference without recourse to direct homophobia? It is much easier for him to become homosocially energised in relation to David, at the 'art femme's' expense, because David is not labelled as gay, and thus any repression of him will not open up *Roseanne*'s apparently progressive agenda to liberal criticism.

There are two occasions in which Dan must face the queer challenge alone. One occurs when Nancy and Marla are visiting on Christmas Eve. The rest of the Conner family is stranded in snow at the diner. The lesbian couple take the opportunity to kiss under the mistletoe: Dan's response is to pretend that it is not happening so that he does not have to engage it, and he looks away. Later on in the episode, while he is basting the turkey, he and Nancy talk about her having children. He suggests that she might have ruined her chances of being a mother now that she is a lesbian, but Nancy says that she and Marla are planning to have kids. Dan asks her to explain how she could do that, 'without being at all specific'. At that moment they both look at the turkey baster, he hands it to her and runs off. In another episode Leon is playing poker with Dan and his buddies. In the course of some routine homosocial exchange of 'babe' stories, it becomes apparent that Dan is not aware that Leon is gay. Leon comes out, and it is the rest of the poker players who engage with this: one says that he knows a gay man in Chicago, called Bill, who Leon might know. Dan's intervention is to finally shut them all up so that they can play cards.

In both instances the interactions measure Dan's distance from queerness (he does not even express any voyeuristic interest in Nancy and Marla) without him having to produce himself in such a way as to accommodate and relate to that queerness. It is always going to be fine to have Roseanne queening and bitching and feuding around with gay men or with lesbians, because representationally Roseanne's femininity will always be more natural, credible and consequently more authoritative (however bombastic and militantly fat, she is a wife, a mother, and she is a woman) than Leon or Scott's 'unnatural' refusal of masculinity, or Nancy's refusal of heterosexuality and men, because that refusal constitutes a negation of the very site through which she may accrue social authority. In one argument between Roseanne and Leon in an episode about their partnership at the diner, she tells him that no 'Mary-come-lately' is going to stand in her way. Such remarks are as near as the show gets to out and out homophobia, and here it is rendered safe as it comes in the context of a bitch-fest. Nevertheless, whenever the character of Roseanne Conner raises the stakes to a direct stand-off about who is the best 'Mary', Leon will always become the somewhat pathetic Mary-wannabe, while Roseanne, with her marriage to Dan behind her, will be the authentic Mary. Roseanne's authority is dependent on the symbolism she accrues by virtue of her blue-collar, white-trash, physically indomitable husband. Bringing her heterosocial affiliations with gay men into too close a proximity to her marriage, would challenge and erode her authority precisely by destabilizing the homosocial mythology of her masculine husband.

Extra-diegetically, as a personality, a media image, Roseanne herself is obviously something of a gay icon, for the reasons I discussed above, and in the context of corporate timidity and greed her political statements about a range of issues, including those that relate to lesbians and gay men, are welcome and diverting. At its best *Roseanne* is an extraordinary piece of television, deriving a witheringly deadpan comedy from synthesizing a *laissez-faire* cynicism with a bombastically passionate enactment of woman-centred authority which is intoxicating in itself, especially to a queer audience, for the reasons I have discussed. If publications such as *Out* and *The Advocate* can utilize *Roseanne* strategically to effect heterosocial and queer advantages, refashioning its representations to find material that provides subcultural sustenance, or material with which to worry dominant faultlines, then this is obviously very exciting. However, I am not sure that *Roseanne's* literal deployment of queerness in itself can sustain the weight of such desires.

Given the nature of the show, it is inevitable that all the principle narratives, and experiences *Roseanne* dramatises ultimately become functions of its eponymous heroine's perspective. This dramatic solipsism is one of *Roseanne's* strengths, given that it makes the show so powerfully woman-centred, and can be used effectively to solicit powerful ideological critiques when that dramatic epicentre is destabilized, as in the confrontation with Mr Williams. However, in relation to *Roseanne's* handling of lesbian and gay issues this solipsism is something of a problem. We have seen how the nominally heterosexual, but queerly signifying character of David is used not only to empower women in the shape of Darlene by portraying them in supportive and authoritative relations with men, but to reinstate a homosocially grounded masculinity in which he is failing, and the other men are colluding. *Roseanne's* knowledge of queerness stalls at those moments when it would be challenging to heterosexuality, or incompatible with the particular character and determination of Roseanne's transgression as 'killer bitch'/feminist. Roseanne has said:

Men who are anything like women are devalued in this society. There's a pecking order in male culture, and at the very bottom, if they're included at all, are women.[38]

This neatly encapsulates the heterosocial enigma *Roseanne* poses. The recognition that the shape of another kind of oppression may be similar to your own, indeed may be a function of your oppression, seems an encouragingly heterosocial understanding. Yet at the very moment of this awareness, we see that this heterosocial knowledge is twisted through the axis of its empathy so that it repositions Roseanne herself as inversely privileged: she becomes even more oppressed. This privilege is naturalised, rendering Roseanne's own heterosexuality ideologically cloaked because her rendering of it lines up with heterosexist hegemonies, and because it does not interrupt the homosocial narrative along the axis of its homophobia. The Domestic Goddess, the Goddess of Retribution, Divine tamer of Faggottry, she is our (flawed) champion of the progressive in the arena of homosociality.

4
Pedro Almodóvar and *Women on the Verge of a Nervous Breakdown*: the Heterosocial Spectator and Misogyny

If the critical attention paid to Tennessee Williams is indicative of the meanings attached to questions of gender identification and homosexuality in a pre-'liberationary' period, then discussion of Pedro Almodóvar brings a contemporary perspective to such questions. As we have seen, for mainstream critics Williams's particular interest in female characterization was a pathological and morbid manifestation of his own inversion. The public rendering of such characterization in performances of Williams's plays was, apparently, a bitter and aggressively vengeful attempt to soil the sanctity of moral decency in female representation. I have argued that such hostile readings are a reactionary attempt to recuperate the unsettlingly denaturalized representations of gender that Williams makes. Hostile critics infer that Williams's work was somehow an attempt to debase everyone else as he himself was debased. I have suggested that in as far as the playwright's compelling characterisations are debased, in that they attempt to fracture the powerful ideological containments erected around gender roles in postwar American culture, then Williams's opponents are correct. Blanche, The Princess and Maggie the Cat, as well as Stanley Kowalski, Chance and Brick, represent queer refractions of gender roles that show an awareness of how central gender identity is for Williams as a homosexual – and furthermore, how central our homosexuality is within systems of gender.

In discussion of Pedro Almodóvar's films the issue of his special relationship with women characters and female actors, and his status as a women's director, is almost universally central: it is the abiding tag with which the Spanish writer and director is understood. Yet as a European art-house or independent filmmaker, the audience and the critical context in which discussion of his work takes place is already located in an apparently liberal, progressive and intellectually engaged context in which gay and lesbian culture is supposed to flourish, and in which the idea of an iconographic relationship between women and gay men, hags and fags, is accepted. Discussion of this audience context may provide an interesting consideration of the possibilities for queer articulation and resistance, and the limits of liberal chattering-class culture, that is, of middle-class liberalism that aspires to radicalism. The terms through which Almodóvar circulates are different to those which were faced by Williams. In many ways it would appear that Almodóvar's films are consumed within a cultural context that is politically and intellectually privileged. If Williams's work was received with a rabid hostility which stringently attempted to foreclose the more challenging and marginal aspects of the plays, then we may expect Almodóvar's work to receive a somewhat more enabling reception among the audiences of art-house cinema and the readers of liberal broadsheets. Given the extent to which audiences have been able to transcend the ideological containments erected around Williams and still make resistant meanings, we might expect much more exciting and radical responses from an audience constituency apparently already predisposed towards an embracing of gay politics and conversant with the terms of homosexual representation.

A Case of public or private?

As well as being a maker of cultural products, someone who creates tangible artefacts, Pedro Almodóvar is a star – a personality, a phenomenon; an entity in himself. That is to say, he is a star for many within that small proportion of the population who are the metropolitan, liberal, urban, probably graduate, heterosexual middle-classes who frequent art-house cinema and who in Britain read the *Guardian*, or possibly the *Observer*, maybe even the *Independent* – the so-called chattering classes, who comprise an intellectual and social/artistic elite in Britain and in the United States. Almodóvar is also a star for those who occupy a space where this group overlaps with a section of urban lesbian and gay culture – queer 'culture vultures': largely students and graduate professionals in education, the arts and the caring professions: middle-class urbanites, or those who aspire towards those values. As largely a product of urban, and often metropolitan spaces, contemporary lesbian and gay culture has a particularly visible investment in the values of the 'chattering classes', witness the particularly high incidence of upward class mobility many lesbians and gay men experience in their gravitation towards commercial and cosmopolitan urban environments – at least in values and aspiration, if not in economic terms.[1]

If Pedro Almodóvar is a star, then his homosexuality is, of itself, an issue of cultural interest. In the context of this study the values and meanings attached to the presence of significant subcultural characters is as important as the negotiations conducted through textual material. Not only are the terms under which important figures circulate significant as a kind of filter through which particular constituencies may decode textual artefacts, but highly visible and successful lesbian or gay celebrities are subcultural myths, in that they actually structure iconographies of queerness. As I suggested earlier, Tennessee Williams has a value in gay culture that far exceeds the literary worth of his substantial body of work: he is a figure around whom new notions of homosexuality and gender have emerged and been contested (for instance in the work of Split Britches and Bloolips in *Belle Reprieve*); key elements of Williams's meaning are transmitted and negotiated through the actual literary work (and its filmic forms as well) but always in a complex dialectic with an aura of the figure Williams is understood to be – itself a highly contested issue, as I have demonstrated. As theorists of popular culture, from Barthes to Richard Dyer, Andrea Weiss and Christine Gledhill have shown, stardom is a discourse with particular resonances in gay and lesbian culture, with a strong and influential history – particularly in relation to film, but also in the theatre.[2]

The place of homosexuality in the *laissez-faire* liberal and intellectual culture addressed by the *Guardian* or the *Observer* is complex and ambivalent. On the one hand such august British journals secure an impression of their fairness, liberalism and reasonableness by distancing themselves from the rabbid, hysterical and overt homophobia of tabloids such as the *Sun*. On the other hand, Michelangelo Signorile argues in the Preface to the British edition of his book *Queer in America* that:

> most of the 'responsible' media refuse to reveal public figures' homosexuality, even when relevant – except, of course, when such revelations play into their homophobic agenda.[3]

Signorile's contention is that all media should report the homosexuality of subjects if relevant to the content of a story, regardless of the stance those subjects may have in relation to lesbian and gay politics (p. xv). His model of the closet is that it is 'a place where gay men and lesbians are forced to live – under penalty of ostracism and, in some cases, even death – since their earliest realization of their sexuality' (p. xi), and outing 'is a refusal by journalists to be complicit with the closet, a refusal to make special arrangements for the closeted when reporting the news' (p. xv). This outing, rather than a punitive act and experience of punishment, should be a liberating experience (p. xv). Signorile accounts for ambiguity around homosexuality in what he calls the 'responsible' or liberal press by suggesting that journalists writing in such contexts cover up 'facts about public figures' homosexuality even when relevant to news stories, because journalists are 'uncomfortable with homosexuality', masking this discomfiture as a 'sympathy for gays' "right to privacy"' (p. xiii).

Clearly such reasoning seems plausible, particularly given the disengenuousness the 'quality' press exhibit in relation to the sensationalization of homosexuality – often maintaining the liberal consensus by reporting on tabloid coverage of sensational stories, thereby situating the responsibility for such scandal with the downmarket press, while continuing to titillate their own readership. However, it seems that it is in relation to this titillation that Signorile's model is a little simplistic: the suggestion that the liberal/quality/responsible press collude with the closet, and that this is the primary tool through which homosexuality is oppressed overlooks the fact that the press actually deploy representations of gay and lesbian culture in order to engender a sense of ethical superiority and an assurance of liberal toleration, and that the metropolitan liberal middle-class culture addressed by such newspapers has a voyeuristic fascination that is in part a consequence of the need to demonstrate and affirm the security of their readership's liberalism. This requirement, then, of homosexual content, if only to demonstrate liberal tolerance, let alone to detail sufficiently explicit material to satisfy the demands of kinky voyeurism, compromises both the rigidity of Signorile's model, and more importantly, the idea of straightforward demonization or suppression of homosexuality by this liberal/intellectual middle-class culture.

An example of this ambiguity appeared in the *Life* 'magazine' section of the weekend *Observer*, in an issue that followed Pride weekend in London in 1995. The cover depicts a gay male couple embracing, decked out in Indian quasi-religious drag (in a fashion popularized by Boy George during his dalliance with Krishna consciousness), replete with nose rings, cropped and dyed hair, and on one of the pair, a head-dress of lillies and gypsophilia. The banner reads 'Pride not prejudice – Coming out in style'. Inside, the piece transpires to be a fashion spread highlighting the wild and wacky outfits some people had worn at the Pride festival. The short text read

At the same time as 100,000 people were camping at Glastonbury, almost twice that number attended what has become Britain's biggest urban festival. Lesbian and Gay Pride, held in Victoria Park in east London, has grown from a small march in 1971 to the huge and diverse event it is today.

Pride represents a milestone in a lot of gay people's lives, providing many of them with their first opportunity to come out.

The festival-goers on these pages demonstrate the wide variety of unstereotypical style statements currently being made in the gay community.[4]

Alongside cropped men in fetish heels or in pink Barbie wear are images of a butch and femme lesbian couple dragged up for their wedding, a lesbian couple and a gay couple in military uniforms, a couple in sailor suits, a femme dyke duo, a black funky-chick, a couple of Sisters of Perpetual Indulgence, a cropped and goateed queer boy and so on. The ambience of voyeuristic titillation is clear in the represented foreigness of the material and in the expositionary tone, highlighted by the mode of address the feature uses – it is not aimed at anybody who might actually have been one of the 200 000 people who attended the event.

Yet such is the anticipated sophistication of the *Observer*'s readership, the tone of the piece is only mildly offensive, taking a somewhat conspiratorial attitude which is allied with the subjects of the piece. The effect of the feature is to highlight the diversity of the Lesbian and Gay Festival (the text even refers to it), and to point out that the event was twice the size of the annual Glastonbury music festival, which received substantial television coverage – thus Pride is accorded some measure of dignity and respect, even superiority to an equivalent (nominally) heterosexual event, even if it is reduced to the level of being merely about display and spectacle: a fashion spread. It could also be argued that the iconography of the principal photography in the feature is somewhat at odds with the up-beat liberalism of the text, if not with the voyeuristic glimpse it offers the domestic chattering classes of a 'wild' subculture. Under large pink letters 'Out and proud' a man in a cropped black fluffy jumper and shiny, tight black pvc jeans is shown on his knees, cropped and dyed head down in his hands, arse pushed into the air, and one leg slightly raised. On his feet he wears outrageous and enormous black pvc platform stilettos, decorated with silver studs. A huge black belt with bold silver details separates his waist from his pale and bare midriff, and the waistband of his designer underpants is just visible. The effect of the image, in terms of the provocative posture (the caption reads 'Dean Stevenson, exhausted after walking in the Pride march: "I did this look to be glamorous".') suggests other exhaustions, while the 'kinkiness' of the pvc and all the black intersects strongly with the image of the extraordinary shoes and the raised up arse to provide an image somewhat at odds with conventional liberal images of Pride – this is an intimate, provocative image, slightly sanitized by the extremity of the attire and the context of the focus on fashion. However, given its association with the headline 'Out and proud' the image is structured by the absence of any facial characteristics – no proud gaze from eyes which meet those of the spectator, no grins of proclamation, just the protruding arse and provocative iconography. The image is quite distinctly post-Queer, not only in terms of the particular aesthetic trappings it deploys – the clashing of fetish, drag and porn codes, but also because it is appearing in a national 'quality' broadsheet (albeit in the weekend 'lifestyle' section) and was obviously knowingly styled to key into recognizable symbols.

It should be clear then, that undertaking an analysis of the *Observer*'s Pride feature purely on the basis of a closet versus liberation model, such as that expounded by Signorile, would not sufficiently account for the functional purposes to which a liberal/broadsheet press utilises the explicit representation of homosexuality and the resultant ripples of discontinuity produced across the terrain of liberal consensus: any representation of homosexuality undertaken by such journals, Signorile suggests, must accord with 'their homophobic agenda' (p. xv). The *Observer*'s Pride feature may have an agenda discontinuous with that of many lesbian and gay Pride participants (but it may not: indeed its agenda may be congruent with that of some lesbian or gay participants, and some heterosexual ones) but it certainly isn't attempting to keep homosexuality in the closet – the text implicitly 'outs' all the subjects photographed, and actually notes the importance Pride has in terms of being a very public space – a festival no less – in which to *come out*. Whatever policing and constraining effects contemporary *laissez-faire* liberalism, in the shape of the broadsheet press, has, those effects are fundamentally dissimilar to the effects operative in the immediate post-Wolfenden climate in Britain, where there was an assumption of secrecy on the part of lesbians and gay men and a public consensus about the abject nature of homosexuality itself.

Liberal titillation and the regime of the couple

An article published in the American lesbian and gay magazine *Out* to coincide with the release of Almodóvar's film, *Kika*, noted recent gossip that had been circulating about the writer/director, which alleged that he had secretly married Bibi Andersen 'once billed as the tallest trans-sexual in Europe.'[5] A British journalist, Robert Chalmers, repeated the gossip in the *Observer* at about the same time.[6] In a *Late Show* special screened to coincide with the opening of *Kika* in England, Almodóvar himself notes that he and Carmen Maura were once almost like an 'official couple', 'like Elizabeth Taylor and Richard Burton, without the jewels'. He is referring to a period in which Maura and the director worked and associated together, through the making of *Pepi, Luci, Bom and other Girls on the Heap* (1980), *Labyrinth of Passion* (1982), *Dark Habits* (1983), *What Have I Done to Deserve This?* (1984), *Matador* (1986), and *The Law of Desire* (1987) up until their last work together on *Women on the Verge of a Nervous Breakdown* (1988). During the making of *Women* the 'couple' became estranged and subsequently Victoria Abril became Almodóvar's favoured female actor. What is notable then, about much of the queer and liberal media interest in Almodóvar, a filmmaker Marsha Kinder has described as having 'done more that any other Spaniard to popularize worldwide the image of a liberated outra-geous Spain',[7] is the preoccupation with his relationships, his bonds, with women – particularly his leading female actors.

Significantly, this preoccupation sits alongside a tacit acknowledge-ment of Almodóvar's homosexuality. In the *Out* article Gooch recounts Almodóvar's frustration with Tom Hanks's reported ambivalence about playing a homosexual in *Philadelphia*: 'You don't have to do anything to play a homosexual. A homosexual is a human being.' (p. 54), and then goes on to compare the writer/director's pop-cartoon appeal with that of other 'grand European bad boys, models of respected irrespect-ability' such as Elton John, Boy George, Thierry Mugler, Jean Paul Gaultier and Gianni Versace, all figures understood by both lesbian and gay, and cosmopolitan liberal middle-class constituencies, to be queer. Robert Chalmers's *Observer* piece contains an instance of Almodóvar's frustration with being 'always "the gay director Pedro Almodóvar"' (p. 24). In both examples the slippage from Almodóvar's bonding with women to his homosexuality is seamless, to the extent that Chalmers makes clear his frustration with the writer/director's impatience about identifying his sexuality. There appears to be an underlying under-standing at work here about the relationship between sexual desire (homosexuality) and identification (bonding with women) and between public consort with women (the appearance of heterosexuality) and private sex with men (the reality of homosexuality). The tenacity of this understanding occupies a special place in circulations of the queerness of Almodóvar and his work. When the subject of Maura, or Abril, or the male to female transsexual Bibi Andersen, arises in media discussion of the writer/director they are invariably positioned as his consort, despite a consensual assumption about his (homo)sexuality. Indeed this director–muse relationship is offered as being emblematic and constitutive of that sexuality.

It appears that in the manner in which the subject of Almodóvar is addressed in gay and lesbian, and mainstream liberal press, the terms of this relationship between the writer/director's sexuality and his identification with women are contested, and that complex tensions are being played out, not only between sexual orientation and gender identification, but also around the conditions of liberal public tolerance. As we can see, Almodóvar is a compelling subject for the analysis of heterosocial affiliations. The ways in which he is handled by both the queer and mainstream press suggest a conventional awareness of the cultural and political significance of gay men's relationships with women. It is also clear that the two contexts through which critical discourse about Almodóvar circulates have radically different agendas, but the ambiguous status of homosexuality in Almodóvar's work and pronouncements raises similar problems for both discourses; problems that are ultimately a function of the liberal–intellectual contexts both inhabit.

For straight liberal commentators the problem arises out of a need to balance the funky perversity of films like *Kika* or *Matador* or *Law of Desire* that is sold as a function of Almodóvar's homosexuality, with the danger of too fully instating the writer/director's work as queer and thus as potentially troubling. Obviously labelling him as queer is important, as we have seen, both for making him kinky and interesting *enough* and for keeping that weirdness at bay, different from heterosexual normality. Here the more outlandish elements of Almodóvar's films can be a function of his perversity; however if he is made too perverse, too strangely non-heterosexual then that queerness becomes threatening and may begin to speak for itself. The consumption of kinky queer culture within a liberal context can thus be seen as something of a faultline within hegemonic arrangements of gender. One key strategy that seems to be used to lessen the anxiety around the faultline, particularly for apparently liberal males, who of course must assimilate queerness within their privileged cosmopolitan millieu with some measure of homosocial panic, is to profile Almodóvar's association or consort with women. Here his strangeness is maintained (he is kinky and hangs out with women all the time, and not with other men, as a properly unified homosocial subject would) but it is a de-sexualized queerness rendered cute and furry because it emphasizes how sensitive and glamorous he is: note the comparisons with a raft of 'European bad boys', all fashion designers and pop stars. In an article in the *Guardian*, Nigel Floyd suggests that

> [Maura and Almodóvar's] partnership seemed made in heaven, Maura's earthy beauty bringing flesh and blood reality to her roles as a bongo-playing nun in *Dark Habits* or a transvestite [sic.] in *Law of Desire*. Yet, like Diego and Maria in *Matador*, their partnership burned brightest at precisely that moment when they began to eclipse one another.[8]

Here, under the sign of divine normality ('made in heaven') Floyd suggests that the director–muse relationship of Almodóvar and Maura is symmetrical to that of a pair of (albeit perversely) heterosexual lovers. Moreover, her earthly beauty, her body, realises his mind, his vision. Thus for Floyd, not only are Maura and Almodóvar an honorary heterosexual couple, but the constitution of their roles within that *menage* coincides with traditional hetero-patriarchal understandings of women as physical and men as cerebral, with women bearing the physical marks of men's cognition. Such accounts make queer Almodóvar available for less anxious consumption by straight, liberal *Guardian* readers; for, although his world view is slightly naughty and dangerously daring (transvestites, bongo-playing nuns, lovers who have a death wish and so on) he can be tolerated, enjoyed even, in Floyd's view because his perspective reflects heterosexual arrangements – even aspires towards them. Afterall, Elizabeth Taylor and Richard Burton, with or without the jewels, were for the time an engagingly daring example of heterosexual coupledom. Grandiose liberal tolerance is secured through an assimilation of the gay director Pedro Almodóvar into the diversely cosmopolitan culture covered in the pages of the *Guardian*, while the values and world view of that urban liberal milieu are protected from any challenge Almodóvar's homosexuality may pose, because, through Floyd's eyes, that homosexuality merely recreates heterosexual models after all. Almodóvar's sexuality is thus rendered only partially visible: implicit and connotated, but not represented in and of itself; what is available to reassure *Guardian* readers that it really is safe to assimilate the wild and outrageous director is a succession of couplings which are rendered so as to ape a publicly hetero-'sexual' orientation: Pedro and Bibi, Pedro and Rosy (de Palma), Pedro and Carmen, Pedro and Victoria. This strategy of assimilation relies on a residual post-Wolfenden structure in which public and private behaviours are separated, one begetting a voyeuristic fascination with the other, while the public front confers reassurances about matters of identity: this is one way in which the liberal slippage towards a reactionary position is effected. Michelangelo Signorile notes this formation, as we have already seen: discomfort around homosexuality is masked, suppressed, in liberal media by 'sympathy for gays' "right to privacy".'⁹

This privileging by liberal discourses of public behaviour in matters relating to the constitution of sexuality attempts to resecure any public behaviour in which heterosexuality itself is not *actively* problematized – thus Almodóvar's private sexual object–choice can become secondary to his public and productive association with women in the minds of the *Guardian*'s tolerant readers. The *laissez-faire* voyeuristic attraction broadsheet analysis has for Almodóvar is insufficiently agile even to attempt to secure him for a radical context or agenda, even if they were disposed to do so. Given the dominance of heterosexual arrangements even the complexly mediated public/private boundaries still operate to privilege public, formalized structures of sexuality: family, marriage, engagement, courtship, parenting, romance and so on, and repress abnormal, problematic arrangements – or at least express them through the filters of condescension and voyeurism that is liberalism. Post-Wolfenden 'toleration' of homosexuality has constituted the notion of the 'private' as a means of control through which the alternative is consigned to invisibility and covert control, and the public realm is normalised – alternatives appearing as just that: *alternatives* to normality – wild and daring spectacles always contextualised within frameworks of propriety. This privileging of public space acts as a sign system which structures private behaviour and identity: public participation connotes normality which presumes private obeisance. The liberal tolerance of the 'enlightened' chattering classes moderates this post-Wolfenden model, in that the public realm does not need to be continually purged of homosexuality: does not need to be closeted in other words, but the strategy still has some currency. If queer Almodóvar can be shown to be preoccupied with such reassuringly normal activities as public consort with women, from within the very site of his wild and perverse world (afterall, the women he bonds with constitute the repertory company of actors in his movies, his work), then not only does the idea of homosexuality not appear threatening, it actually appears to offer an amusing and novel view of one's own normality. Thus, we can see how this cosmopolitan liberalism is a ventriloquization of more authoritative and reactionary interests; it exhibits a slippage away from a sponsorship of radical arrangements, towards a reconfirmation of mainstream hetero-patriarchal models.

From a queer perspective the existence within straight culture of such disparate, conflicting, positions as those represented by the *Sun* and the *Guardian*, for example, enables further control – making assimilation by lesbians and gay men to the latter's powerful, and apparently liberal culture (and clearly bits of it are liberal, or at least ventriloquize liberalism effectively) attractive over the former's truculent reactionism. After all, pandering to the tolerant world of disengaged cosmopolitan liberalism has its benefits: in Britain the assimilationist Stonewall lobbying group hosts an annual Equality show. In late 1994 this event was held at the Albert Hall, where the audience were entertained by the likes of Elton John, Sting, Richard Gere and Alison Moyet; also in attendance, with his wife, was the newly elected leader of the Labour party, the ultra-moderate social democrat, Tony Blair. Hobnobbing with such luminaries feels like validation, even if it is under the terms of liberal humanist consensus – particularly in contrast to the rabid hate-mongering of tabloids like the *Sun*. On the other hand such active foregrounding of queer culture as queer (in this particular space the labelling is necessary to secure the smug reassurance of toleration, unlike other appropriations of queer culture into the mainstream, in which it is unnecessary and inappropriate to identify the origin of the particular artefacts being plundered) brings the work of someone like Almodóvar into relief on a wide scale, foregrounding the ever possible threat that through that visibility he will be associated with challenging meanings – hence the need to attempt to assert stringent control over the circulation of his work in the very same liberal broadsheets which valorize him in the first place.

Queer opportunities

The recuperation of Almodóvar by liberals strategically highlights his relationships with women, and so the terms through which we may handle his heterosocial opportunities are potentially traumatic and are certainly highly mediated by heterosexual hostility, however valorizing and celebratory such hostility at first appears. It would seem that there are two substantial difficulties facing those of us who would wish to disrupt the liberal assimilation of Almodóvar for heterosexual voyeurism so that we may address the queer and dissident possibilities in his work. The first of these is the director's own insistence upon addressing the mainstream, his desire to be a universally addressed artist and his consequent reticence about queer self-identification. Paul Burston, an Almodóvar apologist, notes that the director himself, 'has always maintained that he hates "obvious homosexual expressions", even going as far as to suggest that the homosexual relationship in *Law of Desire* could just as easily have been a heterosexual one.'[10] As we have seen, Robert Chalmers's *Observer* piece contains an instance of Almodóvar's frustration with being 'always "the gay director Pedro Almodóvar"' (p. 24). In an interview in *Out* Almodóvar tells Brad Gooch, 'I could be married in two years, and I don't want anyone saying nothing against that. To be gay is not something that determines my life. It's a part, but not the most important part.'[11] When *The Flower of my Secret* was released in England, *The Pink Paper* ran an article on Almodóvar entitled 'Pedro's Love of Ladies' which draws heavily on general understandings that Almodóvar maintains a special relationship with women in his films. However Mansel Stimpson, the author of the piece, goes on to express disappointment about Almodóvar's attitude to his homosexuality:

> In 1994 his comments made it clear that the man who, as writer and director, brought us such sexually explicit films as *Law of Desire* and *Tie Me Up! Tie Me Down!* was something of a conservative in his attitudes towards being gay. . . . What is clear is that he is particularly apprehensive of the American attitude, which treats sexuality as a label. He sees the tag of 'gay artist' as constricting, and is relieved that gay sensibility is discussed much less in Spain than in the US or over here.[12]

These ambivalences make it difficult for us to be confident that Almodóvar is actually addressing us as a queer constituency. As we have seen, potential anxiety about Almodóvar's sexuality can be allayed by highlighting a reassuring association with women: therefore our second problem in assimilating Almodóvar for heterosocial purposes is that when such hegemonic control has been effected, the meanings attached to the writer/director's work can be moulded, corrupted, reworked. We are then faced with not only the prospect that Almodóvar's heterosocial expressions will become disseminated as heterosexual expressions through media that we are encouraged to feel allegiances with, but also with the prospect of that heterosocial representation becoming understood as misogyny.

In a promotional brochure produced by the UK video distributors of Almodóvar's movies in the run-up to 1994's Yuletide season of consumption, *Pepi, Luci, Bom and Other Girls on the Heap* is described as telling the story of a 'group of women living in a punk-inspired Madrid [who] encounter...the will to forge strong female friendships.' The copy goes on:

> Many find this kind of female bonding and oppression, portrayed through a gay man's sensibility, contradictory in Almodóvar's films. His flamboyance and fluctuations between humour and offensiveness, however, makes the questioning part of the journey.

Here the disclaimer that Almodóvar's view of women is the function of a gay man's sensibility seems to precisely address the cosmopolitan, liberal audience I have been locating: knowledge of the writer/director's sexuality adds kudos to watching his films, while the wacky offensiveness, flamboyance and fluctuations – all codes for the camply hysterical artistic temperament in line with understandings of both the Latin disposition and the effeminate homosexual one – invite a voyeuristic spectacle of satisfyingly grandiose proportions. Almodóvar's *enfant terrible* reputation is something of a bonus for this cosmopolitan audience: rendering a potentially politically incorrect landscape without the hazards of illiberal complicity. In the Almodóvarian world women are oppressed by punk lesbians who piss on them, husbands who smack them around, mentally unstable sex-gods with whom they fall in love while (literally) in enforced bondage, priests in the name of whose love they have become 'women', porn stars who rape them and trash TV that offers up rape as voyeuristic spectacle.

Yet for those who would wish to engage with Almodóvar's work in a more ingenuously radical context, rather than the assimilationism of *Guardian*-culture *faux* radicalism, the issue of the filmmaker's apparent outrageous fluctuations is crucial: clearly it is not satisfactory to sponsor the assimilation of an overt misogynist. Rose Collis, former film reviewer for Britain's *Gay Times*, says of the rape scene in *Kika*:

> But is Almodóvar merely being 'misogynist' – a charge often levelled against him in the past – or is he daring us to find it funny, despite its horror...[13]

Uncharacteristically, British queer journalist Paul Burston makes an acute assessment of Almodóvar's predicament when he says:

> It is worth noting that the straight male critics so quick to point a finger at Almodóvar are usually the same straight male critics who

rush to defend the misogynistic pleasures of your average Hollywood boys' own adventure. And, of course the sensational coverage generated by such scenes tends to distract us from the fact that Almodóvar's films are often a celebration of powerful women.[14]

The price of liberal assimilation is that homosexual culture risks speaking for that liberalism and not for itself: as I have suggested, the sponsorship of Almodóvar by the responsible press may satisfy the conditions of middle class aspirant intellectual liberalism, but it also offers us the opportunity to exploit such visibility for more radical ends. Thus it is important to represent these negotiations as a dialectic: the liberal press have not had a consistently valorizing view of Almodóvar; as his fame has spread, and his *enfant terrible* reputation has become more celebrated, it appears that there has been a concurrent need to question the political and personal appropriateness of the writer/director within the very liberal space in which he acquired visibility. The excess and schlock melodrama celebrated in *Women on the Verge of a Nervous Breakdown* and *Tie Me Up! Tie Me Down!* were lamented as absent from *High Heels* and lambasted as being too excessive, too politically compromising in *Kika*. It is worth noting that film critics, those pundits who make film their especial concern in more specialized periodicals such as *Sight and Sound* in Britain, unfold yet another narrative of Almodóvar's oeuvre, in which it is the films before the first truly commercial offering, *Women on the Verge of a Nervous Breakdown*, which had a 'fresh and challenging vision'; latterly Almodóvar's 'growing sense of professionalism has resulted in a worrying lack of edge, emotional or otherwise.'[15] Such accounts do suggest an insider's expert smugness, but lend an authority to more mainstream, liberal accounts which appear to appropriate the terms of this relationship between Almodóvar's increasing success and popularity and an inverse sense of his worth. As a particularly fraught and contested feature of Almodóvar's work, it is in relation to the faultline representation of women that later liberal questioning has taken place in order to effect hegemonic exclusion of the writer/director.

Clearly it seems that the stress heterosexual, mainstream critics (presumably the audience Almodóvar wants to address for fear of becoming a 'gay artist') place on his relationships with women can also serve more explicitly homophobic purposes than the ability to consume, safely and voyeuristically his wacky and cute queerness. As we have seen with Tennessee Williams, critics who speak from a position of unmediated dominance within hetero-patriarchal systems take

particular relish in bringing attention to the misogyny of gay male heterosocial activity. As I noted, Stanley Kauffman accuses Williams of
'viciousness towards women ... lurid violence that seems a sublimation
of social hatreds', which of course enables Kauffman to have his cake
and gleefully eat it: displaying his own parochial, fatherly concern for
possible oppression of the fairer sex at the same time as manifesting his
own unsublimated hatred of the homosocial abject, particularly when it
is attempting heterosocially to circumvent that homosociality.[16] This
has become something of a standard strategy, and the recuperative
patriarchal impediment at work in Kauffman could surely be seen in
Robert Chalmers's boorish anxiety when he writes of Almodóvar for the
Observer.[17] Chalmers's article, 'Pedro on the Verge of a Nervous Breakdown?' unfolds his own fantasy narrative of Almodóvar's oeuvre in
which '*Kika* is a return to the early Almodóvar formula of shock-
melodrama, a tired strategy which is bound to produce diminishing
returns' (p. 26). This diminishing artistic bite is accompanied, in
Chalmers's fantasy, by the writer/director's increasing petulance and
impatience. Almodóvar's apparent resentment over the interference of
'Anglo-Saxons' becomes not only a marker of his artistic temperament
(itself a not very subtle indication of a pejorative homosexuality), but
an opportunity to instate ideological framing around undifferentiated
and suspicious outsiders. Chalmers lumps together non-Anglo-Saxon
Spaniards, denizens of 'foreign art-house productions', intellectuals,
typified by Paul Julian Smith and the unnamed writer of 'Is the Rectum
a Grave?' and badly behaved gay men (those who compere competi-
tions such as 'General Erections' Chalmers cites from *Pepi, Luci, Bom and
other Girls on the Heap*), in a move which reseals an Anglo-Saxon ethnic
hegemony.

It seems ironic that the exclusion of Smith's overly intellectual (read
effeminate) discourse of diversity is effected through the authoritative
instatement of Spanish homophobia by quoting the *Guardian*'s former
Madrid correspondent. Even at the moment at which Chalmers's jingo-
ism requires him to suggest that Spanish society is more homophobic
than 'ours', any murmur of alignment with homosexuality is displaced
by the confidently hegemonic assertion that '*almost all readers* are likely
to find some unfamiliar material in *Desire Unlimited*'s reading list'.
(p. 26, emphasis added) Thus an inside group of unquestioning liberalism
is invoked, a reassuringly inclusive consensus, unless you happen to be
Spanish, or one who is 'unfamiliar': these are the outsiders through whom
Chalmers's cultural superiority becomes stated, and through whom
Almodóvar becomes identified as a kind of Norma Desmond-cum-Dorian

Gray figure, a pitiable parody of itself, an ageing drag queen whose earlier excesses and debaucheries are taking their toll, and whose lack of normality (non-Anglo-Saxon, homosexual) is leaving him artistically spent, past the gimmick of 'shock-melodrama'. In Chalmers's criminally irony-free fantasy Almodóvar 'on the Verge of a Nervous Breakdown' is frustrated and lonely, but petulant and consoling himself in attempted normality in the pseudo-marriage with the pseudo-woman Bibi Andersen.

Women on the verge of queer sistership?

Women on the Verge of a Nervous Breakdown (1988) is Almodóvar's most successful and famous film. Paul Julian Smith, probably the most widely published 'expert' on Almodóvar is quite emphatic about what I would call the film's heterosociality:

> Almodóvar has been punished by male critics for placing himself so consistently on the side of the woman (on the side of sentiment and of spectacle). In spite of its success, *Mujeres* was awarded neither the Spanish Goya for best director nor the Oscar for best foreign-language film: the prizes went to more 'serious' (more 'masculine') works. While actual women may not thank Almodóvar for his over-identification with feminine stereotypes which they may well wish to challenge, there is cause to welcome that boundary confusion brought about by his cinematic narcissism. It suggests an unfixing of identities (both sexual and national) which can only tend to support that feminism which is committed to social and psychic change.[18]

Yet what form does that heterosocial representation take? How would Smith resolve the tension between his understanding that the film is something feminism should welcome when women may wish to challenge it? Smith is keen to identify Almodóvar as a 'glitch' in the cinematic system because he is 'a Spanish director who has achieved international renown; an openly gay director known for his love of women'; but can such an ambiguously self-presented homosexual deliver the boundary confusion that causes the disturbance of critics in the 'over-identification of a filmmaker with the women in his films.'?[19]

As we have seen, many reactionary straight liberal responses to Almodóvar's work precisely emphasize his interest in women because this brings his imputed queerness into a heterosexual frame, displaying his consort with women as a token of his sensitivity to soften and allow unfettered consumption of his outrageousness. It is clear, then, that the opportunities for claiming Almodóvar as a queer or heterosocially heroic figure are fraught and unstable because our responses are filtered through complex contextual considerations.[20] However, it is because Almodóvar's work lies at such a hectic intersection of ideological, political and representational concerns that his films are so interesting and the stakes so high.

Women on the Verge of a Nervous Breakdown opens with a voice-over by Pepa (Carmen Maura) who tells us that she moved to her apartment with Iván when, for her, the world was falling apart and she wanted to save it, acting like Noah by bringing couples of animals to live on her terrace. She adds that she was not able to save the couple she cared about most, her and Iván. The camera pans down a shape of candy-pink material to a mass of tousled brunette locks. We realise that Pepa is asleep and dreaming, and the shot cuts to a terrace, rendered in dream-like monochrome. We get our first look at Iván and he is a function of Pepa's subconscious. The first thing he does is use fresh breath spray, he then walks along a terrace past a succession of diversely exotic women and speaks a number of melodramatic romantic insincerities ('I cannot live without you') to each as he advances. He is speaking into an elaborate 1950s-style microphone and his voice sounds fragmented, non-naturalistically mechanised. We are immediately presented with a number of contrasts: between Pepa, fuschia pink, intimately voiced and Iván, dully monochrome, vocally artificial and disembodied: Pepa, present in the film's diegetic reality (albeit asleep); Iván a fantasy, a figment of Pepa's imagination. As the opening tableau of Pepa's subconscious gives way to the film's narrative these contrasts become a structuring dynamic. Emotionally Iván's abandonment and irresponsible cruelty are all too proximate for Pepa, leading her to the verge of the title's breakdown; yet physically Iván is elusive, insubstantial, even ephemeral, as Pepa's verging leads her through a farcical series of near-misses and coincidences through which contact with the caddish Iván eludes her. Although *Women on the Verge of a Nervous Breakdown* does not maintain the first person narrative position of the immediate post-opening credit sequence, where we share Pepa's intimate reflections and see her dream directly through her 'eyes', the film nevertheless maintains an equivalence between Pepa's experience within the narrative and our own experience as the audience. As Iván is elusive to Pepa, so he is elusive to us, and we share her frustration at his duplicity and slipperiness. As Pepa wakes from her dream of Iván he is leaving her a message on her answering machine; she runs to the telephone, but is too late. We hear his disembodied voice as she does: the film avoiding a customary cut to Iván leaving the message at his end of the phone. She rings the studio where they work, but he has already left.

Within the narrative of the film, Pepa and Iván are actors. Before Pepa goes to work, we see her with the doctor, who tells her that she is pregnant. Later, at work, Pepa is dubbing her voice onto the soundtrack of *Johnny Guitar*. As we join her, she is the Spanish voice of Joan Crawford in a scene where Crawford's Vienna is having a confrontation with her leading man, played by Sterling Hayden, who has the Spanish voice of Iván, who has dubbed his lines earlier. Pepa's performance of Crawford-as-Vienna runs alongside Crawford's, and their words of barely controlled passion are part of a narrative of desertion and ill treatment at the hands of Iván-as-Hayden-as-Johnny Guitar. So, to the script of a film rife with troubled signification (of Crawford's iconic star quality, of recuperated feminist resistance, of pathological lesbian desire – all of which have activated considerable subcultural queer investment) we watch Carmen Maura acting the role of Pepa as she negotiates the trauma of performing in a film which commentates on the feminine subjection she is experiencing in our film as romantic victim in her relationship with Iván. This deliberate breaking of cinematic naturalism is a powerful device that Almodóvar has also used in *Law of Desire*. This device of filmic refraction has an intensified ironic effect for foreign audiences of *Women on the Verge of a Nervous Breakdown*, particularly English speaking ones, given that Crawford and Hayden's drama in *Johnny Guitar* is enacted in English. As we participate in the literal translation, through over-dubbing, of a cultural text into a new context, the original and familiar artefact of *Johnny Guitar*'s drama becomes especially contingent, potentially inauthentic, and this adds greater impact to our sense of Pepa producing a self-conscious, narrativized effect of herself in her role within a familiar patriarchal drama of male indifference and female suffering. To underline the effect, Pepa is overcome and faints.

Yet even in the midst of such female suffering, a suffering we masochistically share in our principal identification with Pepa, Iván remains elusive, disembodied, a mechanized effect equivalent to the iconic fiction of Crawford or Hayden on the screen in the studio Pepa is working in, while our heroine is present, corporeal, passionate. Her femininity, her suffering, the part she plays in response to male heterosexual infidelity and mistreatment, that is a performance, an act, scripted by her role as a heterosexual woman. Unlike Iván's insincerity which brokers his power and freedom as a man – his refusal to step into the world of emotions and responsibility, Pepa's role-playing is a sign of her entrapment. Crucially, it seems that the representation of Pepa suggests a self-conscious awareness of her performance, especially in the scene where she is overdubbing Crawford, and her fainting suggests that it is the strain of maintaining her performance of stoic powerlessness, in the face of male brutality and refusal to engage emotionally, that produces female hysteria. Hysteria here is an effect of lack of choice. The self-consciousness of Pepa's professional acting allows us to think of her relationship with Iván as a role where she knows she is following a script, but manifests hysterical frustration that she cannot find another one to follow.

This de-naturalization of Pepa's performance of the wronged woman shows how this role is about repressing the effects of mistreatment, maintaining wounded silence, suffering but not hitting back, retaining passivity because men maintain power. Ironically this suggestion of the role-playing necessary to sustain women's position, allied to the Pepa-centred narrative and scopic organization of *Women on the Verge of a Nervous Breakdown*, has the effect of rendering women as more real than men. Iván is but a mechanised, disembodied refraction, potentially damaging, but not present, he displays no self-consciousness, no acknowledgement of role-playing, he is but the voice of absent authority: there is nothing behind the role, no emotional engagement. If hysteria is a sign of the strain of maintaining the role of powerlessness, then I would suggest that *Women on the Verge of a Nervous Breakdown* eventually exploits the faultline such hysteria represents, fashioning it into a gender dissidence which attempts to refuse male control, male rationality.

This sense of women's realness in contrast to the refracted absence, the empty signification of Iván, pervades the film. The receptionist at the studio is interfering and nosy, the pharmacist Pepa goes to for illicit sleeping pills has a lurid pink face from a cosmetic treatment mask she is trying, while the other women in the chemist's shop gossip, commenting rudely on how Pepa doesn't look as good as she does on television. Iván's estranged wife, Lucía, maintains a stolid fury throughout, telling Pepa to 'fuck off'. Women are real and colourful, their insults, judgements and motivations are up front, delivered honestly and unconsciously. Iván is but a monochromatic mask of honeyed subterfuge, he tells Pepa's answering machine 'I don't deserve your kindness' yet he hurts her. Thus far it does seem that *Women on the Verge of a Nervous Breakdown* delivers a conventional patriarchal narrative of relationship breakdown: women emote passionately, occupying the physical space as ciphers of suffering, while masculinity remains emotionally elusive, never really a part of the breakdown, but utterly instrumental, constitutive even, of female behaviour within it. Iván's masculinity is but a parody of patriarchal faithlessness as he exchanges Lucía for Pepa, Pepa for Paulina.

The woman's film as gay film?

The key disjunction with which *Women* initially modulates these conventions is that it offers us little choice but to identify and valorise the corporeal, hysterical space Pepa occupies. Not only is Pepa the film's only significant protagonist, but events and perspectives are continually skewed to portray her affectionately. *Women on the Verge of a Nervous Breakdown* appears to encourage us to revel in the masochistic experience of identifying with such hysteria and emotional trauma. Psychoanalytic film theory, which has represented a powerful, and often residual, phase in the evolution of cinematic studies, would suggest that the organisation of the cinematic frame protects an imputed male spectator from castration anxieties that the narratively subjugated woman embodies; this organisation elicits a sadistic gaze upon the woman which punishes and controls her. The valorised masochistic collusion which *Women on the Verge of a Nervous Breakdown* encourages seems quite different to such sadistic spectatorship. Here the slipperiness and elusivity of Iván acts not only to centralize Pepa in the narrative, but actually makes an identification with a patriarchal representative in the text elusive as well: Iván has an insubstantial textual presence. In this (as in many formal considerations of genre and mode) *Women on the Verge of a Nervous Breakdown* offers a striking contrast to *Pulp Fiction* in its scopic organization and narrative representation of gender. As we saw earlier, *Pulp Fiction* offers aspirant patriarchal spectatorship diverse iconographies of hip masculinity with which to align, and for good measure a couple of abject queers for the purposes of counter-identification; women are mere homosocial foils for male display and exchange. In *Pulp Fiction* the manifestation of women's punishment for embodying the threat of castration doesn't merely reside in the organisation of a sadistic and controlling gaze, but is narratively and comically glorified in the punishment of women, such as in the scene where Vincent administers a terrifying and piercingly phallic injection to Mia's heart with a foot long needle.

We could suggest that *Women on the Verge of a Nervous Breakdown*'s sponsorship of our masochistic identification displaces the sadistic, patriarchal gaze, the object of which is to control castration anxiety, and replaces it with a queered gaze, one which aligns our spectatorship with Almodóvar's heterosocial affiliation with Maura/Pepa: the actress his publicly acceptable consort, the character his own creation. This reading of *Women on the Verge of a Nervous Breakdown* would seem to be compatible with Mary Ann Doane's notion of the woman's film, a genre with a lavish history of gay subcultural investment.[21] Doane suggests that the woman's film attempts to constitute female subjectivity and desire through the sponsorship of fantasies associated with the feminine: masochism, hysteria, paranoia and neurosis. Gay male audiences have tended to access the pleasures of the so-called woman's film through the vehicle of star adoration and identification: witness the cultish veneration of Bette Davis, Joan Crawford, Barbara Stanwyck and others, that has come to define camp spectatorship. We could argue that historically the loose and sometimes vague genre of the woman's film has provided as much pleasure in resistant subjectivity to gay male audiences as it has to female ones.[22] Indeed many of the characteristics of the woman's film have been appropriated as substantial components of gay male gender resistance, although the issue of appropriation is a complex one. The discursive and subcultural association of gay men with landmark woman's films such as *Mildred Pierce*, *Sylvia Scarlet*, *Now, Voyager* and *A Star is Born* could be interpreted as appropriative of what is essentially women's cultural space, but this is a troubled, problematic interpretation.

Clearly the canon of women's films can be significant in many contexts simultaneously and one need not negate another; nor are there substantial institutionalized power differences between constituencies of gay men and of heterosexual women such that either may have the power to enforce the true reading on the other: both are empowered and disempowered in different, but often symmetrical ways, as I have been discussing. An important inducement to the investment gay men have made in woman's films is the understanding about the homosexuality of key Hollywood personnel involved in their production. The homosexuality of George Cukor, the pre-eminent woman's director, has been subculturally appreciated for many years: in *Hollywood Babylon* Kenneth Anger recounts how Clark Gable had Cukor fired from *Gone With the Wind* because he was homophobic and Patrick McGilligan's biography, *A Double Life* recounts the same narrative.[23]

We do not need to fall back on an idea of some essential gay sensibility to see the significance of Cukor's sexuality to gay men's investment in his movies. Camp spectatorship and the parodic, excessive overdetermination it sponsors provides an iconography of reading traces for queer audiences, destabilizing naturalizing discourses and representations with an excess of authenticity, an ironic subversion or an insistence on surfaces and performativity, artificiality. That mode of reading, whether its purpose is to find especial messages or meanings, or merely the presence of another like mind, has been a crucial part of gay subcultural activity through pre- and post-Stonewall periods back to the turn of the century, and possibly before if we accept Rictor Norton's thesis about the mollies (notwithstanding doubts about the continuity of molly culture).[24]

As was discussed in the opening sections, our notions of queerness or homosexuality are constituted and contested through our interaction with subcultures. In the case of George Cukor and the woman's films that came out of postwar Hollywood, it seems fair to say that not only are they the bearers of gay subcultural investment, but that they display and communicate reading traces that exhibit an awareness of subcultural activity that is inherent in the production. Gay men do not have a genetic predisposition to be interested in women, femininity and glamour (many of us, alas, show little interest in such trappings) but these are things that our gay subcultural alignments show us have been important to gay men, and may give us clues as to where we may look for similar gay men to ourselves in a culture that often necessitates our closetedness and discretion. Other gay men in other parts of the subculture, may be in different temporal or spatial locations, with access to the means of cultural production, in filmmaking, art or music, may also lay the foundations of such reading traces as expressions of their interests and also as signposts to other queers and friends in the know. That these markers of camp spectatorship may offer the opportunity for gender dissent, or heterosocial affiliation by gay men, only makes our political and historical investment, as well as our reading skills, more acute. Of course, it remains to be seen whether such queer reading traces fulfil their heterosocial potential politically, but such activity is neither the expression of our essential empathy with femininity, nor of our essential proclivity towards pro-feminism or a progressive gender politics – though it may be.

In *Women on the Verge of a Nervous Breakdown* as in *Now, Voyager*, women's emotional excess may be venerated within the fictional worldorder that is the cinematic diegesis and thus offer gay male audiences camp reading traces; but such feminine hysteria remains meaningful within wider patriarchal culture as a mark of not having control. It is here that tensions between the reading strategies of gay men, and of women, may appear, particularly when gay men may precipitate the celebration of filmic imagery that marks, however sublimely, women's powerlessness in heterosexual relations with men. Of course, the most successful of these films will be those that position such emotional excess as rebellion, as wilfully and determinedly outside the ambit of homosocial authority. Maria LaPlace has made a convincing reading of *Now, Voyager* which integrates understandings of Bette Davis as star icon with feminist film criticism and suggests that the film offers 'a symbolic system in which women can try to make sense of their lives and even create imaginative spaces for resistance, a system which the film ... enters despite itself.'[25]

The concession with which LaPlace concludes her account suggests a degree of selection that makes her reading plausible: this is valuable strategic practice. Clearly the woman's film has a vexed history of meanings for women, regardless of any subcultural activity on the part of gay men. Hollywood aggressively produced and marketed woman's pictures to fulfil what was understood to be a dominant share of cinema audiences, and they have remained enormously powerful sources of pleasure and pride, but also difficulty, as Jeanine Basinger encapsulates:

> the woman's film reminds women that they have a biological function related to their role as women ... love is their true job ... the movies prettied up the woman's biological function as love. ... Over and over again the answer to the question of what a woman should do with herself was wrapped in shiny paper and presented as love.[26]

Consuming women in woman's films as objects for the experience of love, as bearers of romantic pleasure and romantic pain at the hands of men, may be relatively unproblematic for gay male spectatorship, which isn't undermined by being located so far outside authoritative male homosocial subjectivity. Indeed, as I have been arguing, queer heterosocial affiliations precisely strive to achieve this distance from powerful, masculine homosocial formations and revel in such romantic and emotional representation.

However, the meanings of potential identification with emotionally flamboyant, excessively feminine women are different for lesbian and for straight female spectators than they are for gay male ones. For gay men such representations of women are anti-masculine, they are role models for acts of dissent against dominant codes of maleness that gay men are forced to inhabit, and then are punished for inhabiting queerly. Such identifications attempt to reimagine homosexual identity as something other than a mechanism for purifying and policing homosocial power structures with which women are patriarchally exploited and gay men are despised. For straight women, such representation of valorized hysteria may authenticate their experiences of heterosexuality and womanhood as subjects of homosocial activity, by offering sisterly collusion and images of poised transcendence, but ultimately they lock women into heterosexual suffrage – glamorous, gutsy, but still suffering, still gaining cultural privilege by virtue of their subjection to men.[27] For lesbians, such material seems to be unsatisfying in that it confirms a feminine and powerless position women are already forced to inhabit in relation to men. As lesbianism is precisely about resisting participation in relations with men and certainly ones which follow the patriarchal script of heterosexuality, the opportunity to identify with victimized heterosexual women, however glamorous their suffering, is going to be pretty meaningless. As Paula Graham has argued, gay men may be punished within masculine subjectivity, but lesbians are excluded from it:

> femininity is, after all, a relatively privileged category from which lesbians are excluded, but which is also, for women, a mark of subordination to masculine authority, and not a form of resistance to it. ... Even 'excessive' femininity ... still seems to have considerably less appeal to lesbian audiences that to gay male audiences.[28]

So, in the context of gay male culture, I am suggesting that spectacles of female emotional excess act as reading traces, opportunities that we learn about through our membership of gay subcultures, for our anti-homosocial identification. Sometimes these reading traces are a function of gay subcultural investment on the part of producers or directors, and they can act as a nod and a wink to gay audiences conversant with the codes of camp spectatorship. However, even though such identifications may evade complicity with a sadistic patriarchal gaze, the disparity between gay male, straight female, and lesbian readings of such ecstatic masochistic identification may disrupt the heterosocial potential of camp spectatorship; this is not necessarily because such disparity invalidates gay male practice, but because this difference marks ideological tensions. The adoration of spectacles of female emotional excess, where that excess is the breaching of rationality and containment, is an important part of gay male cultural vernacular, but beyond its value as a subcultural language, a kind of community glue, we need to be sensitive to the particular ways in which we line up these identifications with our homosexuality.

Edward II: queer homosociality?

An illustration of these difficulties can be found in the late Derek
Jarman's film *Edward II*, which was released in 1991, but got caught up
in the excitement about so-called New Queer Cinema in 1992 with the
release of *The Hours and Times, Swoon, The Living End, RSVP* and the new
wave of queer activism aimed at *Basic Instinct* and *Silence of the Lambs*.[29]
Edward II is a very striking film for a number of reasons bound up with
Jarman's retelling of Marlowe's drama in the context of Thatcherite
Britain, and the emerging queer politics typified by the newly formed
activist group, Outrage!; Jarman himself writes in notes in the published script, that it sets out to represent a gay love affair by taking 'a
dusty old play and violat[ing] it.'[30] This modernisation of a Renaissance
narrative produces a number of incoherences which would seem to be out
of step with Jarman's apparently radical queerness, which in *Edward II*
seems very much lined up against the gentry and the bourgeoisie,
both of whom are modelled on Thatcherite archetypes: the yuppie, suited
businessman, the handbag-clutching Tory housewife from middle-
England and the crisply khakied SAS-style soldier. Not the least of these
ruptures the film exhibits is that the site of our heroic queerness is in
the heart of the monarchy. The film makes it clear that the ideology of
respectability upheld by state apparatus is incompatible with queerness,
but Edward and Gaveston's continual anxious mediation between gay
love and royal duty somewhat overshadows more radical possibilities of
the new queer agenda. Jarman's own outspoken attitude to his homosexuality and his HIV status made him something of a hero, certainly
for British queer activists (in September 1991 he was canonised by the
Sisters of Perpetual Indulgence), yet Jarman's work as an artist and filmmaker owes more to traditions of bohemian high art classicism than it
does to street politics.

However, *Edward II* is particularly compelling in its handling of camp
spectatorship, and for the way in which it positions gay men and
straight women in adversarial relations. As we might expect, the film is
visually stunning, with most scenes being rendered as painterly tableau,
the characters vividly displayed in front of minimalist stone backdrops.
Each shot displays iconically precise composition, with skin and fabrics,
blood and water, lit to highlight their form and texture, always displayed with a sensitivity to the spectacle of detail. By far the most complex and richly displayed spectacle in *Edward II* is that of Queen Isabella
(Tilda Swinton), Edward's wife. In each of her scenes Isabella shimmers,
resplendent in a succession of fabulous outfits that self-consciously

reference the formulaic excess of female star iconography; in an interview where he talks about *Edward II* in detail, Jarman himself notes that in one particular scene Isabella looks like Joan Crawford, in another that she is a cross between Crawford and Christine Keeler, and in another that she looks like Evita, 'the musical, not the politician'.[31] What have been called a '*Vogue*'s gallery of designer dresses'[32] evoke the spectacles of Audrey Hepburn and Eva Peron, among others, but it isn't just the costumes which plug into such a distinctive visual vernacular, one that has a strong history of gay male identification: crucially it is Tilda Swinton's performance, which manages to capture elements of pastiche and irony but also makes astonishing use of poised stillness that at different points evokes stunned victimisation and sinister evil.

It clearly is not necessary to sift through anecdotal and incidental biographical material in order to situate Jarman as a gay man, but it may be necessary to engage in such subcultural enterprise in order to think about Jarman as the kind of gay man who identifies or aligns himself with women. What becomes clear from Jarman's volumes of memoirs, *Dancing Ledge*, *Modern Nature* and *At Your Own Risk*, is that in his own subcultural milieu he did not have much to do with women at all.[33] The journals suggest a membership of, or movement through, an assortment of artistic cliques, bohemian enclaves and upper- and middle-class gay subcultures, but Jarman's principal interests usually seem to lie in other men, in either sexual or fraternal terms. Clearly the finished product that is the representation of Isabella in *Edward II* is the result of a complex collaboration between the director, his writers, costume designers, photographers, lighting designers, and of course, and not the least Tilda Swinton herself. B. Ruby Rich has noted how 'Tilda Swinton's brilliance as an actor – and full co-creator of her role – invests her character with more weight, and thus more evil, than anyone else on the screen.'[34] I shall return to the issue of evil shortly. At the risk of being overly speculative though, it doesn't seem too bold to suggest that the extent to which Isabella signifies as a camp icon in *Edward II* is an indication of the extent to which such imagery plays a part in urban gay male culture (as understood by Swinton and other workers on the film, as much as by Jarman), rather than an indication of Jarman's own female identification or heterosocial practice. The iconography of the diva or the Hollywood screen siren saturates gay male culture and is naturalized in this context, so that it often functions as a kind of background noise that most men who circulate through urban gay space will be familiar with, even if such representations do not describe or elicit their identification. This familiarity with camp female iconography will also be true for those honorary members of gay subculture – friends, political affiliates, camp followers both male and female, straight–queer chicks and chaps – all of whom may fraternize with gay men and lesbians in gay spaces because the party's funkier, or as a respite from homosocial chauvinism, or as heterosocial political dissent.

One of the most striking images near the beginning of *Edward II*, one notable among many striking images, is of two naked young hustlers who are having sex in Gaveston's bed in France as he receives his call home from Edward. The men themselves represent an iconography of queerness that seems to have become representative of the activist group Outrage!, and the kind of queer politics it represented in Britain in the early 1990s. The men are white, young, smooth and beautiful, their heads are shaved to precision, they are lithe, muscled and masculine, and they are utterly uninhibited, exhibitionistic even, in their sexual practice: in many ways they are a gay ideal that we may aspire to. The couple are also genderless: their matched physicality negating sexual difference, unifying masculinity in a narcissistic union. Not for these two perfect faggots the easy iconography of active and passive that is exhibited in Leo Bersani's reading of Erik and Riton fucking on the roof in Genet's *Funeral Rites*.[35] These studs are raunching around, but their perfectly matched physical type and masculinity, and thrillingly undifferentiated sex acts deflect any understanding of top or bottom or power imbalance, let alone camp spectatorship, effeminacy or female identification. This couple represent one of the ruptures that makes *Edward II* so fascinating. They are an ideal of homosexuality that remains unfulfilled by Edward and Gaveston throughout the film, indeed that they cannot fulfil: the queer hustlers are a product of queer Britain in the 1990s, while Edward and Gaveston are Renaissance sodomites.

Despite their easily identifiable iconographic origins, as possible sites of identification this couple of nameless hustlers have no culture, they are not shown having to integrate their subjectivities and sexuality into a social system, they do not even display the rank and taste that clothes might afford. They are just perfect faggots having a perfect (non)fuck. Their unselfconscious and irony-free eroticism makes a striking contrast to the troubled coupledom of the king and his working-class lover. Edward and Gaveston have vexed conversations riddled with doubt and anxiety, they share the absurdity of constitutional pomp and they share an intimate humour as they dance the tango; but they do not have sex and they do not represent the perfect faggottry of the hustlers who form an ideal of queer sexuality against which we measure Edward and Gaveston. The introduction of the hustlers and the idealization of homosexuality they represent so early in the film allows us to monitor continually the levels of homophobic intervention Edward and Gaveston must overcome in order that they may fulfil that idealisation. However, the hustlers also serve to define homosexuality in purely libidinous terms that efface gender from queerness. This organization of homosexuality becomes more sustained as the narrative of the film develops and Isabella comes to increasingly personify the homophobic obstacles Edward and Gaveston face in becoming perfect queers, where that perfection is a mutual sameness of masculinity. In the book of the film, Jarman celebrates this masculinity, staking his particular claim upon the 'real' lovers: 'Neither Edward nor Gaveston were the limp-wristed lisping fags so beloved of the tabloids. Edward swam in winter, hedged and ditched the fields of his house at Langley. Gaveston was the finest horseman of his age.'[36]

At first it appears that Isabella is deferential and eager towards Edward, craving his attention, but there can be no sexual satisfaction in their relationship and apparently there can be no sisterly solidarity either. Presumably such an affinity would compromise Edward's aspiration to perfect masculine faggottry. Immediately after Gaveston has returned, to be greeted by his lover with titles and power, we watch Edward and Isabella in bed, abortively having sex. The crisp porcelain of Isabella's complexion remains unblemished by any facial expression as her over-tures are coldly rejected by Edward, who appears impatient and repulsed by her. In the published script of the film, which contains Jarman's personal notes, he comments on this scene:

> An unsatisfactory bedroom scene with Tilda and Steven – she thought it might be misogynist, I thought the audience would have some sympathy for her, even if she plays it hard.[37]

A short while later we join Isabella in bed, alone, wracked with jealousy and frustration, but still looking iconographically sublime of course. The military Mortimer entices Isabella to his rebellious cause. After her humiliation by Gaveston, who puts her up against a wall and feints to kiss her, pulling away as the queen in her frustration kisses back, and finally some abuse from her husband, who calls her a 'foul strumpet' for fawning on him, Isabella induces Mortimer to have Gaveston killed. Mortimer comes upon the queen as she is shooting a crossbow at a stag suspended from the ceiling. She's resplendent in full Eva Peron drag, and hysterically gleeful at having thrown off her marital obligations. Later, she returns to the marital bedroom, dripping in strings of effervescent pearls as she brings news to Edward that Gaveston's exile is to be repealed, knowing, as we do, that she has planned with Mortimer for him to be killed upon his return. An exotic and passionate encounter in the corridor cements Isabella and Mortimer's allegiance and immediately afterwards Mortimer stabs Gaveston at a cocktail party in front of Isabella and Edward, who then attempts to banish Mortimer from the court. Thereafter war breaks out between the Thatcherite riot squad of Mortimer's army and Edward's Outrage! activists. While war rages in the background, Isabella, impeccably coiffed, is Eva Peron (the musical) as she addresses the multitude at a microphone. Jarman remains respectful of Marlowe's legacy and ultimately aspirant faggottry is routed, although Edward's unfortunate demise on the end of a poker becomes a paranoid fantasy, while the king escapes at the end alive. (How very queer . . . .)

Edward II seems to illustrate some of the problems that arise when we insufficiently situate homosexuality within the broader field of gender. It seems particularly unfortunate in a film so bristling with the iconographic majesty of Isabella and with self-conscious, state of the art queerness (even Outrage! themselves are on hand as Edward's army), that the interests of women and of gay men can be represented as so antithetical and as so much a function of patriarchal power structures. Indeed, despite her aesthetic glorification, it becomes clear that Isabella herself has little power beyond the symbolic status of her title. Humiliated and rejected by her husband (and her husband's lover), she must make herself an object of exchange, selling her passion and legitimacy to Mortimer, who does have enough material authority to get her on the throne and secure her position. Edward's homosexuality is only a problem in as much as it leads him to reject Isabella, thus producing her scorn, and also in that it offers Mortimer the opportunity to seek power. Otherwise the triangle of Edward, Mortimer and Isabella forms a perfect homosocial system. The passing of Isabella from one powerful man to the other marks the conclusion of their struggle for true patriarchal subjectivity, which is itself marked by ownership of the throne. Edward possesses monarchical power. Mortimer wants power and uses Isabella to get it. The object of their struggle, which is national royal power, symbolised by the throne, is never questioned: queer Edward expects obedience, deference and the trappings of that power as much as Mortimer or the chorus of Thatcherite earls; this queerness declines any critique of state power, or any affiliation with political resistance.

The issue at the heart of the film is about who has the biggest balls to sit in the big chair, not about challenging or resisting complicity with the structures the chair may represent. Early in the film Edward allows his lover to slouch across the throne, later Gaveston larks about on it in the nude, while Mortimer and Isabella later occupy it with pomp and appropriate attire. The basis of Edward's oppression seems to be a recognition that his masculinity is insufficiently ample to justify his ownership of the throne: he never does manage to capture the perfectly unified masculinity of the hustlers and this brings about a dubious alignment between the perfect queerness they represent and institutional state power. Edward's Outrage! army seems to be something of an incoherently incorporated visual gag, rather than indicative of the film's embracing of a queer politics which challenges state power. Indeed, when Edward realizes that he will be impeached if he does not reject Gaveston, he sacrifices his great gay love for the sake of his power and the support of the grubby and grasping earls of middle-England.

However, at least Edward mourns his sacrifice; Isabella, on the other hand seems to become more evil and less sympathetic the further she moves from stunned, frustrated victimisation towards power and fulfilment. Most chilling, and most erotic, is her murder of Kent, Edward's brother, who has helped the rebels for the sake of the monarchy, but who then challenges Mortimer and Isabella's legitimacy as holders of the throne. Isabella is as poised and as perfectly coiffed as ever as she bends down to kiss her brother-in-law's neck. As Kent begins to writhe, we realise that the kiss is too long, too intense; when he starts to struggle and blood pumps out over his throat and her chin it becomes graphically clear that she has gorged the life out of him. Isabella finally steps away, her metamorphosis from 'fawning strumpet' through frustrated wife to homosocial token and finally to malicious vampire is completed. As Ruby Rich suggests, 'For women, *Edward II* is a bit complicated. Since the heroes are men and the main villain is a woman, some critics have condemned it as misogynist.'[38] *Edward II* may be a misogynist film, but only in the extent to which it makes Isabella complicit with a ruthless perfidy and lust for power most usually engendered in men within the state's constitutional autocracy, and which even intoxicates the heroically validated but viciously victimized queers.

Colin MacCabe offers a different interpretation which suggests that *Edward II*'s misogyny is an effect not of a blindness to state power structures, but of Jarman's sexuality itself:

The film is much more unambiguous in its misogyny that any of his other work. In that gay male dialectic where identification with the position of woman is set against rejection of the woman's body, *Edward II* is entirely, and without any textual foundation, on the side of rejection.[39]

There is, of course, considerable disengenuousness in these words, and an implicit naturalization of the author's own heterosexuality and consequent innocence of misogyny. Clearly MacCabe does not have the space or the brief to dissect gay male relationships with women.

Furthermore, his argument has the effect of unifying a gay male relationship with women that is continually balanced between identification and repulsion. It is offensive to suggest that male homosexuality is an effect of a physical repulsion for women: this idea has its modern origins in psychoanalytic and psychiatric practice which until very recently clinically pathologised homosexuality.[40] Clearly many individual gay men are misogynistic, as is much gay culture. Dominant cultures, formed through constant hegemonic renegotiation, are pulling towards patriarchal interests; that means that all counter, resistant, conformist, reactionary and dissident cultures will be formed out of interactions with aspects of that dominant culture. In other words, our society and the knowledges it circulates are misogynistic; this should not surprise us. Such glib accusations deflect analysis of the functions women may have in gay culture, as well as dissection of the *usefulness* knowledges about supposed gay male misogyny have within homosocial systems. There is also something disquietingly homophobic about the assumption that all homosexual men identify with women. It is a basic assumption of this project that such identifications are valuable, but MacCabe's totalising tendency is ill conceived. Not all gay men identify with women, even though, as I have suggested, gay male culture is saturated with the iconography of camp spectatorship such that most will be familiar with the practice. MacCabe's statement is derived from the continuing prevalence of inversionist knowledge about homosexuality, which gay activism has rightly repelled. Third sex accounts of homosexuality work to shore up the authenticity of heterosexual gender roles, and thus patriarchal power. However, accounts such as the third sex models are an attempt to make coherence out of complex and contradictory elements, which arise partly through our own dissident interventions. I would suggest that inversion theories offer us the opportunity to strike back at normative ideologies of gender through the very site of our constraint. Points that require particularly intense policing by dominant authorities are those which elicit dominant anxiety, and thus contain faultlines we must exploit.

However, I have suggested that Derek Jarman's homosexuality, as he ruminates upon it in his biographies, was not meaningful to him in this way; he did not understand his own queerness as a dissident gender identification, but as a form of erotic liberation and bohemian rebelliousness. If the representation of Isabella exhibits a malicious loathing of womanhood, then this occurs precisely because Jarman was not interested *enough* in female identification to elevate her out of normal patterns of homosocial (misogynist) representation. Aesthetically and performatively Isabella represents an almost mathematically precise interpretation of gay male camp iconography, but this imagery is then employed in a narrative which consolidates and naturalizes gay male masculinity to such an extent that it may exchange that female iconography in order to purchase the possibility of homosocial agency and power, symbolized by the throne of England.

Hysteria and heterosocial dissent

If we are to suggest that the markers of camp spectatorship deployed in *Edward II* underwrite homosocial structures, because Isabella's star iconography and sexually repressed hysteria enable her homosocial exchange by gay men as much as sexual objectification would enable her exchange by straight men, then Jarman has unwittingly offered us a critical apparatus with which to assess the heterosocial potential in specific arrangements of camp spectatorship or female identification. This is not to suggest that the iconography of camp spectatorship *necessarily* aligns gay men with straight men by enabling them to enter homosocial bonds through the exchange of women, but *Edward II* shows us clearly how such forms of spectatorship have this (politically undesirable) potential. *Women on the Verge of a Nervous Breakdown* seems to be calling on familiar and identifiable reading traces that invite camp spectatorship: female protagonists, marginalization of men, validation of emotional excess, flamboyant iconography and kitsch aestheticism. These reading traces are substantiated with our knowledge about Almodóvar's sexuality, regardless of the often unhelpful way in which he may comment upon it. Furthermore, such inducements are offered in the context of Almodóvar's circulation through media apparently affirmative to our subcultural interests, where we are encouraged to feel politically comfortable. Liberal broadsheet journalism, as we have seen, may strenuously, but insidiously, attempt to recuperate Almodóvar's aura of camp spectatorship and thus dissipate his potential heterosocial challenges, but such recuperation can never be secure, and in the context of the agility of gay subcultural reading, and the power-ful inducements offered by *Women on the Verge of a Nervous Breakdown*, the film may feasibly retain substantial dissident capacity.

As we have seen, the early parts of *Women on the Verge of a Nervous Breakdown* offers us pleasures we associate with the woman's films of 1930s and 1940s Hollywood. We are invited masochistically to align our identifications with Pepa in her self-conscious manifestation of emotional trauma in the face of her partner's desertion (Annette Kuhn notes that woman's films were often derogatorily known as 'three-handkerchief movies').[41] I have also suggested that the non-naturalistic break in the diegesis offered by Pepa's dubbing of *Johnny Guitar* instates the notion of contingency within the text of *Women on the Verge of a Nervous Breakdown*: its narrative is not universal, but specifically derived from the genre of the woman's film, as is that of *Johnny Guitar*, and the native languages of both films are but one potential point of ethnic or national origin. More importantly, such an instatement of contingency within *Women on the Verge of a Nervous Breakdown* highlights the condi-tionality of Pepa's role-playing of the mistreated heterosexual woman. We come to see her state of hysterical trauma as a cultural response, conditioned in part by a governing patriarchal narrative represented in *Johnny Guitar*, where female dissent and personal authority, to say nothing of the resistance of lesbian identity, becomes crushingly and cloyingly recuperated. The most perfect moment of Pepa's hysteria is when she faints in the studio, ending the session in which she has been dubbing Crawford's voice into Spanish.

What is striking is that it is during Pepa's performance as an actress attempting to represent another woman's hysteria and emotional distress, that she is overcome, and not while she is 'herself' within the trauma she suffers at Iván's hands. It would seem that what is unbear-able is the role of powerless heterosexual woman and not the simple knowledge that some man doesn't love you any more. In the film's press book Carmen Maura comments on the tight skirts and high heels that she has to wear in *Women on the Verge of a Nervous Breakdown*:

> Of course they'll be uncomfortable, but I'll never show it. For some-one like Pepa, high heels are one of the best ways to handle her suffering. If Pepa didn't keep up her looks, her spirits would break down completely.[42]

Significantly the ruptural hysterical excess represented by the fainting, the breakdown in the coherence of Pepa's subjectivity, is produced by performative strain (Pepa-as-Crawford-as-Vienna-as-victim) and not by the strain of her ill-treatment by Iván. It is her powerless role Pepa cannot cope with, not the fact that she is in pain because a man rejected her. This acts as something of a break from the conventions of melodrama and the woman's film, yet continues to maintain Pepa within an emotional framework we recognize as constitutive of these genres, which continues to validate, and indeed propagate, women's (and gay men's) feelings.

After Pepa has procured some illicit sleeping tablets from the pink face-masked pharmacist, she returns home. She moves to the kitchen where we enjoy close up shots of her making gazpacho – all reds and juice and the violent whizzing of the liquidiser. She puts all her sleeping tablets into the jug and tells the gazpacho and us that she is 'sick of being good'. With this decision and the discordance of the blender ringing in our ears, Pepa goes into the bedroom and heaves Iván's suits out of the wardrobe. The soundtrack swells with the magnificently pompous tango of Rimsky-Korsakov's *Sheherezade*, signifying hypnotic passion. Pepa lights a cigarette, but then reminds herself that she shouldn't smoke. So she tosses the matches and cigarettes onto the bed, primal scene of her relationship with Iván, where they catch fire. Woman's passion, igniting in the bed, isn't rational, but it isn't accidental either. The music surges in an intermediate climax. As Pepa walks back to the bed, she is carrying a large plastic tulip of Iván's, which has a pink bloom on the end. The erect tulip detumesces crudely and spectacularly in the heat of the flames and the music, while Pepa stands watching the fire, transfixed, until the smoke starts to choke her. She runs out of the bedroom and returns with the hose from the terrace, with which she douses the fire. Phallic tulips wilt under the heat of a woman's passion, while the crude force of ejaculation is not only cold, like water from a hose, but antithetical to such incendiary passion and to the atmosphere of drama and spectacle. The flames and the music are irrational, wanton, enveloping; the water is sensible, necessary and premature: the fire must be extinguished or the bed and the apartment will be consumed.

Iván's estranged wife Lucía has recently been released from a mental hospital and has engaged the feminist lawyer Paulina Morales to sue Iván for the years that she has lost. It is clear once again that it is Lucía's position of powerlessness in her relationship with Iván that has caused her the mental illness for which she now seeks judicial compensation and not the necessary emotional trauma of desertion. At first Pepa's notion of not being good any more consists of more aggressive attempts to speak with Iván and hold him accountable, but she fails to track him down. Conversely, Pepa seems to be finding it very easy to link up with other people, through a series of Dickensian coincidences which complicate the plot to the point of farcical confusion: her friend Candela arrives at the flat when she cannot contact Pepa by phone because Pepa has ripped it out, Marissa arrives with her boyfriend Carlos because the real estate agent has sent them, and Lucía arrives seeking vengeance because she thinks that Pepa is about to go to Stockholm with Iván. Carlos turns out to be Iván's son. He fixes the telephone, and his mother, Lucía, rings the airport to claim that she has planted a bomb on the plane to Stockholm. Candela is on the run because she gave a home to a Shiite terrorist with whom she was in love and who has now been captured. She attempts to throw herself off the balcony. Eventually the police arrive, investigating the bomb threat telephoned to the airport, but this induces panic in Candela, who thinks that they have come for her. Temporary calmness occurs when all parties drink Pepa's spiked gazpacho which, like Oberon's love potion in *A Midsummer Night's Dream*, induces even the threatening figures of the police to succumb to Pepa's spell.

At first it appears that Lucía is squaring up to compete with Pepa for Iván's affections. However, this interaction does not proceed as we would expect, with each measuring up the other's manifestation of feminine attributes that may appeal to men. Rather, they bond through a shared experience of powerlessness in relation to Iván. Pepa and Lucía reflect on how they both know him as a voice, disembodied, instructive. When Pepa's confusion and suffering has cleared enough, she understands the urgency of Candela's situation and goes to see the feminist lawyer, Paulina Morales, for her advice. We already know that Iván is going to Stockholm with someone, and not with Pepa or Lucía. While Pepa waits to see Paulina she answers the secretary's phone and recognizes Iván's voice. He hangs up, but then she notices a plane ticket to Stockholm on the desk. When Pepa enters Paulina's office, the lawyer looks up, recognizing her, and says 'Of all the nerve'; we now understand that Paulina must be Iván's new lover. Pepa explains Candela's predicament, but Paulina Morales is unsympathetic; her advice is that Candela should turn herself over to the very authorities she fears, so that they can put her in jail: afterall, she says, Candela has committed a crime and must pay. Pepa replies that her friend's only crime was falling in love and being afraid; she adds that she herself would have done the same. Paulina is scornful about Candela and Pepa's 'lovelorn' status. Pepa gets very angry and Paulina tells her to leave or she will call the police. Pepa hits the lawyer across the face. As Pepa leaves, Paulina's secretary asks if the meeting was helpful: Pepa smiles contentedly and replies that she feels much better.

In her encounter with Pepa, it becomes clear that Paulina Morales, feminist lawyer, is allied to the very same male interests of which the other women on the verge of a nervous breakdown are victims, and which they are in various stages of overcoming or understanding. Paulina is not tied to the other women through any experience of emotional trauma, through which she may gain an appreciation of powerlessness in relation to men; indeed, Paulina is sufficiently distant from such an understanding that she actually calls upon the authority of men against another woman. Far from recognizing any difficulty in her gender, as a role that propagates passivity, Paulina precisely gains her power over other women through the degree of her naturalized conformity to such subordination. Pepa has been forced out of Iván's affections as Paulina has insinuated herself into them. It would seem that Pepa's anger, and her deeply satisfying violence when she hits Paulina, is justified in the face of such gender treachery, all the more authentic as Pepa is acting not only for herself, but on behalf of other disempowered women, Candela and Lucía. Paulina is visibly stunned when Pepa hits her, and this shock at our protagonist's violence exhibits a fracturing of the lawyer's naturalised position. This naturalisation of Paulina's status acts as a kind of ideological denial through which she has been able to offset her potential victimization with the degree of her favour and success in a male world, which is represented by the legal system in which she works. The effect of Paulina's treachery deepens when we realize that she is Lucía's lawyer in her suit against Iván, but he is now the lawyer's lover; no wonder the case has not been successful.

After Pepa faints at work she begins to move away from the traditional model of hysteria with which woman's films traditionally make sense of heterosexuality. The scene in which she hits the gender traitor, Paulina, marks the climax of this thematic arc which takes Pepa from the kind of female masochistic icon camp spectatorship venerates, into a substantially more powerful textual position which we may describe as exhibiting Almodóvar's heterosocial bonding with her. In a sense Paulina Morales helps to facilitate Pepa's ascension into a more powerful position. From the moment at which she faints in the dubbing studio Pepa begins to move away from manifesting the spectacle of hysterical behaviour we might expect of a wronged woman. Such spectacles invariably suggest an appropriate deficit of activity as expected of women within patriarchal gender roles. Pepa's transcendence of this passivity is again marked when she tells the gazpacho that she is sick of being good, and when she hits Paulina this transformation seems to have come full circle: hysterical women are the ones that get hit across the face, they do not do the hitting. Pepa gradually emerges from under the weight of manifesting the pain of her mistreatment by Iván, which displays her passivity, and then she proceeds to act for other women. She approaches a lawyer on behalf of Candela, and she drugs the policemen who potentially threaten her friend. Pepa manages to overcome the adversarial conditions of her relationship with Lucía, and the two women find a shared experience of having to display acceptance and love in the face of Iván's refracted duplicity in their relationships with him. At the climax of the film, when Lucía fails to be reconciled to Iván's treachery by such bonding, Pepa intercedes in an attempt to stop her from shooting Iván.

As Peter William Evans has noted in his volume on the film in the BFI Modern Classics series, the closure of *Women on the Verge of a Nervous Breakdown* is ambiguous.[43] We have seen how Pepa has overcome the necessary display of her hysteria, we have seen her intercession on behalf of Candela, and her control of the potential chaos at her apartment when all the coincidental and farcical elements of the narrative collide (with the exception of Iván), which becomes complete when the policemen succumb to the narcotic effect of the gazpacho. However, Lucía tears the fabric of this unity and harmony by taking the policemen's guns and pointing them at Pepa. The two women are the only remaining conscious figures. Lucía asks Pepa what it was that she had to tell Iván. Pepa tells her that she has nothing to say to him now: 'I just want to forget him and you should do the same.' Lucía says that she had forgotten him in the hospital, but then one day she heard his voice on the television telling a woman that he loved her: she didn't recognize his face, only his voice. Lucía behaved as if she was cured and was released from the mental hospital.

> *Pepa*: If you're cured, stop aiming at me.
> *Lucía*: But I'm not cured. I faked it and I fooled them. I can only forget him by killing him.

Lucía suggests that now Pepa knows, they should drink a toast. The tension mounts as both women raise glasses of the drugged gazpacho; a series of reverse shots establish eye contact between the women. Lucía breaks the deadlock by throwing her gazpacho into Pepa's face. While Pepa runs to the kitchen in distress to wash the juice out of her eyes, Lucía escapes with the guns, hijacking the boyfriend and motorbike of

Pepa's neighbour, Ana. Pepa and Ana follow in the Mambo cab and the two women commiserate with each other about their fate at men's hands. Ana is jealous of the fact the Lucía is sitting on the bike seat; Pepa reminds her that Ambite, her boyfriend, is being held at gunpoint. Ana shrugs this off, he is unfaithful and she is going to get some money and buy his motorbike: 'With a bike, who needs a man?' Lucía is enjoying herself enormously, cackling into the wind as she fires the gun at the pursuing Mambo cab, entreating Ambite to go faster or she will shoot him. Pepa arrives at the airport after Lucía and finds Iván's ex-wife putting on her glasses and pulling out a gun ready to shoot her prey. Pepa pushes a luggage trolley at Lucía and watches it as it knocks over the potential assassin, who fires the gun into the air, causing panic. Pepa faints. She revives in Iván's arms with Paulina looking on disdainfully, but pushes him away and tells him to let go. She tells him to instruct Paulina to go away. He dithers and Pepa does it herself. The lawyer retreats. Iván may be incapable of action, but he remains capable of honeyed rhetoric: he tells Pepa that he is ashamed and that he has treated her badly. She tells him that all she wanted was to talk to him. He asks her to say what she needed to say, but it is too late. We know that the withheld information concerns Pepa's pregnancy. Pepa admits that at any time before their meeting she would still have told him, but not any more. She only came to save him from Lucía, now she wants to go. She turns away and returns to her apartment.

Here at the end of *Women on the Verge of a Nervous Breakdown*, Pepa's romantic restraint is the equal of any heroine of any woman's film, even that of Bette Davis's Charlotte Vale in the sublimely melodramatic *Now, Voyager*. Yet the meaning of Pepa's restraint does not lie in some noble sacrifice, a self-denial for a liberal morality; her restraint appears to be a heterosocial triumph. Peter William Evans suggests that 'our cravings for a happy ending are frustrated' but his hegemonic 'our' nominates and naturalises an audience looking for patriarchally inscribed heterosexual romance.[44] In as much as Pepa's reconciliation with Iván would undermine that resistance fashioned from her hysteria, then the ending of *Women on the Verge of a Nervous Breakdown* does offer satisfying completion. Yet there remain some fundamental ambiguities here which may remind us of the difficulty we face in maintaining consistent textual dissent. Pepa, and indeed Lucía, remain embedded within narratives of heterosexual romance: given that the narrative structure of *Women on the Verge of a Nervous Breakdown* is organized upon the premise of Iván's elusiveness, it would seem appropriate that the conclusion of this arc would bring the erstwhile lovers face-to-face for some kind of reckoning. *Women on the Verge of a Nervous Breakdown* seems to offer us three different kinds of resolution with Iván represented by Pepa, Lucía and Paulina.

The lawyer gets her man, and is leaving the scene of the problematic diegesis with him. Yet her romantic conquest is a hollow one that we are not encouraged to identify with: Paulina Morales is a gender traitor, and worse, has not been on the verge of a nervous breakdown, indeed has colluded with those forces which would bring other women to that verge. We are supposed to find her famous feminism ironic in the light of her gender treachery, but such humour undermines gay heterosocial investments in female bonding by belittling women's activism. That the lovers are leaving Madrid, glorified heart of Almodóvar's oeuvre, underlines her marginalization. The film's ending does marginalize Iván within the structure of personal affiliations, as our heterosocial expectations demand: Pepa does dismiss him. However, she has come to the airport to save Iván, and not, as we may hope, to save Lucía from the consequences of shooting Iván, in what could have been an act of sisterly bonding between the women. As Lucía is escorted away, Pepa ignores her and tells Iván that she came to prevent his assassination. Here, then, Lucía is but the means to bring Pepa and Iván together so that they may play out a final scene in their romance. It is Lucía, with her glorious relish of the motorcycle chase and her vivid, purposeful pursuit of Iván who embodies the film's sponsorship of hysteria as rebellion against homosocial vanity and complacency, but her version of narrative completion is marginalised and she is carted off to the mental hospital. Anyway, we could see Lucía's need to kill Iván as an indication of her ongoing infatuation from which she has not recovered. Pepa and Lucía, potentially heterosocially united in homosocial defiance in their bonding and in their assassination of Iván, end up leaving the airport separately, Lucía escorted by the police, with her plan thwarted by her potential ally. Iván lives to fly off with the gender traitor.

This conclusion, with its heterosocial disappointments and emotive good-byes, resuscitates a conventional account of female hysteria as emotional weakness in the face of abandonment and frustrated romance, which back-tracks somewhat on the efforts made earlier to identify hysteria as the effect of maintaining a powerless gender role. Lucía knows that her only freedom comes not with the knowledge that her love relationship with Iván is over – she already knows that – but with his death and thus with her release from having to continually endure the pain of his choice and power, and her passivity. To that end,

Pepa's rescue of Iván recuperates Lucía's audacious dissidence. We may rejoice in Pepa's brushing-off of Iván's ludicrous disengenuousness, and that she is able to maintain restraint, but this is a much weaker, more rational conclusion of her relationship with Iván than murdering him would have been. The incendiary passion, brilliantly underscored with Rimsky-Korsakov, that burns Pepa's bed and threatens to consume the apartment, which seemed to represent an embracing of hysteria but also a refusal of passivity, is here extinguished in the rationality of Pepa's dignity and restraint. Such an uncompromising resolution of Pepa and Lucía's verging breakdown as Iván's glorified murder would certainly alienate the mainstream liberal audience Almodóvar seems so concerned to address, at the expense of a more specialised and radical one; clearly this is not a risk the writer/director is willing to take.

In the ending of *Women on the Verge of a Nervous Breakdown* it seems that the manifold disparate factors which make up the context of the film's production and consumption coalesce. Knowledge of Almodóvar's sexuality and his particular interest in women lead us through a narrative which does offer many of the pleasures associated with camp spectatorship, both for audiences of gay male queens, and for diverse appropriative or heterosocially aligned camp followers. The narrative perspective would seem to confirm the director's affiliation with women by sponsoring Pepa's perspective, while the scopic organization of the film decentres male protagonism, which makes it difficult for an imputed male spectator to gain sufficient leverage to enter into an exchange of women through a textual patriarchal representative. However, this is often true of many melodramas and so-called woman's films which choose not to address a male spectator. At its most successful *Women on the Verge of a Nervous Breakdown* manages to fuse such woman-centred interests with a continuing acknowledgement of its appeal to camp spectatorship, thus offering the conditions for heterosocial bonding.

In the final scene of the film we see Pepa arriving home to the shambles of her apartment, after she has left the airport. Candela, Carlos, Marissa, the telephone repairman and the policemen are all still sleeping, and there is broken glass and spilled gazpacho all over the floor, the bed is a burnt-out wreck and the telephone is disembowelled. Marissa is sleeping out on the terrace, while her erstwhile fiancé is curled up with Candela on the couch. Pepa steps over the mess and notes that 'the repairman is a doll, but I better save him for Marissa.' She joins Marissa out on the terrace as she wakes up. Pepa confides that she is pregnant and Marissa gives up her chair. Marissa then confides that she had a dream which has left her no longer a virgin. The two women are sharing their distaste for virgins as the credits roll.

Under the influence of Pepa's magic potion, the gazpacho (which with its violent red seems to evoke her passion, and was whizzed together under her spell, 'I'm sick of being good') what emerges at the end of *Women* is a set of bondings that transcend the adversarial relations sponsored by homosocial systems. *Edward II* shows us that the trappings of camp spectatorship alone do not safeguard gay men's relations with women from reproducing these bonds, which work to sustain patriarchal authority. Similarly the portrayal of Paulina in *Women on the Verge of a Nervous Breakdown* shows us how the exchange of women within homosocial arrangements often sets up competitive relations between women themselves for the limited advantage of male patronage. *Women on the Verge of a Nervous Breakdown* brings Pepa to an epiphanal moment which fractures the normativity of her breakdown, exposing the powerlessness of her romantic obsession for Iván, which locks her into suffrage. Such fracturing does not give her power, it can't: she remains subject to male power, and in a way we can see the inexorability of her meeting with Iván at the end of the film as symptomatic of this. Yet there are diverse ways of inhabiting a position which retains significant structural powerlessness, and during her combative encounters with Paulina and Lucía, and in her protectiveness of Candela, Pepa seems to develop a more resistant attitude towards the relations in which her gender role is manifested.

Our (gay male) pleasure in masochistically identifying with Pepa's romantic pain leads us through the same epiphany. Our knowledge about Almodóvar, circulated through a liberal press anxious to instate his associations with women, and the markers of camp spectatorship with which Pepa is represented (the lurid kitsch of her outfits, her deft handling of phallic tulips, telephones and feminist lawyers) elicit gay male camp spectatorship. This queer gaze upon Pepa may initially be manifested through a pleasurably masochistic identification, but such pleasure does not become recuperatively entrenched. A gay male gaze upon Pepa does not pin her into a punishing scopic relay where our homosocially induced instability may be disavowed through her suffering. We could say that this is the predominant effect of the use of camp spectatorship in *Edward II*, but for all its ambiguity, our identification with Pepa in *Women on the Verge of a Nervous Breakdown* remains structurally distinct from Jarman's ambiguous handling of female representation. In watching *Edward II* those gay men whose principal textual investments usually lie in identification with women have a significant problem, in that the very possibility of plausible queer subjectivity is organized as being antithetical to the interests of empowered womanhood. Edward and Gaveston's security and happiness, their integrity as a plausible couple, falls in direct proportion to the ascendance of Isabella. In *Women on the Verge of a Nervous Breakdown* there is no such split in identificatory positions: plausible anti-homosocial subjectivity and camply empowered womanhood are both unified in Carmen Maura's character. Pepa's self-conscious enlightenment about how her tormented romantic infatuation has normalized her subordinate gender role, leads to her subsequent empowered activity in the punishment of the gender traitor, the bonding with other women and the assistance of fellow victims of male power (Lucía and Candela). This gender enlightenment and bonding activity express both her empowered womanhood and her heterosocial alignment at the same time. Unlike the empowerment sought by Paulina Morales, which must be traded for desirability in male eyes and sponsorship of male interests (punishment of Candela), Pepa's resistance is not a function of her exploitation of the structural subordination of identities proximate to her own. Indeed the strategies by which she resists her own subjection to the homosocial narrative complement and enhance gay male homosocial resistance derived through an identification with her. We can see a striking contrast not only within different female characterizations in *Women on the Verge of a Nervous Breakdown*, but between Pepa's complementary heterosocial dissent, her refusal to be homosocially exchanged or complicit with the homosocial exchange of others, and the more problematic alignment made by *Roseanne's* domestic goddess with homosocial mechanisms. As we have seen, there seems to be a reluctance in *Roseanne* to step away from the privileges heterosexual women may accrue in relation to lesbians or gay men through their circulation in homosocial systems. The character of Roseanne Conner assiduously exhibits a refusal to be homosocially exchanged herself, but is willing to court queer culture as a naturalised homosocial subject so as to trade on homosexual abjection and perversity in order to accrue trendiness and normativity.

To date *Women on the Verge of a Nervous Breakdown* has been Pedro Almodóvar's most celebrated work, so much so that it has recently warranted a volume all to itself in the British Film Institute's prestigious Film Classics series. The joyous, almost flippant account it offers of a resistance of homosocial mechanics seems to have given the writer and director his greatest success yet, as Paul Julian Smith has noted.[45] It is ironic that Almodóvar attains his most substantial, much sought after, mainstream recognition at the moment at which he is most appreciated subculturally. As I inferred in the earlier discussions about Almodóvar's circulation through liberal press, his subsequent work, while it may often offer more acute reading traces of camp spectatorship (the astonishingly lurid sets and the towering transsexualism of Bibi Andersen in *Kika*, for example, or the fantastically knowing enactment of diva mannerisms by Femme Letal's drag act in *High Heels*) has also struggled to stabilise effective heterosocial representation. The infamous and protracted rape scene in *Kika* offers a familiar staple of gay pornographic fantasy in a startlingly erotic and farcical form, set up to disquiet our voyeuristic desires by refracting them through Andrea Scarface's television programme, but in doing so it confuses camp flagrancy with manipulative victimization. Similarly, Almodóvar's continuing desire to signify in mainstream contexts, and his personal alignment with glamorous and famous heterosexual coupledom, has led to some troublingly homosocial arrogance in his exchange of Carmen Maura as his identified consort and muse, for Victoria Abril in the first instance, and more recently for Marisa Paredes. This passing on of favours from one woman to another too closely replicates the kinds of treatment women experience within homosocial systems: having to win and maintain favour with men in order to attain social credibility; especially as Almodóvar, as an internationally renowned *auteur*, wields considerable power in relation to the careers of actresses whom he may, or may not choose to fete with his adoration. Such reactionary activity suggests that gay men may find it difficult to sustain heterosocial dissidence in the context of their own continuing oppression, where the inducements to acquire shreds of homosocial authority are potent, but destructive to alliances of trust built up through heterosocial activitiy with heterosexually resistant women (be they lesbian or straight).

Almodóvar's most recent film, *Live Flesh*, which has also been his most acclaimed for some time, seems to further consolidate the homosocial identification the writer/director has been pursuing. Strikingly for an Almodóvar film, the central protagonists of *Live Flesh* are men, a homosocial archetype: police partners. David is cuckolding his partner Sancho, who is a drunk. During a tense confrontation, it appears that Victor, who is stalking Elena, shoots David, causing his paralysis and putting him in a wheechair. Years later, while David and Elena are living in a loveless marriage, it transpires that Sancho shot David as revenge for his relationship with Carla, Sancho's wife. Women are the vehicles through which relations between the men are driven. Elena's frustration with her marriage to David (and the film makes unpleasant and inaccurate associations between sexual impotence and using a wheechair) provides the opportunity for him to seek some kind of redemption through a confrontation with Victor, the cause of his disability. Carla's frustrated marriage to Sancho pushes her into a relationship with the young and beautiful Victor, just released from prison where he was incarcerated for shooting David (a crime that we know he didn't commit), but this relationship merely provides the opportunity for a further confrontation between Sancho, the real cause of David's disability (and Carla's husband) and Victor. Victor is not only the redemptive agent for the women, but is the manifestation of masculine virility on behalf of the incompetent Sancho and the impotent David.

The ironies and Dickensian coincidences which structure the narrative of *Live Flesh* are, however, as near as the film gets to manifesting the kinds of queer motifs of camp spectatorship that we expect from Almodóvar.[46] Instead the film rests on homosocial romanticism between men: when David learns that he has been disabled by his partner, and not by Victor, this offers the opportunity not for revenge, but for the production of greater intimacy between them. Similarly the film's climactic showdown between Sancho and Victor; while it enables a resolution of Victor's hatred of the man whose crimes he has paid for, is scopically more concerned with phallic iconography, as Victor's virile, cuckolding crotch is made equivalent to the dramatic device of Sancho's pistol.

As ever, opportunities through which we may exploit faultlines are shifting and elusive. It is clear that Almodóvar cannot be consistently claimed for his heterosocial potential. Nevertheless, identification with Pepa in *Women on the Verge of a Nervous Breakdown* not only satisfies many of the desires of camp spectatorship, but politically aligns gay male investments with the project of empowerment and resistance of women within heterosexuality. The film exhibits a marked effort to resist slipping into becoming merely an opportunity for self-indulgent wallowing in a masochistic consumption of the spectacle of women's anguish. Almodóvar's successes in *Women* are relatively modest and as we have seen, they subsequently become elusive in his work, but in the way in which the film enhances a resistance of homosocial practice by encouraging a coalition of straight female and gay male interests, he circumvents an antithesis engineered for patriarchal interests, and he models a pattern for our heterosocial dissent.

Conclusion

Fag Hag: a cautionary tale?

Ever since this world began,
There is nothing sadder than,
A one-fag fag hag
Looking for the fag that got away.[1]

Robert Rodi is a gay writer who has published a series of novels that, with varying degrees of hilarity and cynicism, expose and celebrate key archetypal figures in metropolitan gay subculture: *Fag Hag*, *Closet Case*, *Drag Queen* and *Kept Boy*.[2] *Fag Hag* narrativises a relationship between the generously proportioned Natalie Stathis, and a poetically beautiful gay man, Peter Leland. Natalie and Peter spend their weekends trawling the gay bars of Chicago, Natalie tagging along while Peter looks for Mr Right:

> she beamed a smile that pleaded, 'Notice me!' She pressed herself, all hundred and seventy-odd pounds, through crowds of taut, muscular young men and, through sheer flamboyance, attracted the attention of a few of them. And as she talked to them, using every ounce of feminine wile and wit at her disposal, they laughed in delight and flattered her and sometimes even kissed her, but never, never, once, not even for a moment, did they stop looking over her shoulder for something better.[3]

Each time Peter embarks on a new relationship, Natalie loses her consort, but is prevailed upon to counsel her friend through the tribulations of his romantic liaison. In the course of giving this support she uses her considerable insight and guile to disrupt Peter's path to true love so that he may return to her side. Natalie faces her greatest challenge when Peter meets Lloyd Hood and falls in love with this gun shop owning gay survivalist. Peter deserts his sidekick, realigning his behaviour and tastes with those of his new lover, whose house he moves into. As the novel progresses, and moves into realms of blacker and blacker comedy, Natalie resorts to more extreme tactics to attempt to dismay Peter's infatuation. When planting a bug on the lovers' headboard fails to reveal any friction that she may profitably exploit, Natalie attempts to instil in Peter a gun phobia by disguising herself, breaking into the house and holding her erstwhile consort at gunpoint with a weapon purchased from Lloyd's emporium. Finally, when this tactic fails, because Lloyd is prepared to sacrifice his business for his lover, Natalie kidnaps Peter, and intends to keep him in her basement (which she has converted into a luxurious prison cell) until he confirms his undying love for her: this does not happen. Eventually Lloyd rescues Peter, by which time Natalie has sunk to such depths of madness that she retires to a sanatorium, to be released in the novel's epilogue, cured of her fag haggery and independently spirited.

Taken at face value this product of and for gay subculture seems to offer a dismal reflection of the contemporary state of relationships between women and gay men. *Fag Hag* would appear to punish women for maintaining an intimacy with gay men which those men rely on and take for granted. While Peter is rewarded with his prince charming and the promise of living happily ever after, Natalie's obsession leads to mental instability and estrangement from those few people with whom she shared any intimacy. Thus, a presumptive reading of *Fag Hag* may suggest, with some credibility, that an imputed gay male readership would identify against Natalie, the fag hag, delighting in her descent into ruthlessness and madness as signs of her failure to assimilate herself into gay subculture, or as punishments for not being a gay man. There is sufficient material in the novel to support this reading. Consumed as a product of gay subculture, but read without a familiarity with the filters of irony that are a prevailing condition of queer reading strategies, *Fag Hag* would seem to uphold and valorize gay male misogyny.

However, *Fag Hag* seems to reflect the faultline conditions in which relations between women and gay men are conducted, and as a result throws up incoherences which open up more interesting possibilities. This presumptive reading cannot account for the way in which the novel's authorial interest is a function of Natalie's point of view: the narrative is constituted not only by following her actions, but the emotional resonances this narrative induces are empathic reflections of

her experience. When Peter moves in with Lloyd, we are invited to associate with Natalie's loneliness and sense of betrayal and futility, and not
with Peter's smug fulfilment. The integrity of the first, hostile, reading
of *Fag Hag* rests on the potential implausibility of a gay male novelist
encouraging a largely gay male readership to identify with a heterosexual woman in her battle *against* a gay man. This identification with
Natalie by gay male readers would seem especially unlikely as her
struggle could be interpreted as one whose aim is the annihilation of
his very gayness: her apparent aim is to replace Peter's male lovers with
herself, and form a heterosexual coupling with him. However, that
counter-identification becomes more probable in the extent to which
Peter is held up as the lofty, unattainable apex of gay male desirability
and in so far as he manages to achieve marital pair-bonding with Lloyd
in the most unselfconsciously smug fashion possible, and with a right-
wing man at that, whose very essence is antithetical to the concept of
gay subculture. At a disastrous dinner party during which Natalie
attempts to expose tendencies in Lloyd that will be unattractive to
Peter, a tactic which fails because Peter has so thoroughly sublimated
his own interests to Lloyd's, the survivalist explains his lack of interest
in subcultural or communal affiliations; he tells her:

> I'm a man, Natalie; I'm capable, I'm intelligent, I'm strong, I've got
> my wits. There's no reason I should *want* to depend on anyone but
> myself. (p. 101)

Not only does this self-satisfied coupledom eschew any sense of communality, but in his monogamy Peter has rejected the gay spaces of
Chicago's scene (as well as Natalie's heterosocial relations) for the company of Natalie's prejudiced brother Calvin, who responded with shock
when she told him his gun merchant was gay:

> 'Goddam! That's what I thought! I can't believe that guy's a fag.'
> 'He's a homosexual, Cal,' she said, 'But he's definitely *not* a fag.
> Trust me, there's a difference.' (p. 114)

If this novel's gay men do not provide any critique of smug middle-
class monogamy and the heterosexual values it underwrites, *Fag Hag*'s
fag hags exhibit little reticence about mounting such a critique. As
Jennifer, Natalie's boss and confidant tells Calvin's pregnant wife,
Vera: 'Bad case of sperm poisoning you've got there.' (p. 290) From a
subcultural perspective, we might acknowledge the faultline nature of

Fag Hag's representations, and see in it a challenge to the kinds of knowledge and experience that comprise the background noise of gay environments that I referred to in the discussion of Jarman's familiarity with the codes, if not the purpose, of female identification (Chapter 4). As Natalie acknowledges, the label 'fag hag' is applied to women 'derisively' (p. 96). Yet as the narrative progresses Rodi draws out a tension between this derided fag hag and the kinds of icons of femininity beloved of gay male identification. Natalie questions the extent of her manifestation of what gay men understand in their labelling of fag hags: 'A silly indulgence, of no importance – not beneath notice, but not much above it, either?' (p. 96). Towards the end of the novel, after she has held up Peter at gunpoint in a Ninja Turtle mask, her van has broken down and the police are on the way, Natalie needs an urgent ride home to avoid discovery. She climbs into a van full of late adolescent young men who are hysterically policing each other homosocially. The boys pressure one particularly fey comrade, 'Fredo, into taking Natalie into the back of the van and having sex with her. Natalie's familiarity with gay affectation enables her to immediately realise that 'Fredo is gay and deeply confused. Natalie saves him from humiliation, using her maturity to protect him from the authority of homosocial intimacy. She pretends to have sex with the youth, hyperbolising his virility; then she tells him:

> these guys are clowns. You don't need them. You're perfect the way you are, and when you figure out what that is, don't be afraid to be it. Okay? (p. 195)

This is an affectionate, valorising portrayal of Natalie's heterosocial commitment to bonding with gay men that does not rest on her denial of homosexuality in men, or in her attempts at 'conversion', but which is empowering and enabling of the young man's homosexuality and protective of it in relation to his ventriloquism of opportunistic homosociality.

If Natalie is a heterosocial heroine, it is not merely for her care of fawn-like baby-queens:

> She peered into her future and tried to see herself in a week, a month, a year; but there was nothing but darkness, no matter how far she projected.
>
> She licked and swallowed the blood from her hand. Fuck the future; darkness was just fine with her. (p. 266)

This kind of delicious malevolence specifically appeals to gay men as it constitutes a perverse rejection of the kind of rational subjectivity men are institutionally organised as personifying, and gay men are punished for queering:

> He was going to have a fight on his hands. He'd have to scrape her flesh and blood off that basement door before he opened it. And God help him if she got him *first*.
> It was petty, it was demeaning, it was evil. It was what she wanted more than anything. (p. 276)

Not withstanding Natalie Stathis's textual womanhood, we have seen that this kind of irrational rejection of homosocial subjectivity is not a strategy that is very effective for women; they are already denied access to rational social authority. Glorifying in enacting demeaning and petty behaviour as acts of dissent is a familiar gay male negotiation of homosocial legislative ideology. It is the oppressive *proximity* of male subjectivity which circumscribes gay men, so that our queerness may function as a policing mechanism. In order for our presence to be sufficiently disquieting, it is necessary that gay men should share a degree of male power: heterosocial gender dissent perverts that subjectivity by flirting with the abjection, the lack of subjectivity, experienced by women in male homosocial culture. Similar flirtatious affectations of femininity do not activate dissent for women because such performances constitute their necessary negotiation of male power in heterosexuality in order to gain vicarious privilege.

Given the nature of Natalie Stathis's homosocial dissent, and her patronage of baby-fags, it seems unlikely that a preferred reading of *Fag Hag* would encourage gay male hostility towards her. She protects gay men from an apparent sense of altruism (she has nothing to gain by saving 'Fredo) and she activates the same kind of 'bitch diva' dissent gay men valorise. Yet if we are encouraged to empathise and identify with Natalie, can we claim a consistent project for the novel which would reconcile its mode of address and its narrative, which tells of a straight woman's attempts to convert a gay man and ruin his homosexual relationships, with its intended audience and the identification it elicits from that audience? Does this project serve prejudicial, heterosexist purposes and ask us to become complicit with them? On the contrary, it would seem that *Fag Hag* attempts to enact a critique of how gay male culture exploits women, at the same time as engendering gay male empathy with that exploitation, so that we may be able to take some responsibility.

Despite her apparently evangelical heterosexuality, Natalie Stathis does not exhibit any collusion with male homosocial interests. Quite the reverse. We have seen how she attempts to protect 'Fredo from the more vicious effects of homosocial ridicule. There are no heterosexual men with whom she shares any degree of intimacy, let alone through whom she may acquire social privilege, or gain cultural capital enough to exert homosocial leverage upon Peter's homosexuality. Indeed, until Peter pair-bonds with Lloyd, his and Natalie's relationship is specifically constituted as resistant to heterosexual norms and values. The nature of Natalie's desire for Peter is complex and contradictory. This desire is certainly not to settle down and reproduce conventionally sponsored marital monogamy in order to accrue authoritative credibility: it is Peter and Lloyd who do that, their normativity emphasized by their socializing with the dreadful Calvin and Vera. Natalie acknowledges that her desire for Peter does not follow prescribed fantasies of hetero-sexual romance:

> The last movie she'd watched was *An Officer and a Gentleman*...she tried to replay it with Peter and herself in the starring roles, but gave that up at once; it was silly and embarrassing. Such flourishing, grand passion would certainly never be part of their relationship. (p. 76)

Indeed her desire for Peter, while recognizing and valorising his erotic appeal, is manifested largely as a turn away from heterosexual men. Natalie asks herself why she pursues Peter:

> Was it because a beautiful, exciting, funny gay man who doesn't want to sleep with you is better than a dull, plain, predictable straight guy who does? As far as Natalie was concerned, that was more or less the case...virtually all the slow inconsiderate *hetero-sexual* men she ever met had paunches and bad table manners and loved to wear disfiguring clothing bearing the hideous logos of inane sports franchises. (p. 76)

It would seem, then, that Natalie's evangelical zeal in her pursuit of Peter could not be described as heterosexual, in that the relationship her desire generates does not uphold male power by reproducing homosocial narratives. Natalie's desire for Peter certainly enshrines a considerable degree of smugness about the glory of male homo-sexuality: she is afterall a function of Rodi's gay male imaginary. While

Natalie is portrayed as unrealistically admiring of gay men, as *Fag Hag*'s readership we are not necessarily encouraged to align ourselves with this unremittingly positive perspective on gay male behaviour. If Natalie's attempts to bond with Peter are resistant of homosocial narratives, then Peter's treatment of Natalie exhibits his commodification of her in line with the extent of his male power and the access this gives him to social legitimacy, confirmed by Calvin and Vera's acceptance of him and Lloyd.

The title *Fag Hag* is provocative precisely because it promises the recirculation of a derisory representation of women from a gay male perspective. We have seen how useful the presumption of gay misogyny is for those male interests which retain considerable structural power: heterosocial affiliations between gay men and women constantly negotiate that hostile intrusion. Yet despite being published by such a large concern as Penguin (admittedly under the more marginal imprint of Plume), *Fag Hag* manifests a specific, focused, level of subcultural address. The publication of Rodi's novels by Penguin may indeed indicate the profitability of a constituency which benefits from a material proximity to male power. Despite these factors, which may lead us to expect that Rodi's novel would deliver merely a gleeful recirculation of bitchy stereotypes and lazy misogyny, *Fag Hag* actually offers a witty and incisive commentary on gay men's relationships with women. Peter's desertion and commodification of Natalie is constantly framed as callous, smug, and a turn not only away from his friend, but from a more exuberant expression of his sexuality. When Natalie breaks into the lovers' house in disguise and holds Peter at gunpoint, he has been living with Lloyd for some months. Before she makes her presence known she observes her object of desire as he watches five minutes of that gay institution, *The Golden Girls*. It is with his own authorial voice that Rodi notes that Peter watches the show 'without laughing' (p. 187), which is a fairly considerable indictment of his current lifestyle. Such betrayals are not handled by Rodi with the same kind of delight with which he details Natalie's scheming to break up Peter's relationships, nor his enthusiasm for her descent into ever more extreme behaviour in order to punish Peter's desertion. It would seem, then, that we could make a reading of *Fag Hag* which would suggest that it challenges the commodification of women in gay culture, but more than that, which invites gay male readers to speculate on the dissident potential of bonds with women, a potential often disregarded and betrayed by our assimilationist ventriloquism of marital (homosocial), heterosexual relationships.

Fag Hag's deliciously malevolent didacticism offers an opportunity to draw together many of the themes that this book has addressed, which is why I have introduced it here in the conclusion. The initial intentions of this work were involved with questioning the nature and purpose of gay male culture's interest in women: *Fag Hag* makes an investment in relationships with women – which we may now understand as heterosocial bonds – by drawing out the value of such relationships from our familiarity with the subcultural commodification and exchange of women. *Fag Hag* quite literally aligns such commodification with powerful homosocial interests, in Peter and Lloyd's socialising with Calvin and Vera, in such a way as to enable us to see the assimilationism of our continuing disregard for women and the potential heterosocial affiliations we may make with them.

Clearly, producing such proximate and familiar representations of the commodification of women by gay men is risky: representing the kinds of knowledge which are sponsored or upheld by powerful, hegemonic interests is a precarious dissident strategy; *Fag Hag* is, as a result, uneven, with a narrative which is sometimes unclear about its authorial investments. While we may see that the novel licenses a degree of heterosocial commentary, it does also allow an endorsement of conventional gay mores. There are occasions when Rodi slips into a more spiteful narration of Natalie's descent into filth and madness which ridicules her. Nevertheless, there are considerable opportunities for us to draw out the similarities in the effects of homosocial exchange and gay male exchange. In Peter's desire for romantic fulfilment in a relationship with a man, and in his deprecated indifference to his relationship with Natalie, *Fag Hag* challenges gay men to reconcile the competing and often contradictory elements of our political, emotional and cultural investments. Fags and hags can be queer sisters.

Fags, hags and gender dissent

In the first chapter's analysis of *A Streetcar Named Desire* and the critical culture which has shaped our context for reading that play, we were able to see how closely aligned the interests of women and of gay men can be. Unpicking inversionist knowledge allows us to see how much ideological work goes into concealing the functional place homosexuality has in the reproduction of gender systems that uphold patriarchy and capital through homosocial male bonds. Yet not only in *spite* of inversionist accounts, but *because* of their investment in our gender dysphoria, *Streetcar* offers cultural resistance by insisting on our ability to comment on gender systems, and offers political dissent by denaturalizing gender roles as effects of homosocial work. This denaturalization, along with the conditions of homosexual representation in America in 1947, which necessitated Williams's closetedness, enables an extraordinarily powerful indictment of heterosexual women's powerlessness, at the same time as portraying the seductiveness and circumscribed privilege of femininity. *Streetcar* is striking in that it offers a gritty, pro-feminist materialist critique of heterosexuality and a screaming exaltation of the performative guile of Blanche's femininity, and manages to hold both kinds of representation in a compelling oxymoronic flourish. The second chapter offered a detailed examination of the narratives and conditioned phobias that constitute male homosocial bonds. These bonds work to maintain the security of male interests, and to enable a structure of knowledge with which to stabilise men's ownership of capital and the racial and class distinctiveness of successive generations. Men's authority is constituted in homosocial narratives as power over women, in both quantitative and functional terms: men have more power than women and directly control women by making notions of womanhood functions of masculinity. I have argued that understanding our homosexuality purely as a non-reproductive sexual pleasure, cruelly legislated against by an intolerant or ignorant state apparatus, is an inadequate structure of knowledge, and will not allow us to gain access to the kinds of dissidence we can see in Williams's work. We must be able to exploit our position in gender systems: homosexuality, constituted by homosocial doctrine as a threateningly proximate abjection, acts to adjudicate male bonds. This chapter suggested that many of the problems inherent in the conflicts between these sexual politics and politics of sexuality, are attributable to the shape of homosocial mechanisms, which work to seduce marginal interests into assimilation. I went on to elaborate heterosocial bonds as a precarious, but promising arrangement by which gay men and women could bond and in the process of that bonding enact dissent against homosocial systems. Chapters 3 and 4 drew together the knowledge accumulated through the first two by examining in detail texts which seem to make the heterosocial move described in Chapter 2, and which were read to privilege gender as the opportunity for gay male dissent, in line with the knowledges about that category opened up by *Streetcar*. *Fag Hag* cautions us to be more considerate about an affiliation that *Roseanne*, slash fiction, *Women on the Verge of a Nervous Breakdown* and *Streetcar* show us has considerable dissident potential.

Despite the claims I have made about the ways in which gender ambiguity, gender dissent and cross-gender identification are implicated in a whole range of gay self-identifications, I am aware that currently such notions, which we might typify as modes of gender dysphoria, are associated with transsexualism or more recent transgendered positions, and not with homosexuality. However, in as far as transgenderism seems to represent a radical engagement with the kinds of damage and punishment experienced by those who cannot reconcile their identity with the expectations of a hostile gender system, then perhaps we could see homosexuality and transgender as alternative responses to similar conditions. (An alternative to both would be a conformist, or assimilationist (as opposed to radical) engagement with the kinds of damage and punishment afflicted by normative gender systems: we may describe this engagement as heterosexuality.) Of course, there are transsexuals who experience their dysphoria as a biological mistake, and seek reassignment therapy as a way of fulfilling a biologically authentic, naturalized gender role to correct that mistake.[4] However, there also seems to be an ever more confident transgender movement which disputes the binary notion of gender that is naturalized in heterosexuality.[5] One expression of this recognition is the double inversion undertaken by some transsexuals, not only of their gender, but of their orientation, so that a queerness may persist in the chosen gender alignment. Such a secondary inversion would indicate both the effectiveness of queer self-identification as a disruption of gender normativity, and also the extent to which transgender positions are themselves a function of dissident discourses produced historically in gay subculture by a range of differently identifying lesbians, gays, cross-dressers, drag queens, butches and femmes.

However, despite the similarities between homosexual and transgender dissent, there remain considerable difficulties in alliances between the two movements. Many lesbians and gays see the gender dysphoria of transsexualism as a homophobic reproduction of natural gender categories, whereby same-sex desire can only be tolerated through an inversion of gender that heterosexualises that desire.[6] There have also been a number of disputes between butch lesbians and female to male transsexuals over questions of gender dysphoria and political space. Aware of the need to protect newly emerging cultural spaces and political articulations, some FTMs have been highly critical of the assertions by butch lesbians of their concurrent female embodiment and gender dysphoria, which is seen as an appropriation of transgender discourse.[7] Such disputes in part arise because of the impoverished conditions within gay and lesbian culture for discussing the gendered implications of lesbian and gay identities (butch *and* femme, male *and* female), and this is a major problem for our culture, as I have been arguing throughout. However, it is clearly problematic to suggest that lesbian identities, which have always negotiated gender transgressions are now appropriating transgendered discourse. The two movements share a heritage.

It is clear that not all formations of identity will promise effective political dissent. Many gay and lesbian formations unfortunately remain hostile not only to the notion of gender dysphoric transsexualism, but to gender dysphoria as a condition of homosexuality. Emphasizing sex-based versions of homosexuality, where our only difference from straight normativity lies in our sexual practice, seems to have become a dominant mode of gay civil rights discourse, where we ask for lower ages of consent, or the opportunity to become open members of the armed forces, or for the opportunity to have our relationships administered by state institutions, on the basis of achieving equality with heterosexuals. What does gender dissent, with its unsettling connotations of pathological third sex identities, have to offer such lesbians and gay men, whose political project is to seek equality within existing social formations?

Heterosocial bonds are clearly going to be of little use to those gay men whose social and economic security naturalizes their performance of masculinity. For these kinds of gay men their material access to power balances out their cultural disadvantage as abject functions of homosocial knowledge to such an extent that they may effectively understand themselves as 'good citizens'. It seems unlikely that we would expect an involvement in the messy, distressing and disruptive business of radicalism when the inducements not to are so powerful and pleasurable.

We can see the effects of this kind of understanding in the assimilationist politics of Andrew Sullivan, discussed in Chapter 3. He displays what appears to be a naive surprise that gay men continue to be denied the same kinds of civil rights accorded to their heterosexual brethren, and sees gay marriage, gay military and equal ages of consent as our rights as otherwise institutionally privileged subjects. Such articulation necessarily identifies us with the kinds of oppressive and powerful systems which continue to diminish the life opportunities of other marginal groups. Is this really the kind of complicity that we want? For these kinds of gay men there is no advantage in understanding their queerness as anything other than an erotic disposition, oppressed as a function of ignorance and squeamishness, but hedonistically exalted in the libidinous eroticism of gay subculture to such an extent that it closes the gap between their exclusion as homosexuals and their otherwise respectable masculine citizenship. We can see a more thoughtful and contorted version of this kind of thinking in Mark Simpson's work, which we looked at in Chapter 2. Here the naturalization of the desirability of gay masculinity is so complete as to stretch out into an appreciation of heterosexual manhood as a misguided representation of queerness itself.

Here, and in Leo Bersani's *Homos*, the ironic phallic doubling gay clone culture often celebrated, which played on the tension between an acknowledgement of our constitution as dickless faggots and our unmediated sexual obsession with the penis (we have got one, and *he has* got one too . . .), loses its transgressive flourish and becomes an assimilationist hankering for the elusive homosocial subjectivity sexual indifference promises. The security of that subjectivity is elusive for heterosexual men, never mind queers, as we have seen. Patriarchal regimes precisely gain their vehemence from the anxiety homosocial narratives produce in potential male subjects, which necessitates the constant display of their exchange of women and a suppression of homosexuality. However pleasurable, privileged and materially secure such negotiations of prejudice are, they will never challenge the very power base that is the source of that prejudice.

As we have seen, the disgust and oppression produced by heterosexual cultures about homosexual eroticism are functions of the place queerness has in ideologies of gender, rather than being due to inadequate levels of awareness or patronage. The circumscription of their libidinous activities experienced by assimilationist, affluent, white, middle-class, well educated, professional gay men who can pass as masculine, is caused by the functional effects this legislation produces in heterosexual male subjects who must repress the queer threat and its proximity to them. Such an awareness may comfortably elude privileged gay men because their very performance of gender is a denial of those signs which indicate the presence of demonized faggottry. Double incomes, double dicks, no kids and access to metropolitan facilities can feel like good citizenship despite legislative difficulties. These men are not fags, just as women who relish the privileges of marriage and the humiliations of male objectification are not hags. There is no advantage for assimilated gay men in making heterosocial bonds with women, or enabling some other form of gender dissent, unless that heterosocial affiliation enables a commodified exchange, as it seems to do in Pedro Almodóvar's public consort with female or transsexual members of his repertory company. In order to activate their dissident potential, heterosocial bonds necessitate a rejection of male homosocial affectations

of authority and an empathic affiliation with the realm of the commodified: an active identification with women, against (gay) men's gender
privileges.

Despite the fact that it merely confirms our awareness of how hegemonies function, it is ironic that the most materially and socially prosperous manifestations of homosexuality are those which are furthest
from an appreciation of the institutional source of our oppression.
These libidinous negotiations of prejudice are not only assimilationist,
they actually naturalise performances of masculinity and the male
power that such performances broker. They are unlikely to facilitate an
understanding of what constitutes the intolerable in homosexuality,
and thus they are self-defeating. The more subtle ways of displaying
masculinity gay men find, the more we may attempt to 'queer' dominant performances of masculinity, the more we effect a proximity
between queerness and masculinity, then the more we underpin homosocial power by bringing the threat of queerness closer to homosocial
subjects whose naturalized masculinity is a function of homosexual
panic and the ruthless commodification of women. Aspiring to
masculine power, authority and legitimacy, maintaining an identification of desire to be and to have masculinity, reproduces the structure of
homosociality, a structure which enforces the castigation of homosexual eroticism as a function of its commodification of women. That
aspiration not only undermines the dissident potential of homosexuality in its assimilationism, but invigorates the very system which is the
source of our disempowerment, and collaborates in the continuing
powerlessness and exchange of women. Such concerns may not be con-
sonant with attempts to flourish as respectable, materially prosperous
citizens: there is a profound challenge in attempting to implicate our
more successful and incorporated gay men in political engagements
and social responsibilities that undermine their levels of comfort and
assimilationism.

If hags and fags are 'sisters', then we are indeed queer ones. The sistership we have the potential to share by virtue of our mutual oppression
within hetero-patriarchal regimes, is 'queered' as a function of the way
our identities are circumscribed by the homosocial narratives that
uphold those regimes. Yet if that queering of our homosocial potential
is an obstacle to bonds between women and gay men, it also marks the
dissident potential of an affiliation that by definition threatens the
integrity of male homosocial subjectivity, by eclipsing the power of that
subjectivity through the very axis of its structural integrity. Homosociality exists as that which is circumscribed by homosexual panic and

exploitation of women. As heterosocial relationships make considerable demands upon both women and gay men who participate in them in order that their dissident effectiveness may sustain, they also often work, as we have seen, to threaten each member of the bond under the most vulnerable term of their identity. Heterosexual women acquire social credibility precisely through their naturalized connection to heterosexual male authority: that is, the kinds of behaviour they enact in order to preserve their heterosexual privilege are understood as natural expressions of their womanhood. There would seem to be little value for women who wish to sustain their heterosexual privilege in de-naturalizing that which is the very opportunity for gaining access to rational cultural credibility. The effect, in relationships which strive for heterosociality, of this reluctance to de-naturalize femininity and gender role-playing, is to 'queer' gay men's unnatural, often feminised gender performances. Gay men who female identify, are thus often cast, in heterosocial relationships, as unnatural women, inferior and subject to disenfranchisement by the 'proper' feminine performances of straight women. Similarly, if gay men do not accede their male authority in heterosocial bonds with women, by enacting that disempowering identification with the commodified realm of the feminine, then they risk entering into those heterosocial relationships on the same terms in which women experience conventional homosocial relationships with men, where there must take up deferential roles as functions of sexual indifference. We can see the effects of the former tendency in *Rose-anne's* Leon, the Mary-come-lately; and we can see the effects of the latter tendency in Pedro Almodóvar's public consort and exchange of women who are subject to the director for their livelihood. As we have seen, despite Roseanne Conner's heterosexuality, *Roseanne* offers considerable heterosocial potential, as does *Women on the Verge of a Nervous Breakdown*; our successes, however, will always be hard won and plagued by assimilationist tendencies which draw us back towards patterns which are sponsored by dominant authorities.

We may suggest that the success of heterosocial relationships with straight women may for gay men be related to their investment in queer sistership with lesbians. For it is through relationships with lesbians that gay men really have the opportunity to challenge their own gender power. Relationships with straight women are often fraught because the terrain upon which those connections are made is always mediated – that is, it is not a queer one, not one in which heterosexuality as a given, natural phenomena is problematized. Furthermore, some relationships between gay men and straight women promote the notion of gay men's sensitivity which offers respite for women from straight men (such as those represented in *My Best Friend's Wedding* and *The Object of My Affection*). Such relationships implicate gay men in a homophobic collusion with straight women's repression of the political and cultural challenge lesbianism offers to heterosexual privilege and objectification.[8] Gay men's relationships with lesbians are conducted under the mutual acknowledgement of queerness, such that the gender performance of each is equally and celebratedly unnatural. Relationships between gay men and straight women seem to be perpetually negotiating the structuring absence of straight men and this locks us, as we have seen, into a perpetual dialectic with homosocial triads which produce a mutually alienating asymmetry. Each agency of disempowerment remains active in relation to the other: queerness remains perverse in relation to heterosexual women, who remain sexually indifferent in relation to (gay) maleness. It seems very difficult to engage a public affiliation with the 'otherness' across the triadic structure of homosociality without re-presenting that 'otherness'. As we have seen, in *Roseanne*, queers still seem to be the playthings of natural folks, and in *Fag Hag* the withdrawal of gay men's attention leads to madness, however ironically it may be presented.

Queer sistership with lesbians may liberate gay men from the homosocial trap. On the one hand a mutual recognition of queerness prevents any pathologisation of performances which are unnatural, as it also prevents gay men from assuming the stance of the oppressed martyr on the liberally inverted hierarchy of oppression. In heterosocial relations with women, both sets of identities are jostling for small residual faultlines within homosocial systems: it is because of this that relations between women and gay men are often adversarial, even when those relations are striving for heterosociality, as we saw with the 'theoretical fag hags' of *Attitude*. Shared queer culture with lesbians makes it very difficult for anyone to lay cultural claim to the essential 'truth' of identity. Although some lesbian feminism does challenge expressions of gay male female identification, that challenge is framed, as we have seen, in the context of a de-naturalization of male power and heterosexuality. In relation to this kind of political culture gay men's empathic alignment with the female realm of the commodified will not threaten the basis of lesbians' social privilege, as it often does in relation to straight women. Furthermore, in bonds with lesbians gay men will be able to more fully escape a reactionary entrapment by homosociality and be able to more deeply challenge the foundations of their male gender roles. Lesbianism is woman-centred and is organized as a resistance of those structures which impel women to act in the interests of men. In heterosocial relationships with lesbians, gay men will be challenged where they are strong and often culpable, that is as subjects who often ventriloquise patriarchal values. The mutual acknowledgement of the inauthenticity and contingency of gender performance would seem to be a precondition of heterosocial bonds with lesbians: we are all queers, and nobody can pretend that that they are a real girl (or boy): other than our same-sex desire, that is what we share.

The advances available to gay men through civil rights activism are achievable and nearly won. While we must remain vigilant against the growth of the ultra-right and maintain our presence as lobbyists and politicians at local, national and international levels, we must also remember that we are queer and that this is something tremendous, that we have our own cultures and that assimilation is cultural death. Our frequent political insistence on our *tolerability* has serious implications that undermine our own alliances of sistership, communality, support, resistance and excessive glamour which define us as gay men. We must remain able to conceive of our identities not only as functions of sex and desire, of privacy, domesticity and commodification, but of gender dissent, subcultural affiliation and the identification with fellow fags, hags and sisters.

We must remember how alluring it is to be fags, queens, screaming sisters, to be effeminate, to be fabulous, intolerable, emotional, hysterical, unreasonable, to be bitch goddesses, twisted divas, mincing Marys, and *stop* pretending to be real. There is a place for making advances in our civil rights, but we must not allow ourselves to be fooled into thinking that this means that becoming good citizens is worth aspiring to, or possible. It isn't.

Notes

Introduction

1. Michael Bronski, *Culture Clash: The Making of Gay Sensibility* (Boston: South End Press, 1984), p. 2.
2. Martin Duberman, *Stonewall* (New York: Plume, 1994).
3. Throughout this work I have tried to be historically accurate about the use of terminology with which people attracted to their own sex, and people who publicly identify as such, have labelled themselves, and have been labelled by powerful social institutions, such as the psychiatric profession. The term 'homosexual' has carried with it connotations of the pathologisation by those medical professions that have used it, and has as a result, been used with some caution by gay men and lesbians themselves; however, the term is also useful for references that cover disparate historical moments and political alignments: in these instances I have used it. 'Gay' refers to those formations of identity which arose out of the Gay Liberation Movement that emerged as the subcultural organization of anger unleashed in the Stonewall riots of 1969. 'Queer' refers either to generally disparaging notions of homosexuality before Stonewall (although, like 'Faggot' and 'Queen', 'Queer' the term also has a celebratory context for pre-Stonewall homosexuals), or to particular political formations of homosexuality made since the early 1990s. Each of these contexts will be elaborated upon in the relevant chapters.
4. Ibid, p. 103.
5. It is clearly important to note some definitions upon which I am resting these discussions and the ones that follow. I take sex and sex difference to refer to the physical and physiological distinctions between different sorts of people that we refer to as men and women. Sexual orientation is the choice of sexual partner, not necessarily a function of sex and gender, but is often understood as such. I understand gender to be the manifestation of a role which negotiates the differential access to cultural and social power ascribed to sex difference, usually organized in terms of heterosexual formations of femininity and masculinity, and not necessarily related to sexual orientation, but often understood as such. In as far as each of these terms arises out of a culture which is not inert, then obviously each becomes dependent on the other. Once you shift one term, cultural knowledge – all the knowing that we have – shifts or inverts all the others. I take it as axiomatic that gender is an ideological formation arising out of a contest between powerful narratives that naturalize a hetero-patriarchal relationship between sex, orientation and gender, and resistant, oppositional and dissident arrangements which disrupt, displace and interrogate this naturalization. Particular enactments of gender roles are not the exclusive purview of either biological physical sex, or of any sexual orientation,

although powerful ideological formations would make such an understanding precarious and necessarily an act of dissent against hetero-patriarchal naturalization.

6. Dennis Altman, *Homosexual Oppression and Liberation* (New York: Avon, 1971), p. 118.
7. Bronski, *Culture Clash*, op. cit., p. 95.
8. Richard Dyer and Derek Cohen, 'The Politics of Gay Culture', in Gay Left Collective (eds), *Homosexuality: Power and Politics* (London: Alison & Busby, 1980), p. 178.
9. Ibid.
10. Corey K. Creekmur and Alexander Doty, 'Introduction', in Creekmur and Doty (eds) *Out in Culture: Lesbian, Gay and Queer Essays on Popular Culture* (Durham and London: Duke University Press, 1995), pp. 3–4. Note again how discussion of the Stonewall riots necessitates, for queer commentators, the ubiquitous commentary about Garland's funeral.
11. Dyer and Cohen, 'The Politics of Gay Culture', op. cit., p. 178.
12. Richard Dyer, 'It's being so camp as keeps us going', reprinted in Dyer, *Only Entertainment* (London and New York: Routledge, 1992), p. 136.
13. Richard Dyer, *Heavenly Bodies: Film Stars and Society* (New York: St. Martin's Press, 1986), pp. 141–94.
14. See Lisa Frank and Paul Smith (eds) *Madonnarama: Essays on Sex and Popular Culture* (Pittsburgh: Cleis Press, 1993) and Michael Musto, 'Immaculate Connection', reprinted in Creekmur and Doty (eds), *Out in Culture*, pp. 427–36. My own MA dissertation written in 1991 and titled 'Queer Icons: Women, Stardom and Gay Subculture' attempted to investigate gay men's investment in star iconography by situating Madonna in the context of the adoration of earlier icons like Judy Garland and Marilyn Monroe.
15. As indicative, see Andy Medhurst 'Pitching Camp', *City Limits*, 10–17 May 1990; Medhurst, 'Batman, Deviance and Camp', in Roberta E. Pearson and William Uricchio (eds) *The Many Lives of the Batman: Critical Approaches to a Superhero and his Media* (New York: Routledge, 1991); Medhurst, 'Camp', in Medhurst and Munt (eds) *Lesbian and Gay Studies: A Critical Introduction* (London: Cassell, 1997); Jonathan Dollimore, *Sexual Dissidence: Augustine to Wilde, Freud to Foucault* (Oxford: Clarendon Press, 1991), pp. 307–25; Alexander Doty, *Making Things Perfectly Queer: Interpreting Mass Culture* (Minneapolis: University of Minnesota Press, 1993), pp. 1–16; Jack Babuscio, 'Camp and the Gay Sensibility', in Richard Dyer (ed.) *Gays and Film* (London: BFI, 1977); Andrew Britton, 'For Interpretation: Notes Against Camp', *Gay Left*, 7, pp. 11–14.
16. Alan Sinfield, *The Wilde Century: Effeminacy, Oscar Wilde and the Queer Moment* (London: Cassell, 1994); Roger Baker, *Drag: A History of Female Impersonators in the Performing Arts* (London: Cassell, 1994); Kris Kirk and Ed Heath, *Men in Frocks* (London: Gay Men's Press, 1984); Marjorie Garber, *Vested Interests: Cross-Dressing and Cultural Anxiety* (New York: Routledge, 1992).
17. Alexander Doty, *Making Things Perfectly Queer*, op. cit., p. 7.
18. Mary Daly, *Gyn/Ecology: The Metaethics of Radical Feminism* (Boston: Beacon Press, 1978, pp. 14–17.
19. Ibid, p. x.

20. Douglas Crimp, 'Right On, Girlfriend!', in Michael Warner (ed.) *Fear of a Queer Planet: Queer Politics and Social Theory* (Minneapolis: University of Minnesota Press, 1993).
21. Ibid, p. 309.
22. Ibid, p. 318.
23. Alan Sinfield, *Faultlines: Cultural Materialism and the Politics of Dissident Reading* (Oxford: Oxford University Press, 1992).

1   From pathology to gender dissent: Tennessee Williams's *A Streetcar Named Desire*

1. John Peter, 'Desire's Cruel Devices', *Sunday Times*, 5 January 1997.
2. Alistair Macaulay, 'Neurotic Undercurrents in New Orleans', *Financial Times*, 2 January 1997.
3. Charles Spencer, 'This Stately Streetcar Fails to Move', *Daily Telegraph*, 1 January 1997.
4. Kate Clanchy, 'Arts Review', *Scotsman*, 7 January 1997.
5. Alistair Macaulay, 'Neurotic Undercurrents in New Orleans', op. cit.
6. Philip C. Kolin (ed.), *Confronting Tennessee Williams's 'A Streetcar Named Desire'* (New York: Greenwood Press, 1993); Ronald Hayman, *Tennessee Williams: Everyone Else is an Audience* (New Haven & London: Yale University Press, 1993).
7. Lyle Leverich, *Tom: The Unknown Tennessee Williams* (London: Hodder & Stoughton, 1995).
8. David Benedict, 'Tennessee Williams and His Women', *Independent*, 15 June 1994, Section 2, p. 23.
9. Molly Haskell, *From Reverence to Rape: The Treatment of Women in the Movies*, 2nd edn, (University of Chicago Press, 1987), p. 248.
10. Alistair Macaulay, 'Neurotic Undercurrents in New Orleans'.
11. John Gross, 'A Princess Goes Potty', *Sunday Telegraph*, 5 January 1997.
12. Michael Coveney 'A study in blush pink', *Observer Review*, 19 June 1994, p. 10.
13. David Savran, *Communists, Cowboys and Queers: The Politics of Masculinity in the Work of Arthur Miller and Tennessee Williams* (Minneapolis: University of Minnesota Press, 1982), p. 116.
14. In Karla Jay and Allen Young (eds) *Out of the Closets: Voices of Gay Liberation* (New York: Pyramid, 1974), p. 70.
15. Derek Jarman, *At Your Own Risk: A Saint's Testament*, (ed.) Michael Christie (London: Vintage, 1993), p. 55.
16. Howard Taubman, 'Modern Primer: Helpful Hints To Tell Appearances from Truth', *New York Times*, 28 April 1963, Section 2, p. 1.
17. Stanley Kauffman, *Persons of the Drama: Theater Criticism and Comment* (New York: Harper and Row, 1976) quoted in Michael Bronski, *Culture Clash: The Making of Gay Sensibility* (Boston: South End Press, 1984), p. 126.
18. Stephen S. Stanton (ed.) *Tennessee Williams: A Collection of Critical Essays* (Englewood Cliffs, N.J.: Prentice Hall, 1977).
19. Stephen S. Stanton 'Introduction' in Stephen S. Stanton (ed.) *Tennessee Williams: A Collection of Critical Essays*, p. 1.

20. In his essay 'Selected Memories of the Glorious Bird and the Golden Age', Gore Vidal details the extensive and vitriolic hostility to Williams in the period 1945 to 1961, which predated Stanton's liberal toleration.
21. Stanton, 'Introduction', p. 4.
22. Alan Sinfield, 'Un-American Activities', in Sinfield, *Cultural Politics – Queer Reading* (London: Routledge, 1994), p. 42.
23. Ibid.
24. Haskell suggests that 'it is from the male in them that the women acquire their hyperactive libidos . . . the scenes . . . between Marlon Brando and Vivien Leigh in *A Streetcar Named Desire* are powerfully sexual, in the flexing, posturing fascination of homosexual pornography for a repressed or 'closet' seductee.' *From Reverence*, op. cit., p. 248.
25. Tennessee Williams *Memoirs* (London: W.H. Allen, 1976): 'so incontinent was my desire for the boy that I would wake him repeatedly during the night for more lovemaking. You see, I had no sense in those days – and nights – of how passion can wear out even a passive partner . . . Kip said to me, 'Last night you made me know what is meant by beautiful pain.' (p. 55); Williams tells how the go-go boys in a bar in New Orleans all have clap in the ass and so you shouldn't penetrate them (p. 75); tells how he 'screwed' a gay marine seven times in one night; how he refused a sailor who wanted to fuck him (p. 79); how he doesn't like to be topped (p. 97); how a hustler he met was inexperienced and would not 'turn over', but who later said, 'Mr. Williams, if you'd like to, you can bugger me tonight.' (p. 154).
26. See Gert Hekma, '"A Female Soul in a Male Body": Sexual Inversion as Gender Inversion in Nineteenth Century Sexology', in Gilbert Herdt (ed.) *Third Sex, Third Gender: Beyond Sexual Dimorphism in Culture and History* (New York: Zone Books, 1994); George Chauncey, 'From Sexual Inversion to Homosexuality: Medicine and the Changing Conceptualization of Female Deviance', *Salmagundi*, 58–9, Fall 1982–Winter 1983; and Tim Edwards, *Erotics and Politics: Gay Male Sexuality, Masculinity and Feminism* (London and New York: Routledge, 1994), p. 19.
27. Hekma, 'A Female Soul in a Male body', op. cit., p. 220.
28. Ibid, p. 221.
29. Chauncey, 'From Sexual Inversion To Homosexuality', pp. 114–46.
30. 'The sexologists and boy-love advocates made the masculine/feminine binary structure even more necessary and central while, at the same time, doing little to clarify its confusions', Alan Sinfield, *The Wilde Century: Effeminacy, Oscar Wilde and the Queer Moment* (London: Cassell, 1994), p. 118.
31. Richard von Krafft-Ebing's *Psychopathia sexualis mit besonderer Berucksichtigung der contraren Sexualempfindung: Eine klinisch-forensische Studie* was published in 1886; Karl Heinrich Ulrichs's 'Vier Briefe' *Jahrbuch fur sexuekke Zwischenstufen* was published in 1899: see Gert Hekma, 'A Female Soul in a Male body', op. cit., p. 542.
32. E.M. Forster 'Terminal Note' to *Maurice* (London: Penguin, 1972), p. 217.
33. John Fletcher 'Forster's *Maurice* and the scapegoating of Clive' in Joseph Bristow (ed.) *Sexual Sameness: Textual Differences in Lesbian and Gay Writing* (London: Routledge, 1992) in which he outlines the confusions and tensions in the Platonic texts themselves about the ethical and social meanings of sexual and non-sexual relations between men.

34. Ibid. p. 90.
35. See Alan Sinfield, *Literature, Politics and Culture in Postwar Britain* (Oxford: Basil Blackwell, 1989): 'Homosexuality was a further reason for commitment to the life-style of the leisure class, where its practice was most possible. There was more toleration than elsewhere, one might evade difficulties through the deployment of money or influence, and one was well-placed to gratify and impress lower-class young men – whole groups of whom, guardsmen for instance, learned how to play the scene.' (p. 65) This association of homosexuality with the leisure classes has subsequently been challenged by Murray Healy in *Gay Skins* (London: Cassell, 1996).
36. See Sinfield *The Wilde Century*: 'At that point [after the trials of 1895], the entire, vaguely disconcerting nexus of effeminacy, leisure, idleness, immorality, luxury, insouciance, decadence and aestheticism, which Wilde was perceived, variously, an instantiating was transformed into a brilliantly precise image' (p. 3).
37. Forster, *Maurice*, p. 33. Further references to *Maurice* will be given in the text.
38. Forster, *Maurice*, p. 214; this also has the effect of securing the power relation embedded in their respective class identities – Clive's concern here is meant to be at least partly parochial.
39. Edward Carpenter, 'Self-Analysis for Havelock Ellis', reprinted in David Fernbach and Noel Greig (eds) *Selected Writings: Volume One: Sex* (London: Gay Men's Press, 1984), p. 290.
40. Francis King, *E.M. Forster* (London: Thames & Hudson, 1978), p. 80.
41. See Jeffrey Weeks, *Coming Out: Homosexual Politics in Britain, from the Nineteenth Century to the Present* (London: Quartet, 1977), pp. 68–70 for an account of Edward Carpenter's bourgeois background and the romanticized politics he developed of the working classes.
42. '[homos] have cast off, I noticed, most of the swish and camp that made them . . . unattractive to me' Williams, *Memoirs*, op. cit., p. 50.
43. See Alison Hennegan, 'Introduction' to Radclyffe Hall, *The Well of Loneliness* (London: Virago, 1982) among others for detail about this; we could suggest it as an instance of Foucault's reverse discourse.
44. See Alan Sinfield *Faultlines: Cultural Materialism and the Politics of Dissident Reading* (Oxford: Oxford University Press, 1992): 'faultline stories are . . . the ones in which the conditions of plausibility are in dispute. . . . The task for a political criticism, then, is to observe how stories negotiate the faultlines that distress the prevailing conditions of plausibility. [. . .] No story can contain all the possibilities it brings into play; coherence is always selection.' pp. 47–51.
45. Eve Kosofsky Sedgwick *Epistemology of the Closet* (Hemel Hempstead: Harvester Wheatsheaf, 1991), p. 3.
46. See Michael Bronski *Culture Clash: The Making of Gay Sensibility* (Boston: South End Press, 1984) and Jack Babuscio 'Camp and the Gay Sensibility' in *Gays and Film* (ed.) Richard Dyer (London: BFI, 1977) for an elaboration of the gay sensibility, and Joseph Bristow 'Being Gay: Politics, Identity, Pleasure' in *New Formations*, No. 9, Winter 1989, for a critique of these notions. Not all of the cultural expressions I note here were initially acceptable: some, such as pornography and sadomasochism, were highly controversial

within alliances of gay men and/or lesbians. The contestations over the issues divided many groups within the sexually dissident margins, and led to the sexual politics/politics of sexuality split that is the context for my discussions in the next chapter. However, by the time of a pre-queer period, all these forms have become understood as expressions of gay culture and identity: often their problematization has centralized their importance.

47. John D'Emilio *Sexual Politics, Sexual Communities: the Making of a Homosexual Minority in the United States 1940–1970* (Chicago: Chicago University Press, 1983), p. 240.
48. This notion of the parity between Queer politics and Liberationary politics is disputed by Greg Bredbeck in 'The New Queer Narrative', *Textual Practice*, Vol. 9, No. 3, 1995, pp. 477–502, who argues for the distinctiveness of the two movements.
49. National Lesbian and Gay Survey, *Proust, Cole Porter, Michelangelo, Marc Almond and me: Writings by gay men on their lives and lifestyles from the archives of the National Lesbian and Gay Survey* (London: Routledge, 1993), p. 7.
50. Ibid, p. 110.
51. John M. Clum, '"Something Cloudy, Something Clear": Homophobic Discourse in Tennessee Williams', in R.R. Butters, J.M. Clum and M. Moon (eds), *Displacing Homophobia* (Durham, NC: Duke University Press, 1989); and Clum, *Acting Gay: Male Homosexuality in Modern Drama* (New York: Columbia University Press, 1994), p. 149.
52. Clum, *Acting Gay*, op. cit., p. 150, emphasis added.
53. For example, Mark Lilly, *Gay Men's Literature in the Twentieth Century*, London: Macmillan, 1993, pp. 105–15, discusses how Williams's homosexuality is metaphorically refracted through, among others, Laura's lameness in *The Glass Menagerie*.
54. Clum, 'Something Cloudy, Something Clear', op. cit. and *Acting Gay*, op. cit., p. 150. Further references to *Acting Gay* will be given in the text.
55. Eve Kosofsky Sedgwick *Between Men: English Literature and Male Homosocial Desire* (New York: Columbia University Press, 1985); Craig Owens 'Outlaws: Gay Men in Feminism' in Alice Jardine and Paul Smith (eds) *Men in Feminism* (New York and London: Routledge, 1989).
56. Neil Bartlett *Night After Night* (London: Methuen 1993), p. 14.
57. Tennessee Williams *A Streetcar Named Desire* (London: Penguin 1959), p. 183. There is an interesting discrepancy between the text of the Penguin edition and that of the New Directions text *The Theatre of Tennessee Williams* (1971) which includes the line 'the boy I had married and the older man who had been his friend for years' which is omitted in the former.
58. Gregg Blachford 'Male Dominance and the gay world' in Kenneth Plummer (ed.) *The Making of the Modern Homosexual* (London: Hutchinson, 1981), p. 187.
59. Judith Butler, *Bodies that Matter: On the Discursive Limits of 'Sex'* (New York and London: Routledge, 1993).
60. Judith Butler, *Gender Trouble: Feminism and the Subversion of Identity* (New York and London: Routledge, 1990).
61. Sheila Jeffreys, *The Lesbian Heresy: A Feminist Perspective on the Lesbian Sexual Revolution* (London: The Women's Press, 1994), p. 97.

62. Ibid, p. 118.
63. See Maddison 'All Queered Out' *Red Pepper,* No. 9, February 1995.
64. Judith Butler *Gender Trouble,* op. cit., p. x.
65. In his review of a British Conference in 1994, *Troublesome Visibilities,* which was advertised as 'Reviewing Queer Theory and Gender Performance', and in which he was a participant, the influential British gay journalist Paul Burston bemoaned the absence of straight men and suggested that a transsexual spoke as though they were on *The Oprah Winfrey Show;* he also pointed out that to lament the absence of a black male speaker 'was strangely out of synch with notions of non-fixed subjectivities'. (*Troublesome Visibilities,* London 30 April 1994; Burston's report appeared in *Time Out* 11–18 May 1994, p. 90).
66. See Hilary Harris, 'Toward a Lesbian Theory of Performance: Refunctioning Gender' in Lynda Hart and Peggy Phelan (eds) *Acting Out: Feminist Performances* (Ann Arbor: University of Michigan Press, 1993), p. 273.
67. Bette Bourne, Peggy Shaw Paul Shaw and Lois Weaver, *Belle Reprieve.* In *Gay and Lesbian Plays Today,* (ed.) Terry Helbing (Portsmouth, NH: Heinemann, 1993), p. 8. Further references to *Belle Reprieve* will be given in the text.
68. Harris, 'Toward a Lesbian Theory of Performance: Refunctioning Gender', op. cit., p. 261.
69. Ronald Hayman, *Tennessee Williams: Everyone Else in an Audience* (New Haven and London: Yale University Press, 1993), p. xiii; Mark Lilly, *Gay Men's Literature in the Twentieth Century,* op. cit., p. 114; C.W.E. Bigsby, *A Critical Introduction to Twentieth Century American Drama, Volume Two: Williams, Miller, Albee* (Cambridge: Cambridge University Press, 1984), p. 60.
70. Donald Spoto *The Kindness of Strangers: The Life of Tennessee Williams* (London: The Bodley Head, 1985), p. 44.
71. *A Streetcar Named Desire* (London: Penguin, 1962), p. 115. Further references to this edition of *Streetcar* will be given in the text.
72. Sander Gilman, 'Black Bodies, White Bodies: Toward an iconography of Female Sexuality in Late Nineteenth-Century Art, Medicine and Literature' in James Donald and Ali Rattansi (eds) *'Race', Culture and Difference* (London: Sage, 1992), p. 174.
73. Lionel Kelly, 'The White Goddess, Ethnicity, and the Politics of Desire' in Philip C. Kolin (ed.) *Confronting Tennessee Williams's A Streetcar Named Desire* (New York: Greenwood Press, 1993), p. 121.
74. Gilman, 'Black Bodies, White Bodies', op. cit., p. 176.
75. Angela Davis *Women, Race and Class* (London: The Women's Press, 1982), p. 174.
76. Williams, *Sweet Bird of Youth* (London: Penguin, 1962), pp. 66–67.
77. Derek Jarman, *At Your Own Risk,* op. cit., p. 55.
78. One of Taubman's list of signs of unwanted homosexuality in American theatre was 'the male character who is young, handsome, remote and lofty in a neutral way . . . be on guard for the male character whose proclivities are like a stallions', 'Modern Primer: Helpful Hints To Tell Appearances from Truth', op. cit.
79. Charles Spencer, 'This Stately Streetcar Fails to Move', *Daily Telegraph,* 1 January 1997.

80. Michael Billington, 'Persistence of a Bleak Vision', *Guardian*, 31 December 1996.
81. Bigsby, *A Critical Introduction to Twentieth Century American Drama*, Volume Two, p. 60.
82. Sheila Gish, 'Tennessee Williams and his Women', *Independent*, 15 June 1994.
83. John Peter, 'Desire's Cruel Devices', op. cit.
84. Alistair Macaulay, 'Neurotic Undercurrents in New Orleans', op. cit.
85. Michael Billington, 'Persistence of Bleak Vision', op. cit.
86. *Streetcar*, p. 148, emphasis added.
87. For an audience with knowledge of Williams's biography, there is an additional point of connection here: his sister Rose suffered a similar fate for behaviour that was related to her alleged lack of sexual modesty; see Williams's *Memoirs*.

    Donald Spoto sheds a different light on this, and suggests that Rose was the victim of sexual abuse at the hands of their father and that her mental health problems were a consequence of bearing the responsibility of silence, having been disbelieved once by their mother, Miss Edwina. (Spoto, *The Kindness of Strangers*, op. cit., pp. 59, 61) It has been suggested that the scenario which unfolds in *Suddenly Last Summer* was inspired by Williams's guilt over Rose's eventual lobotomy. In the play Catherine will be lobotomized for bearing witness to her cousin Sebastian's procuring of young boys for sex: it is interesting to reflect that in writing a narrative purportedly attempting to cathart the predicament of his sister – one that preoccupied him until his death – he seems to guiltily substitute a sexual identity symmetrical to his own for the abusive behaviour of his father.
88. The description is Boss Finley's, from *Sweet Bird of Youth*, p. 67.
89. Gore Vidal, *Palimpsest: A Memoir* (New York: Random House, 1995), pp. 155–6.

2 Heterosocial Tendencies

1. Sheila Jeffreys is indicative of the radical feminist position: her most recent work, *The Lesbian Heresy: A Feminist Perspective on the Lesbian Sexual Revolution* (London: The Women's Press, 1994) is a furious diatribe against Foucauldian feminism and what she terms 'lesbianandgay' theory. Examples of the so-called libertarian feminists include such sex radicals as Susie Bright and Pat Califia, but probably also stalwarts of critical theory, such as Judith Butler.
2. Gayle S. Rubin, 'Thinking Sex: Notes for a Radical Theory of the Politics of Sexuality' in Carole S. Vance (ed.) *Pleasure and Danger: Exploring Female Sexuality* (New York: Routledge & Kegan Paul, 1984) and 'The Traffic in Women: Notes on the 'Political Economy' of Sex' in Rayna R. Reiter (ed.) *Toward an Anthropology of Women* (New York: Monthly Review Press, 1975).
3. Rubin, 'Thinking Sex', op. cit., p. 309.
4. Michel Foucault, *The History of Sexuality* (New York: Pantheon, 1978), p. 106, cited by de Lauretis, 'Sexual Difference and Lesbian Representation' (*Theatre Journal*, 40, 1988) in discussion of Rubin, 'Thinking Sex' (Ibid, p. 307).
5. Such is the impact of post-Foucauldian theory that even those activists or theorists who object to the centrality of sexuality and desire based notions

of identity and politics must engage with its agenda; Jeffreys' *The Lesbian Heresy*, op. cit., is an example.

6. In Britain 'Queer' politics appeared to be very much a function of metropolitan and artistic subcultural activity in London, principally. The supposed coalescence of lesbians, gay men, people of colour, bisexuals, heterosexuals, sadomasochists, drag queens, fetishists and transsexuals, now appears quite momentary, and although promising, always seemed dominated by relatively institutionalised journalists and artists and those whose identities were already the most culturally validated – men, white people, the heterosexually privileged; with the occasional exceptions of those whose outrageousness was momentarily voyeuristically celebrated in the quality press or mainstream cosmopolitan culture (I shall return to this celebration in the chapter on Pedro Almodóvar). The trajectory of Queer politics in America has been similar, but was always founded in different conditions, where the HIV/AIDS emergency has been considerably more acute, lending an urgency to political militancy and coalition. And, as I noted in the previous chapter, gay or queer politics in America have culturally specific expectations that are a function of the ideological importance of the Constitution: the call to a Queer Nation in the States has an entirely different resonance than it would elsewhere.

7. Jana Sawicki, 'Identity Politics and Sexual Freedom: Foucault and Feminism' in Irene Diamond and Lee Quinby (eds) *Feminism and Foucault: Reflections on Resistance* (Boston: Northeastern University Press, 1988); and also in Sawicki, *Disciplining Foucault: Feminism, Power and the Body* (New York and London: Routledge, 1991).

8. Ibid.

9. Caroline Ramazanoglu and Janet Holland, 'Women's sexuality and men's appropriation of desire', in C. Ramazanoglu (ed.) *Up Against Foucault: Explorations of some tensions between Foucault and feminism* (London and New York: Routledge, 1993).

10. See Ramazanoglu and Holland, 'Women's sexuality and men's appropriation of desire', p. 239, for further discussion of this.

11. Sandra Lee Bartky, *Femininity and Domination: Studies in the Phenomenology of Oppression* (London: Routledge, 1990), p. 65.

12. Domna C. Stanton, 'Introduction: The Subject of Sexuality' in Domna C. Stanton (ed.) *Discourses of Sexuality: From Aristotle to AIDS* (Ann Arbor: University of Michigan Press, 1992), pp. 1–46.

13. An extreme example is Louise J. Kaplan's work, *Female Perversions* (London: Penguin, 1993).

14. Leo Bersani, *Homos* (Cambridge, MA and London: Harvard University Press, 1995), p. 113. Further page references will be given in the text.

15. One could speculate that the missing figure here is Oscar Wilde, often included with the others as the epitome of witty transgressive immorality. It would be unfair to Bersani to condemn him for not considering Wilde, but it is interesting to note that of all of them, he is probably the least easily recuperable to a masculinist agenda, given that his trial is identified as the moment at which the notions of homosexuality and effeminacy first coalesced.

16. In his contribution to the volume *Constructing Masculinity* (eds) Maurice Berger, Brian Wallis and Simon Watson (New York: Routledge, 1995), entitled

'Loving Men', Bersani notes that: 'In that tension [between our 'political alignments' and our 'phantasmatic investments'] lies an important moral dimension of our political engagements. But to be aware of the tension means being aware of both sets of determining factors, and perhaps especially of those identifications and erotic interests it is not always gratifying to acknowledge.' (p. 117).

17. Teresa de Lauretis, 'Sexual Difference and Lesbian Representation', reprinted in Henry Abelove, Mich le Aina Barale and David M. Halperin (eds) *The Lesbian and Gay Studies Reader* (New York and London: Routledge, 1993).

18. Ibid, p. 143.

19. In *The Persistent Desire: A lesbian femme/butch reader* (Boston: Alyson, 1991), Joan Nestle talks about her own experiences of homophobia from other lesbians because of her identification as a femme. Elsewhere in the collection, butch lesbians express similar experiences.

20. I am here specifying gay male identification rather than lesbian identification, not because I believe lesbian practice to be tremendously different, or any less important than that of gay men, but because of the intrinsically different power relations in the two sets of identifications. It is precisely my intention to assess the effects of gay male practice on the constitution of gender authority and gauge the potential radicalism (or reactionism) in gay male practice. Nor do I wish to gesture at the existence of specific lesbian practices, while pretending I would rather they went away. Many studies tokenistically gesture towards difference without ever attempting to resolve the complexities it raises. At those points at which lesbian cultural practice throws gay male practice into relief, confusion or suspicion I intend to try and maintain a commitment to handling such complexity.

21. Eve Kosofsky Sedgwick *Between Men: English Literature and Male Homosocial Desire* (New York: Columbia University Press, 1985), p. 3; subsequent page references will be given in the text as BM.

22. Teresa de Lauretis, 'Film and the Visible' in Bad Object Choices (eds) *How Do I Look? Queer Film and Video* (Seattle: Bay Press, 1991), pp. 223–64; see also Terry Castle, *The Apparitional Lesbian: Female Homosexuality and Modern Culture* (New York: Columbia University Press, 1993), pp. 67–73.

23. Craig Owens 'Outlaws: Gay Men in Feminism' in Alice Jardine and Paul Smith (eds) *Men in Feminism* (New York and London: Routledge, 1989), p. 223.

24. Owens' reading of Irigaray could be disputed. The seminal essay 'Sexual Difference and Lesbian Representation' by Teresa de Lauretis (*Theatre Journal* 40, 1988; reprinted in Abelove, Barale and Halperin (eds) *The Lesbian and Gay Studies Reader*, New York and London: Routledge, 1993) takes as its theoretical grist a distinction de Lauretis precisely identifies in Irigaray's work between homosexuality and hommo-sexuality. For de Lauretis, this distinction expresses the paradox of sexual (in)difference, in which lesbian desire is inconceivable within the terms of sexual difference – a binary with no dialectic, no subject position other than that of the male, no desire other than that of the male, no sexuality other than male sexuality ('hommo-sexuality'). De Lauretis argues that these are the terms of heterosexuality, terms through which the possibility of lesbianism is effaced. Within de Lauretis' deployment of Irigaray, male phallic homosexuality does become visible (and distinct from male bonding), if only by connotation. She

identifies a paradox between hommo-sexuality and homosexuality, one that we could name as homosociality, but the implication of her positing of this proximity is the emergence of a gay male who is disenfranchized from the system of sexual indifference neither by his hommo-sexuality, his masculinity and maleness, nor by his narcissistic desire in others (*hommes/homos*) for that hommo-sexuality. Ironically, then, we see that the only terms of male homosexuality are masculine ones: it is perhaps this phallocentric construction of gay male sexuality that Owens objects to. It is ironic to note the similarity between what Owens appears to object to in Irigaray and Showalter's work, and the celebratory nihilistic phallicism Bersani admires in Genet's considerations of fascism.

25. Leo Bersani, 'Is the Rectum a Grave?' in Douglas Crimp (ed.) *AIDS: Cultural Analysis Cultural Activism* (London and Cambridge, MA: University of Massachusetts Press, 1988), p. 212.

26. Tania Modleski, *Feminism Without Women: Culture and Criticism in a 'Postfeminist' Age*, (New York and London: Routledge, 1991), pp. 62–3.

27. Ibid.

28. Other than Leo Bersani, Mario Mieli is one of the few gay male writers to have candidly and explicitly considered gay male anal eroticism and its relation to male heterosexual anxiety, in his book, *Homosexuality and Liberation: Elements of a Gay Critique*, (London: Gay Men's Press, 1980), pp. 137–45. Mieli's work is a fabulous melange of a queen's subcultural world view and dense theoretical readings: 'The point is, that if you get fucked, if you know what tremendous enjoyment is to be had from anal intercourse, then you necessarily become different from the 'normal' run of people with a frigid arse.... Of all the aspects of homosexuality, I would say that the one heterosexual men fear above all is anal intercourse.' (p. 139).

29. The phrase is Sedgwick's own: she uses it in pointing out Marjorie Garber's effacement of complex negotiations of homo/heterosexual oppression and resistance in cross-dressing; Eve Sedgwick and Michael Moon, 'Divinity: A Dossier, A Performance Piece, A Little-Understood Emotion', in Eve Sedgwickt (ed.) *Tendencies* (New York and London: Routledge, 1994), p. 223.

30. Julia Penelope, 'Heteropatriarchal Semantics: Just Two Kinds of People in the World', *Lesbian Ethics* 2.2, 1986, p. 59.

31. Mary Daly, *Gyn/Ecology: The Metaethics of Radical Feminism* (Boston: Beacon Press, 1978) p. 357 and p. 359; subsequent page references will be given in the text, and identified as G/E.

32. David Van Leer 'The Beast of the Closet: Homosociality and the Pathology of Manhood', *Critical Inquiry* 15, No. 3, Spring 1989, p. 605; subsequent page references will be given in the text, BC.

33. Richard Dyer, *Brief Encounter* (London: BFI, 1993), pp. 11–12.

34. Andy Medhurst, 'Karaoke Treatment', *Sight and Sound*, Vol. 4, No. 4, April 1994, p. 32.

35. Paula Graham, 'Girl's Camp? The Politics of Parody', in Tamsin Wilton (ed.) *Immortal Invisible: Lesbians and the Moving Image* (London and New York: Routledge, 1995), p. 168.

36. Ibid, p. 177.

37. Mark Simpson, *Male Impersonators: Men Performing Masculinity* (London: Cassell, 1994), p. 4 (emphasis in original).
38. Lynne Segal, *Straight Sex: The Politics of Pleasure* (London: Virago, 1994), p. 199.
39. See Allan Hunter, 'Same Door, Different Closet: A Heterosexual Sissy's Coming-Out Party' in Sue Wilkinson and Celia Kitzinger (eds) *Heterosexuality: A Feminism and Psychology Reader* (London: Sage, 1993), pp. 150–69, for a consideration by a heterosexual man of the disjuncture between dominant faction membership and the inability to display appropriate manliness.
40. See my 'Small Towns, Boys and Ivory Towers: A Naked Academic' in Jan Campbell and Janet Harbord (eds) *Temporalities: Autobiography in a Postmodern Age* (Manchester: Manchester University Press, 2000) for further discussion of the difficulties associated with the commodification of gay male identities in urban spaces.
41. Editorial, *Attitude*, No. 1, May 1994, p. 7.
42. For an account of the emergence of these publications, see my 'A Queered Pitch', *Red Pepper*, February 1995, p. 27.
43. Ruth Picardie, 'My date with kd lang', *Attitude*, No. 8, December 1994, p. 49.
44. Suzanne Moore, 'Merchant semen', *Attitude*, No. 5, September 1994, p. 51.
45. Angela Lambert, 'Close to you', *Attitude*, No. 12, April 1995, p. 51.
46. Suzanne Moore, 'You don't have to be gay around here . . . but it helps', *Attitude*, No. 1, May 1994, p. 61.
47. Ibid.
48. Suzi Feay, 'Will the real miss thing please stand up?', *Attitude*, No. 3, July 1994, p. 57.
49. See Richard Dyer, 'Is a gay man always a girl's best friend?', *Attitude*, No. 15, July 1995, p. 114, for a consideration of gay male misogyny among female identifying constituencies.
50. Suzi Feay, op. cit., p. 57.
51. Suzanne Moore, 'You don't have to be gay . . . ', op. cit., p. 61.
52. Ibid.
53. Henry Jenkins, *Textual Poachers: Television Fans and Participatory Culture* (New York: Routledge, 1992); Constance Penley, *NASA/Trek: Popular Science and Sex in America* (London and New York: Verso, 1997).
54. Jenkins, Ibid, p. 192.
55. Much of this work is available on the internet. For general archives of slash fiction of all types see 'Slash Fiction on the Net' http://members.aol.com/ksnicholas/fanfic/slash.html, 'Slash Revolution International' http://www.frii.com/~xangst/sri/index.html; for fiction by explicitly gay men and lesbians, as well as straight women, see the Slashkink Archive http://www.geocities.com/SoHo/Gallery/8743/slashkfict.htm; for explicitly lesbian slash see 'Obsession's Homepage Presents: The Xena Warrior Princess Lesbian Fanfiction Index' http://www.obsession14.com/XenaRotica/fanindex.html.
56. See the Slashkink news group SlashKink@eGroups.com, 'Is it just me?' 4/1/99–5/1/99 and 'Are they gay?' 6/1/99.
57. 'Britta's Slash Page' http://www/tommyhawksfantasyworld.com /britta/.
58. ASCEM (L) is 'alt.startrek.creative.erotica.moderated' http://come.to/treksmut/.
59. *The Taming of Tom Paris*, Britta's Slash Page, op. cit.

3   *Roseanne*: Domestic Goddess as Heterosocial Heroine?

1. In *Lesbian Studies: Setting An Agenda* (London and New York: Routledge, 1995) Tamsin Wilton makes the following assessment of Simon Watney's argument in his *Policing Desire: Pornography, AIDS and the Media*: 'Gay men ... who see gay male sex in a homophobic culture as intrinsically radical, and for whom the assertive and defiant expression of sexuality has developed as the backbone of the collective cultural struggle to survive AIDS, have denounced a monolithic 'feminism' as life-threatening in its erotophobia and prudery'. (p. 102).
2. Celia Farber, 'Don't Tread on Me', *Spin*, May 1996, Vol. 12, No. 2, p. 40.
3. John Lahr, 'Dealing with Roseanne', *The New Yorker*, 17 July 1995; Kevin Sessums, 'Really Roseanne', *Vanity Fair*, February 1994; Celia Farber, 'Don't Tread on Me', *Spin*, May 1996, Vol. 12, No. 2.
4. Farber, 'Don't Tread on Me', p. 41.
5. *Out*, No. 29, February 1996.
6. *Out*, No. 24, July/August 1995.
7. Peter Galvin, 'Her life as a woman', *The Advocate*, 24 January 1995, p. 52, emphasis in original.
8. Tim Allis, 'The Faces of Straight America', *Out*, No. 24, July/August 1995, p. 70.
9. Sue Carswell, 'Roseanne for Queen of the Universe', *Out*, No. 29, February 1996, p. 114. In the 1997 season, during which *Roseanne* has dramatised the difficulties faced by the Conner family now that they are multi-millionaires, Roseanne's screen mother, Bev Harris, has admitted that while her now dead husband was having sex with her she would fantasize about the photographs in her illicitly consumed copies of *Playboy*.
10. It should be noted however, that *Roseanne*'s identification of the Conner family's class identity has been subject to considerable change, even disengenuousness, throughout its run. By the time of the 1995 season Roseanne runs her own business and is no longer quite so oppressively positioned as she once was. See Janet Lee, 'Subversive Sitcoms: *Roseanne* as Inspiration for Feminist Resistance', *Women's Studies*, Vol. 21, 1992; and Kathleen K. Rowe, 'Roseanne: Unruly Woman as Domestic Goddess', in Horace Newcomb (ed.) *Television: The Critical View* (Oxford University Press, 1994). Furthermore, at the beginning of the 1996/97 season the Conners win the Illinois State lottery and become multi-millionaires, which at the least represents an abandonment of the show's realism, if not its commitment to working-class politics. This shift in the fortunes of the Conners does not appear to have been popular. In the UK Channel 4 moved *Roseanne*, in the middle of its season run, from its prime time position in the schedule on Friday nights at 10 p.m. to a late-night mid-week slot, on Wednesdays at 11.30 p.m.
11. Lahr, 'Dealing with Roseanne', p. 51.
12. Roseanne Arnold, *Roseanne: My Lives* (London: Century, 1994), pp. 91–5, 107–10, 111–30.
13. Lahr, 'Dealing with Roseanne', p. 54.
14. Lisa Schwarzbaum, 'All the Rage', *Entertainment Weekly*, 21 April 1995, No. 271, p. 24.
15. Galvin, 'Her life as a woman', p. 52.

16. Schwarzbaum, 'All the Rage', p. 24.
17. Ibid.
18. Mick Bowes, 'Only When I Laugh', in Andrew Goodwin and Garry Whannel (eds) *Understanding Television* (New York and London: Routledge, 1990) p. 129.
19. For Roseanne's body image see, among others, Sessums, 'Really Roseanne', *Vanity Fair*, February 1994. For considerations of the connections between homosexuality and sickness and deformity, see Simon Watney, 'Sex, Diversity and Disease' in S. Watney (ed.) *Policing Desire: Pornography, AIDS and the Media* (Minneapolis: University of Minnesota Press, 1987); Stuart Marshall, 'Picturing Deviancy' in Tessa Boffin and Sunil Gupta (eds), *Ecstatic Antibodies: Resisting the AIDS Mythology* (London: Rivers Oram Press, 1990); and Paula A. Treichler, 'AIDS, Homophobia, and Biomedical Discourse: An Epidemic of Signification' in Douglas Crimp (ed.) *AIDS: Cultural Analysis/ Cultural Activism* (Cambridge MA: MIT Press, 1988), among others.
20. Carswell, 'Roseanne for Queen of the Universe' front cover, op. cit.
21. On 'killer bitch' see Galvin, 'Her life as a woman', op. cit., p. 54; for 'Goddess of retribution' see Janet Lee, 'Subversive Sitcoms: *Roseanne* as Inspiration for Feminist Resistance', *Women's Studies*, Vol. 21, 1992.
22. For Roseanne's attack on Streep and Foster see Lahr, 'Dealing with Roseanne' op. cit., p. 58; for attack on feminism see Lahr, Ibid. p. 47; for employing men writers not women, see Sessums, 'Really Roseanne', p. 46.
23. Schwarzbaum, 'All the Rage' op. cit., p. 26.
24. Allis, 'The Faces of Straight America', op. cit., p. 70.
25. It doesn't seem irrelevant that Mariel Hemmingway famously played the object of Woody Allen's Lolita complex in his film *Manhattan* in 1979.
26. Eve Sedgwick, *Between Men, English Literature and Male Homosocial Desire* (New York: Columbia University Press, 1985), p. 89.
27. Carswell, 'Roseanne for Queen of the Universe', op. cit., p. 114; my emphasis.
28. Ibid.
29. *Roseanne*'s sharper eyed viewers may note that Elgin is the home of Lips, the gay bar: funny how Elgin seems to be the proximate, but not *too* proximate scene of diverse nefarious activities...
30. Leo Bersani, *Homos* (Cambridge, MA and London: Harvard University Press, 1995), p. 113.
31. *The Advocate*, 16 July 1996.
32. Andrew Sullivan, *Virtually Normal: An Argument About Homosexuality* (London: Picador, 1995), p. 183.
33. Ibid., p. 185.
34. Homocult, *Queer With Class: The First Book of Homocult* (Manchester: MS ED (The Talking Lesbian), 1992).
35. Ibid. (Note that Homocult's publication does not contain page numbers.)
36. I am thinking here of those texts, many of which are listed in Paul Rouen, *High Camp: A Gay Guide to Cult Films*, Vol. 1 (San Francisco: Leyland, 1994) a representative selection of which have made it into mandarin criticism in the works of Richard Dyer, Paula Graham, Alex Doty, Andy Medhurst, Michael Bronski, Andrea Weiss and others. See Dyer, *Heavenly Bodies: Film Stars and Society* (New York: St. Martin's Press, 1986) (especially pp. 141–94); Dyer, *Only Entertainment* (New York and London: Routledge, 1992) (especially

pp. 65–98, 135–48, 159–72); Dyer, *The Matter of Images: Essays on Repres-entations* (London and New York: Routledge, 1993) (especially pp. 19–51, 52–72); Dyer, *Brief Encounter* (London: BFI, 1993); Graham, 'Girl's Camp: The Pol-itics of Parody', in Tamsin Wilton (ed.) *Immortal, Invisible: Lesbians and the Moving Image* (London and New York: Routledge, 1995); Graham, 'Looking Lesbian: Amazons and Aliens in Science Fiction Cinema' in Diane Hamer and Belinda Budge (eds) *The Good, The Bad and the Gorgeous: Popular Cul-ture's Romance with Lesbianism* (London: Pandora, 1994); Doty, *Making Things Perfectly Queer* (Minneapolis: University of Minnesota Press, 1993); Medhurst, '*Victim*: Text as Context', *Screen* Summer 1994; Andy Medhurst, 'One Queen and His Screen', in Emma Healey and Angela Mason (eds) *Stonewall 25: The Making of the Lesbian and Gay Community in Britain* (London: Virago, 1994); Medhurst, 'That Special Thrill: *Brief Encounter*, homosexuality and authorship', *Screen* Summer 1991; Bronski, *Culture Clash: The Making of Gay Sensibility* (Boston: South End Press, 1984) (espe-cially pp. 92–109); Andrea Weiss, 'A Queer Feeling When I Look at You', in Christine Gledhill (ed.) *Stardom: Industry of Desire* (London: Routledge, 1991); Weiss, *Vampires and Violets: Lesbians in Film* (London: Penguin, 1993).

37. A small, but noteworthy detail: in the spoof black and white 1950s episode of *Roseanne*, the character of David is transposed into the French exchange student Davide who minces around in an artist's smock and rakishly tilted beret. Even the most heterosocially incompetent should not have much of a problem decoding *that* iconography.

38. Galvin, 'Her life as a woman', op. cit., p. 54.

4   Pedro Almodóvar and *Women on the Verge of a Nervous Breakdown*: the Heterosocial Spectator and Misogyny

1. Obviously these issues are complex. Despite the upward class mobility many gay men and lesbians undergo as a necessary part of their integration into metropolitan gay subcultures, many lesbians and gay men continue to earn less than their middle-class heterosexual counterparts, partly because we are more likely to take jobs in less prestigious and materially rewarding circumstances, but where it may be easier for us to be queer. See Alan Sin-field, *Gay and After* (London: Serpent's Tail, 1998). For an account of how aspiring towards middle-class artistic values is related to the emergence of gay male identity, see Derek Cohen and Richard Dyer 'The Politics of Gay Culture' in *Homosexuality: Power and Politics*, edited by Gay Left Collective (London: Allison & Busby, 1980); for a consideration of how the search for signs of lesbian existence and desire engenders an interest in literature and the arts, see Alison Hennegan 'On Becoming a Lesbian Reader' in Susannah Radstone (ed.) *Sweet Dreams: Sexuality, Gender and Popular Fiction* (London: Lawrence & Wishart, 1988).

2. Roland Barthes, *Mythologies* (London: Jonathan Cape, 1972); Richard Dyer, *Heavenly Bodies: Film Stars and Society* (New York: St. Martin's Press, 1986) and *Stars* (London: BFI, 1979) and 'It's being so camp as keeps us going' in *Only Entertainment* (London and New York: Routledge, 1992). See also: Andrea

Weiss, 'A queer feeling when I look at you: Hollywood stars and lesbian spectatorship in the 1930s' in *Stardom: Industry of Desire* edited by Christine Gledhill (London and New York: Routledge, 1991); Quentin Crisp, *How to Go to the Movies* (New York: St. Martin's Press, 1989); Alex Doty, *Making Things Perfectly Queer: Interpreting Mass Culture* (London and Minneapolis: University of Minnesota Press, 1993); Lisa Henderson 'Justify Our Love: Madonna and the Politics of Queer Sex' in *The Madonna Connection: Representational Politics, Subcultural Identities, and Cultural Theory*, edited by Cathy Schwichtenberg (Boulder and Oxford: Westview Press, 1993); Wade Jennings 'The Star as Cult Icon: Judy Garland' in *The Cult Film Experience: Beyond All Reason*, edited by J.P. Telotte (Austin: University of Texas Press, 1991).

3. Signorile, *Queer in America: Sex, the Media and the Closets of Power* (London: Abacus, 1994), p. xv.

4. 'Out and Proud', photographed by Gavin Evans; fashion by Lucinda Alford and Karl Plewka, *Observer Life*, 9 July 1995, pp. 38–41.

5. Brad Gooch, *Out*, May 1994, p. 56.

6. Robert Chalmers, 'Pedro on the Verge of a Nervous Breakdown?' *Observer*, 5 June 1994, p. 24.

7. Marsha Kinder, 'Remapping the PostFranco Cinema: An Overview of the Terrain', *Quarterly Review of Film and Video* 13, 4.

8. Nigel Floyd 'The New Man from La Mancha', *Guardian*, 5 December 1991. Note that Maura's character in *The Law of Desire* is a post-operative transsexual and not a transvestite.

9. Signorile, *Queer in America*, p. xiii.

10. Paul Burston, 'Genre Bender' in Burston, *What are you looking at? Queer Sex, Style and Cinema* (London: Cassell, 1995), p. 141.

11. Brad Gooch, 'The King of Kink', *Out*, May 1994, p. 57.

12. Mansel Stimpson, 'Pedro's Love of Ladies', *The Pink Paper*, 19 January 1996, p. 18.

13. Rose Collis, 'Pedro Almodóvar: Putting the Boo back in Taboo', *Gay Times* 90, July 1994, p. 16.

14. Paul Burston, 'Through the Keyhole: Interview with Pedro Almodóvar', *Attitude*, July 1994, p. 66.

15. David Thompson, 'High Heels' review in *Sight and Sound*, Vol. 1, No. 12, pp. 61–2.

16. Stanley Kauffman, *Persons of the Drama: Theater Criticism and Comment* (New York: Harper and Row, 1976).

17. Robert Chalmers, 'Pedro on the Verge of a Nervous Breakdown?', *Observer*, 5 June, 1994.

18. Paul Julian Smith, *Desire Unlimited: The Cinema of Pedro Almodóvar* (London and New York: Verso, 1994), p. 101.

19. Smith, Ibid, p. 100.

20. Not the least of these contextual considerations is Almodóvar's nationality. One significant advantage of Smith's work is his expertise in Hispanic culture, language and history. Unless I am directly quoting I have chosen to use the English translations of titles of the films as an indication of the specific and partial context of my reading, which pretends no particular expertise in Spanish culture. I heed the admonition Smith gives to 'foreigners [who] cannot expect Almodóvar to subscribe to forms of

resistance which evolved in response to the triumph of the British and North American Right in the 1980s; and if they are serious about respecting cultural difference they must pay more attention to a nation whose under-standing... may well be more sophisticated than their own.' In cultural criticism there is a considerable tension between a residual investment in authenticity (yet which we necessarily and strategically re-instate in order to make intelligible concepts such as identity: heterosexual, man, British and white; nation) which left-wing politics usually respects in order that the margins of power may speak to identify the conditions of their lives, and an investment in postmodernism, through which authenticity has been discredited, which seems to have had the effect of proliferating everything and specifying nothing. We may suggest that postmodernism is an effect of American (and Anglo) globalisation. It is not my intention to attempt to represent the authentic Almodóvar – to uncover the true reading of his work, nor to naturalize the English Anglo-Saxon origins of my own identity. Almodóvar is an international commodity, as he is an important artefact within marginalized and often politically progressive queer subcultures. An authentic Spanish context is not the only one in which Almodóvar may be validly consumed; indeed we may suggest that the metropolitan system is available in Madrid and Barcelona, as much as it is in London. It seems to me that the question is about recognizing the potential for power imbaances, and for a blindness to the partiality and culpability of one's own position.

21. Mary Ann Doane, *The Desire to Desire: The Woman's Film of the 1940s* (Bloomington: Indiana University Press, 1987).
22. A lot of critical work has been done on women's pleasures in the women's film, see: Jeanine Basinger, *How Hollywood Spoke to Women 1930–1960* (London: Chatto & Windus, 1994); Jackie Stacey, *Star Gazing: Hollywood Cinema and Female Spectatorship* (London and New York: Routledge, 1994); Judith Mayne, *Cinema and Spectatorship* (London and New York: Routledge, 1993); Christine Gledhill (ed.) *Home is Where the Hearth Is: Studies in Melodrama and the Woman's Film* (London: BFI, 1987); see also, Christine Gledhill, *Stardom: Industry of Desire* (London and New York: Routledge, 1991). For commentary on the generic limitation and complexities of the woman's film, see Mary Ann Doane, 'The Woman's Film' reprinted in Gledhill, (ed.) *Home is Where the Hearth Is*, Ibid, p. 284.
23. Kenneth Anger, *Hollywood Babylon* (Paris: JF Pauverte, 1959); Patrick McGilligan, *George Cukor: A Double Life* (London: Faber & Faber, 1992).
24. Rictor Norton, *Mother Clap's Molly House* (London: Gay Men's Press, 1992). For discussion about the continuity of the molly subculture, see Alan Bray, *Homosexuality in Renaissance England* (London: Gay Men's Press, 1982); Randolph Trumbach, 'London's Sodomites: homosexual behaviour and western culture in the eighteenth century', *Journal of Social History*, 11, 1977–78; Alan Sinfield, *The Wilde Century: Oscar Wilde and the Queer Moment* (London and New York: Cassell, 1994).
25. Maria LaPlace, 'Producing and Consuming the Woman's Film', in Christine Gledhill (ed.) *Home is Where the Hearth Is*, p. 165.
26. Basinger, *A Woman's View: How Hollywood Spoke to Women 1930–1960*, pp. 17–18.

27. It is important to note, however, that most feminist criticism of the woman's films recuperates them as sites of women's pleasure and importance. Very few, if any, feminist film critics locate their pleasures within structures of heterosexuality and most emphasize the opportunities of subjectivity that the woman's films offer, rather than dwelling on analysis of the masochistic pleasures they enshrine.

28. Paula Graham, 'Girl's Camp? The Politics of Parody', in Tamsin Wilton (ed.) *Immortal Invisible: Lesbians and the Moving Image* (London and New York: Routledge, 1995), p. 178.

29. For discussion of *Edward II* in this context, see B. Ruby Rich, 'Homo pomo: The New Queer Cinema' in *Sight and Sound*, Vol., 2, No. 2, September 1992, and in *Women and Film: A Sight and Sound Reader*, Pam Cook and Philip Dodd (eds), (London: Scarlet Press, 1991).

30. Derek Jarman, *Queer Edward II* (London: BFI, 1991).

31. Mike O Pray, 'Damning Desire', *Sight and Sound*, Vol. 1, No. 6, October 1991, p. 10; Jarman, *Queer Edward II*, p. 124 and p. 148.

32. *The Time Out Film Guide*, ed. Tom Milne (London: Penguin, 1993), p. 205.

33. Derek Jarman, *Dancing Ledge* (London: Quartet, 1984); *Modern Nature: The Journals of Derek Jarman* (London: Vintage, 1992); *At Your Own Risk: A Saint's Testament* (London: Vintage, 1993).

34. B. Ruby Rich, 'Homo pomo: The New Queer Cinema', op. cit., p. 169.

35. See Leo Bersani, *Homos* (Cambridge, MA & London: Harvard University Press, 1995).

36. Jarman, *Queer Edward II*, op. cit., p. 30.

37. Ibid, p. 20.

38. B. Ruby Rich, 'Homo pomo: The New Queer Cinema', op. cit., p. 169.

39. Colin MacCabe, 'Throne of Blood', *Sight and Sound*, Vol. 1, No. 6, October 1991, p. 12.

40. For discussion about homosexuality as hostility and fear of women, see Kenneth Lewes, *The Psychoanalytic Theory of Male Homosexuality* (London and New York: Quartet, 1989), p. 67 and p. 51.

41. Annette Kuhn, *Women's Pictures: Feminism and Cinema*, 2nd edn (London and New York: Verso, 1994), p. 209.

42. Quote reprinted in Peter William Evans, *Women on the Verge of a Nervous Breakdown*, (London: BFI, 1996), p. 70.

43. Ibid, p. 73.

44. Ibid, p. 72.

45. Smith, *Desire Unlimited: The Cinema of Pedro Almodóvar*, p. 101: 'There seems little doubt that *Mujeres* is Almodóvar's most popular work. It remains at the time of writing the only Spanish film to have grossed more that one thousand million pesetas in the domestic market; and it was sold to Spanish television for the unprecedented sum of two hundred million pesetas. The commercial success of *Mujeres* abroad was also exceptional, making Almodóvar the biggest-grossing foreign-language director in the US for 1989.'

46. Since this manuscript has gone into production Almodóvar has released what is arguably his most heterosocially identified work yet, in *All About My Mother*. See: Maddison, 'All About Women: Almodóvar's heterosocial dynamic', *Textual Practice*, 14, 2, July 2000.

Conclusion

1. Robert Rodi, *Fag Hag* (London and New York: Penguin, 1992), p. 95.
2. Robert Rodi, *Closet Case* (London and New York: Penguin, 1993); *Drag Queen* (London and New York: Penguin, 1995); *Kept Boy* (New York: Dutton, 1996).
3. Rodi, *Fag Hag*, op. cit., p. 1.
4. See, for example, Caroline Cossey, *My Story* (Winchester: Faber, 1992).
5. See, for example, Zachary I. Nataf, *Lesbians Talk Transgender* (London: Scarlet, 1996) and Kate Bornstein, *Gender Outlaw: On Men, Women and the Rest of Us* (London and New York: Routledge, 1994).
6. See Nataf, *Lesbians Talk Transgender*, pp. 33–47.
7. For an account of these debates see Judith Halberstam and C. Jacob Hale, 'Butch/FTM Border Wars: A Note on Collaboration', Judith Halberstam, 'Transgender Butch: Butch/FTM Border Wars and the Masculine Continuum' and C. Jacob Hale, 'Consuming the Living, Dis(re)membering the Dead in the Butch/Ftm Borderlands' all in *GLQ*, Vol. 4, No. 2, 1998.
8. In a *Kilroy* discussion programme, aired 9 June 1997 on BBC1, on fag hags and their desire of gay men, a common theme was the intolerability of conventional heterosexuality for women, yet there was no discussion of the possibility of lesbian alternatives. Such an absence was seemingly a function of female homosocial homophobia and gay men's vanity in their attractiveness to women.

Index

Abril, Victoria, 144, 180
Advocate, The, 105, 126
AIDS, 11, 65, 206 *n*.6, 210 *n*.1
Albee, Edward, 17
All About My Mother, 215 *n*.46
Allen, Woody, 211 *n*.25
Allis, Tim, 105
Almodóvar, Pedro, 13, 138–61, 169–81
   and female consorts, 145–7,
        153, 193, 195
   and ambiguity about
        own homosexuality, 144–5,
        148–9, 153
Altman, Dennis, 5
anal penetration, 67–8, 75–81, 98–101
Andersen, Bibi, 144, 153, 180
Anger, Kenneth, 158
Arnold, Tom, 107
Attitude, 94–7, 101, 196
authorial transvestism, 15–16, 19, 32

Babuscio, Jack, 199 *n*.15, 202 *n*.46
Baker, Roger, 199 *n*.16
Baldwin, Alec, 51, 61
Barthes, Roland, 140, 212 *n*.2
Bartky, Sandra Lee, 66
Bartlett, Neil, 35–7
Basic Instinct, 162
Basinger, Jeanine, 160, 214 *n*.22
Beadle-Blair, Rikki, 2
Belle Reprieve, 40–3, 70, 140
Bersani, Leo, 67–70, 75–6, 86, 91, 164,
   193
Bigsby, Christopher, 44, 50
Billington, Michael, 50
bisexuality, 19, 65
Blachford, Gregg, 37
blackness, 45–9, 55, 61, 79–82,
   109–11
   see also ethnicity; race; whiteness;
      national identity
Blair, Tony, 148
Blake's 7, 97

Bloom, Claire, 62
Bornstein, Kate, 216 *n*.5
Bourne, Bette, 40–3
Bowes, Mick, 211 *n*.18
Boy George, 141, 144
Brando, Marlon, 16, 36, 49, 51, 81
Bray, Alan, 214 *n*.24
Bredbeck, Greg, 203 *n*.48
Brief Encounter, 87–9
Bright, Susie, 205 *n*.1
Bristow, Joseph, 202 *n*.46
Bronski, Michael, 7–8
Burston, Paul, 149, 204 *n*.65
Burton, Richard, 144, 150
butch, 21
Butler, Judith, 38–40, 205 *n*.1

Califia, Pat, 205 *n*.1
camp, 9, 29, 33, 65, 66, 90–1,
   158–9, 163–4, 169,
   178, 180
Carpenter, Edward, 23, 25
Carswell, Sue, 106, 120
Case, Sue Ellen, 67, 69–71, 91
Castle, Terry, 207 *n*.22
Cat on a Hot Tin Roof, 17, 35
Chalmers, Robert, 144, 149, 152–3
Chauncey, George, 22, 201 *n*.26
class, 10, 24–6, 48, 52, 54–5, 58–60,
   104, 107, 138–40, 147, 163,
   210 *n*.10, 212 *n*.1
Clinton, Bill, 105, 126
Clum, John, 31–5
Cohen, Derek, 7
cold war ideology, 17, 19, 20
   see also national identity
Collis, Rose, 150
Cossey, Caroline, 216 *n*.4
Coveney, Michael, 16
Crawford, Joan, 155–6, 158, 163
Creekmur, Corey, 8
Crimp, Douglas, 11
Crisp, Quentin, 213 *n*.2